A MILE IN HER BOOTS

WOMEN WHO WORK
IN THE WILD

D1525491

A MILE IN HER BOOTS

WOMEN WHO WORK
IN THE WILD

Edited by

JENNIFER BOVÉ

SOLAS HOUSE
AN IMPRINT OF TRAVELERS' TALES
PALO ALTO

Credits and copyright notices for the individual articles in this collection are given starting on page 299.

We have made every effort to trace the ownership of all copyrighted material and to secure permission from copyright holders. In the event of any question arising as to the ownership of any material, we will be pleased to make the necessary correction in future printings. Contact Travelers' Tales, Inc., 853 Alma Street, Palo Alto, California 94301. www.travelerstales.com

Art Direction: Stefan Gutermuth
Cover Photograph: © Erik Jacobson
Page layout: Cynthia Lamb

Distributed by: Publishers Group West, 1700 Fourth Street, Berkeley, California 94710.

Library of Congress Cataloging-in-Publication Data

A mile in her boots : women who work in the wild / edited by Jennifer Bové.— 1st ed.
    p. cm.
   Summary: "A collection of true stories by women who do a variety of outdoor jobs, from smoke jumping to biology, river running to professional falconry, horse packing to atmospheric science, and more"— Provided by publisher.
   ISBN 1-932361-37-5 (pbk.)
   1. Women—Employment—United States—Anecdotes. 2. Outdoor life—United States—Anecdotes. I. Bové, Jennifer, 1973–

HD6095.M49 2006
331.40973—dc22
                2006007590

First Edition
Printed in the United States
10 9 8 7 6 5 4 3 2 1

Table of Contents

Introduction

There must have been a couple of big rocks stashed some-where in my backpack, someone's idea of a joke. That's all I could imagine because, seriously, I was struggling. Halfway up Killer Hill, a steep grade above Conboy Lake National Wildlife Refuge, I forced one leaden foot in front of the other as I moved toward the lookout from which I could observe sand-hill cranes in the lakebed below. The climb was never easy, but suddenly it seemed impossible, prompting sweat and fatigue and even nausea. I could hardly even feel the crisp spring breeze that normally would have buoyed me up the trail. Finally, I had to stop, rest the spotting scope and its tripod on a stump, and drop the pack from my shoulders to check out its contents. Binoculars, field notebook. No rocks. Planting my hands on my knees, I bent over with a sigh. Morning was wan-ing, and at this rate, there was no way I was going to catch up.

A ringing chorus erupted from the valley floor. Cranes were trumpeting a day-breaking territorial announcement to anybody who'd listen, and I knew they would venture out into plain sight for just a fleeting hour before the heat of the day set in and pushed them back into the cover of trees and brush until dusk. I had to get up to that lookout, above the wall of fir that obscured my view, while the birds were still flaunting their brightly-colored leg bands for me to see through the scope. Those bands were key to revealing all kinds of important in-formation: which individuals had returned from seasons past, who was mating with whom, and where the pairs were establishing nests. I had to get my data; that was the whole reason I was scaling Killer Hill at all.

Just then, I spied a little nutshell between my boots, cupped open to the sky. I sat down in the dirt and picked it up. It was an acorn shell from an Oregon white oak, barely big enough to sit atop my pinkie finger. As I studied it and tried to quell the ache in my gut, some latent voice of instinct spoke up, and a most peculiar thought began to take shape in my brain: *I'm pregnant.* Pregnant? Even though I could hardly fathom it, I knew right then that it was true, without so much as a plus sign on a plastic test strip as evidence. And the funny thing was that I wasn't particularly shocked or terrified at the realization in spite of the fact that this event was something, if anything, I'd planned against all my life. Somehow, sitting there in the wilds of southern Washington with Mt. Adams rising up across the valley with her own fiery volcanic seed in her belly, it was almost like I'd just let myself in on a special secret, and since nobody in all the world—not even my husband—knew this secret yet but me, I was free to just simply revel for a moment in the sweet surprise of it. The wee bud inside me might be just about the size to fit in the acorn shell, I thought.

Eventually, I stood up, dusted off my jeans, and shrugged the pack on again. I took a deep breath and tried not let myself consider the impact that all of this would have on my work. I'd spent the better part of six years breaking in my identity as a field biologist. It was just getting comfy—soft and form-fitting like a good pair of boots. This was where I wanted to be, out here in the middle of nowhere with more bears and sharp-shinned hawks in earshot than people by far. Wilderness had seeped in through my pores and found fertile ground where it could spread root and flourish. I wasn't ready to leave, not now, not ever. But, my concern seemed a bit premature. After all, I hadn't actually *seen* a plus sign yet. The day was still young, the cranes were still calling, and I had a job to do. I tucked the tiny nutshell into my pocket and continued on up the hill.

As it turned out, I was pregnant with my first daughter, and it did take some getting used to. But once I'd settled into the course of change, and once I finally got the nerve to spill the news to the guys I worked with, I understood that I didn't have to spend the next eight months in a housedress with my bare feet propped up; I could still wade wetlands, wield a machete, and hike Killer Hill—just a bit more slowly. And even though I would stay home to raise my baby, I wasn't sentenced to leave the wild when I delivered her. How could I possibly leave it? Wilderness was my identity, ground in deep like dirt within the rings of my fingerprints. And it wasn't simply because I'd walked its woody paths or dipped into its sacred water; it was because I'd gritted my teeth, pulled muscles, worn blisters, and exhausted myself *working* in it. My blood, sweat, and tears had grown akin to pinesap, elk musk, and rain. And so it really wasn't until I became a mother that I learned that wilderness was not just the place where I worked, nor can it be bound by any kind of strict definition like distances to roads or the diversity of creatures within. Wilderness is a state of mind that so many of us enjoy in places, expansive or small, that still harbor elements of nature in its native condition. This mindset is a vital part of who I am, of who my children will be— thanks, in large part, to having spent my formative years immersed in the untamed outdoors. No ordinary job that I know of could offer such a durable sort of sustenance.

In 1980, eminent wildlife ecologist Anne LaBastille published a groundbreaking collection of historical observations and contemporary profiles called *Women and Wilderness,* which documented the burgeoning phenomenon of women living and working in the wild. "Across our continent, women are entering the traditionally male bastions of wilderness work and life," LaBastille wrote. "Sometimes alone, sometimes with families, they are proving beyond doubt that women do have wilderness in them."

And, indeed, they do—now more than ever. Twenty-five years after LaBastille broached the subject, I set out to assemble an unprecedented anthology of writing by modern women who have abandoned the bounds of society to earn a living in a wide spectrum of outdoor professions and who could attest, in their own words, to their proclivity for wild work. I sent out a call for stories to myriad individuals and organizations, a few of which included the Outdoor Writers Association of America, Women in Natural Resources, Women in Fire Service, Women in Fisheries, The National Wild Turkey Federation, and The Wildlife Society. My criteria for submissions were unrestricted, leaving room for interpretation by women in every imaginable wilderness-oriented occupation—the wilder and more remote, the better. I encouraged lively, engaging tales that revealed something about a woman's relationship to wilderness within the context of her job. The experiences could be funny, tragic, harrowing, enlightening; any subject was fair game. Of particular interest were the influences that led women to wilderness work, the ways nature has affected them, and the ways they feel they have affected nature.

In response to my request, *A Mile in Her Boots* bloomed, offering the collective expression of thirty women who have ingrained themselves in the natural world as a way of life. Their professions are varied, ranging from smoke jumping to biology, river-running to professional falconry, horse-packing to atmospheric science, and more. Some of the contributors are well-established authors, while others are new to the literary world, but all present compelling tales of their experiences afield.

As you wind your way through the book, you'll get to know this diverse and intriguing group of women, each of whom extends her hand and welcomes you to explore the rough-hewn details of her trade. Rescue a nest of hatchling sea turtles amid a swarm of nude bathers on a Hawaiian beach with Judy Edwards; fire up a chainsaw and buck fallen trees with Ana Maria Spagna in the Washington rainforest; fish for a little trouble with MaryJane Butters, one of the first female backcountry rangers hired by the U.S. Forest Service; set out spur-of-the moment to a remote Pacific archipelago to study lizards with Maggie McManus; track a pair of fugitive Montana mountain men with Susan Marsh; and keep moving on, as fire lookout Karla Theilen urges in her gripping story of survival. Twenty-seven more adventures await.

Each experience in this collection is unique and each perspective deeply personal, but the creed is the same throughout: we choose to work outdoors because the wild is unshakable in us. We are what we do. It's not about showing up the guys we work with or even trying to fill their size-12 Danners®; it's about the pure feat of breaking ground within ourselves. As Deborah McArthur so determinedly writes in the luminous final essay of the book, "We know who we are. We're wilderness women."

Come, turn the page, and walk a mile in our boots.

—JENNIFER BOVÉ
Ellensburg, Washington

* * *

Camp Cookie Packs Up and Goes Home

THERE'S BEEN NO RAIN, MUCH LESS SNOW, SINCE March. Each hoofbeat of each horse and mule kicks up a mini explosion of trail dust that merges into a Pig Pen cloud enveloping the packstring, hunters, and guides. Me, I'm riding drag, the outfit's new camp cook. This will be the best part of my day. Later, I will actually have to, as the job description implies, cook.

New-job jitters have kept me sleepless for two nights, and if it weren't for choking on trail dust, I might doze off on top of old Grouchy. Grouchy was a chestnut when we started out from base camp, but now, along with the blacks and bays and grays, he's gone claybank.

One of the hunters is shooting photos. They will be monochromes, I think, like blank sheets of parchment paper, or maybe they'll develop all in sepia and we will be captured there in a dusty time warp image: "Packing in to Elk Camp, Turn of Century."

One of the New Jersey hunters twists around in his saddle to talk to me. I grin, risking grit-filmed teeth.

He has his kerchief tied over his nose and mouth and his

eyes are hidden behind mirrored sunglasses. Ray-Ban bandanna bandito. "Hey, Cookie, what's for supper?" he calls.

My grin dries up. Anyone who knows me knows I can't cook, and the only reason I do cook is so I can work with the stock. Fortunately, no one here knows me.

It's a family legend, my fear of frying. I've worked five seasons of fishing trips in the Bob Marshall Wilderness of Montana as a wrangler, cook, and sometimes packer, and I haven't poisoned anyone yet, but that's not been enough to convince me I can cook. Most of the food has been prepared back in civilization by real cooks, and I just heat it up.

But here in hunting camp, I will have to cook from scratch and bake apple pies in a little converted propane barbequer. I have never baked an apple pie before and am convinced the propane oven will blow up in my face. I've already heard horror stories from the other cook, who works a different camp. She lit a match to a propane leak. *Foom!* Her face only blistered up a little.

Swell.

It's 6 P.M. when we reach camp—three canvas wall tents and an electric horse corral. I'm longing to help unsaddle, unmanty and feed the stock, but I sigh and force-march myself into the cook tent, the boss on my boot heels. My mouth gapes open as I survey my domain.

Trail dust like a volcanic explosion of buckwheat pancake flour coats the Last Supper-sized table, the stoves, the kettles, the buckets, the Coleman lanterns, the canned goods. True grit.

"Oh, Lawdy-do!" I hear myself croaking. I've never before used that expression and wonder whence it came. Maybe I'm channeling some long-dead grouchy camp cookie who expired in a fiery *foom* of propane gas.

"You aren't going to quit on me, are you?" the boss asks. It hadn't really occurred to me, but once uttered, it seems an appealing suggestion. I picture myself escaping on foot, dragging my saddle and a fifty-pound duffel bag.

I resign myself to cook-tent captivity, and throw myself into cleaning, unpacking grub, toting water from the creek and frying chicken in a cast-iron skillet. The famished guides and four hunters wander in and out to check on my progress. I've built a fire in the woodstove, and each visitor seems to have a different idea of how the stovepipe damper should be set. It dawns on me over the next month of my servitude that there are no TV remote controls in elk camp, thus the men are forced to fiddle with the damper instead.

It's after 10 P.M. by the time I've finished the dishes. One guide takes pity on me and helps make a dozen sandwiches for tomorrow's lunch. Each person has marked his preferences on a sandwich order form—a little square of paper that lists bread, cheese, condiment and meat choices, peanut butter and jelly. The boss has already instructed me on how to construct the PB&J sandwich. "Lots of peanut butter, on both pieces of bread. Jelly in the middle." He must have heard I can't cook.

I let the guide make the meat sandwiches whilst I plaster great gobs of Jif onto bread. I wonder if I should smear peanut butter on both sides of both pieces of bread, but restrain myself. My eyelids are drooping but I keep on slathering. PB&J sandwiches take on rocket science complexity. Back in my summer job in Montana, everyone made his own lunch each morning. I have been spoiled, I guess, but I still think it's a fine idea and a good general philosophy of life: You make your own sandwich, then you eat it. Or not.

The guide and I retire to our cots by 11 P.M. I reek of Jif and trail dust. "You know," I venture, now that the boss is not in earshot, "I don't know what I am doing here. I hate getting up early and I hate to cook."

Bill—at least three of the guides are named Bill, making sandwich orders an even murkier nightmare—nearly falls out of his cot laughing. I hadn't intended to be funny, but I have to laugh, too. What *am* I doing here? I don't get to so much as saddle a horse. The other cook has warned me off ever "doing the guys' work for them." Packing and wrangling are what I love, but this outfit wants nothing but a kitchen witch. Well, maybe I'll finally learn to cook.

I lie awake all night, anticipating the 3:45 wake up.

That makes three nights without sleep. Then I'm up building fires, lighting lanterns, mixing hot cakes, and frying spuds, bacon, and eggs. I haul water, make coffee, set the table. The hunters stagger in, wolf it all down, stuff ten-pound peanut butter-and-jelly sandwiches into their packs and set out into the morning darkness, a two-hour ride from where they will wait for the dawn and the elk.

I wash the dishes, then go back to bed—the greatest privilege of the cook. But I'm restless and up again soon, splitting kindling, baking muffins and a cake (the oven has not blown up yet!), peeling spuds, making more sandwiches (I'm horrified to see an imminent paucity of peanut butter), putting an elk roast in, filling the temperamental white gas lanterns and trying to swab some of the dust off the pots and tablecloth. I dust and damp wipe over and over and still produce rivulets of mud everywhere.

I'm in a critical stage making supper when Piggy the mule busts down the corral gate. I turn off my boiling pots and sprint outside. I head off the rest of the stock and secure the gate, but Piggy is history, a one-mule stampede on her way to base camp. I'm itching to track her down, but I trudge back to tend supper. Some Bill or other will find the Pig eventually. I'm upset over the runaway mule, but still, the brief stint of corralling horses is the highlight of my long day.

✳

The starving hunters return after dark, homing in on the lanterns I've lit and hung for them. They troop in, adjust the damper, jabber about the elk they've seen. No bulls yet, but everything is rosy anticipation. My elk roast dinner is a ravenous success. After more dishes and breakfast prep, I fall into my cot and announce to the Bill who shares the cook tent with me, "This is probably heresy in the state of Idaho, but I hate spuds. I hate to peel 'em. I hate to cook 'em, and I hate to eat 'em."

Bill by now is beginning to think I'm the strangest kind of camp cook the boss has ever hired. We swap a couple Montana wrangling stories, I cheer up some and as I'm finally drifting off to sleep, I think of a line from "Camp Granada" (*Hello mother, hello father*): I've been here one whole day!

By day seven, I've baked my first apple and peach pies, lost ten pounds and run out of Jif. The boys have bagged one elk and everyone's pretty happy, even the boss, who orders me never, ever to say again that I can't cook—those pies were blue ribbon quality But he can't resist adjusting the damper a tad, and then he says, "I know you're going to tell me I *told* you to make 'em that way, but those peanut butter sandwiches of yours have way too much peanut butter on 'em and not enough jam. A person can't hardly swallow 'em."

"I told you I can't cook," I mutter, but not so he could hear me.

On day eight, I ride out to base camp with Bill. He even lets me lead a packhorse. A light snow has settled the dust, and I'm free of the cook tent, breathing clean snowy air. We hit base camp, and I jump in to help Bill unpack and unsaddle the mules. *Whoopee*, he doesn't tell me not to.

"Nancy, you get up here and sort through your coolers and quit doing the guys' work for them!"—this from the other cook, who is screeching at me from the cook shack.

I sigh. Lucy Ricardo had less trouble getting to sing down at Ricky's club.

For my second hunt, the boss ships me out with a lanky guide named Bob, two hunters and yet another Bill-guide.

Thus freed of direct boss pressure and peanut butter anxiety, I relax several notches and have a fine time trading packing stories with Bob on the steep climb up an old mining road toward yet another 8,000-foot-high hunting camp. The spudhead packers of Idaho call us Montana wranglers "flatlanders." When Bob learns I can pack, he perks up and says I can help pack water up to our camp. It's about a half-mile trip down to the water from the tents to a spring that they've rigged with black pipe and a water trough.

The other cook has warned me about this. "It is the guys' job to pack the water up." Fortunately, the other cook is far away and can't spoil my fun.

My second day in camp, I team up with Chief, a pig-eyed Appaloosa. I lead him down to the water, slowly fill four water jugs from the hose, lift them into Chief's pannier, and pack 'em to camp. I pay Chief off in apples and everyone is happy, especially Bill, who gets out of water duty.

Our two hunters are doctors, which I find comforting until I find out they are an anesthesiologist and a dermatologist. "Swell," I mutter, "if anyone gets a terminal case of acne and needs to be put to sleep, we'll be in good shape."

At supper one night, the two docs and the two guides launch off on a discussion of childbirth, epidurals, and how long their wives were in labor, etc., ad nauseam, followed by an exchange of baby photos. This blessed-without-children tomboy hides behind the dishpans and wishes for a change of subject. Some macho hunt camp this turned out to be.

Despite a corneal infection from an old scratch, the dermatologist downs an elk the third day of the hunt. His eye injury, compounded by the smoke and dust of living in a wall tent, is acting up so much that he and his partner decide they'd better call the hunt off and ride out to town. Bill packs them and the elk out, and Bob rides over to the boss's camp for instruction. I have one blessed night alone in camp. I don't have to cook, and for the first time since I arrived I have time to read a book and look at the stars. The trees set in close and to the north so that I can't see the Big Dipper, and I feel I'm in a foreign land where the constellations are all wrong. Mick is the only horse left in the corral, and he whinnies long and lonesome through the night. I get up every two hours to check on him and slip him a flake of hay.

We are both happy to see Bob and the mule string ride up in the morning. The boss has sent orders to break camp. *Yahoo!* I get out of four days of cooking and can finally do something I'm good at. In my summer job, we have a progressive camp and have to move most every day. I throw myself into dismantling cots with such energy that tall Bob tells me to slow down. We've got two days to get the job done.

We start cutting the hay ropes that hold the guide tent to the poles. I'm hacking away with my dull Leatherman, telling myself to be careful and not cut myself, when from the other side of the tent, Bob hollers and cusses and sends me for the first-aid kit. I fetch it and Bob appears, holding his bleeding arm.

"What did you do?"

"Cut myself," he understates. He has a hole in his left forearm about two inches across and one inch deep. "Is that a tendon, do you think?" he asks quite calmly as he peers into the wound.

I bend my head over the gash. "Yeah, I think it is," I say, a lot calmer than I feel. Most of my pathetically inadequate first-aid training goes galloping out of my mind. About all I can remember is *kiss it and make it better*, but I figure Bob will slug me if I try that one.

"Get the Clorox," Bob says. It's bite the bullet time. Bob washes his filthy hands as best as he can, while I pour hot water and Clorox into the washbasin. I dig out a roll of gauze and some antiseptic ointment and offer Bob what might be a sterile cotton ball to swab with.

Bob and I wrap up the wound and make nervous jokes about how his elk-gutting knife probably didn't have too many germs on it. I inquire about his last tetanus shot. He's current but says he'd like to get to a doctor that night and so there's a change in plans. We'll pack what we can and ride. He puts his arm in a sling to keep himself from using it. I'll have to help him pack the mules.

I work hard to keep a delirium of glee from spreading across my face. Bob might take it wrong that I'm delighted to be doing something more glamorous than cutting eyes out of spuds.

Bob sits down and gets real quiet. His face looks pale under the beard, and I'm thinking maybe he's fixing to faint. "Are you O.K.?" I ask.

"I'm thinking," Bob says. He's planning his loads—how much gear can we pack out on six mules, what's going to balance with the guide tent, etc. I grin with relief. I'm glad to be packing, but I don't much want to have to pack Bob's six-foot-six carcass out as one of the loads.

We both fly into dismantling cots, tables, and guide tent. I manty a couple loads, reveling in the half hitches and packer knots. It's like coming home for me, or discovering a common language in a foreign country. Bob gets more done with one arm than most folks could with two, but he leaves much of the rope pulling to me. I grin up at him. "I bet you're glad I've been on a pack trip before."

"Yeah, I guess I am."

We carry heavy tent poles and lean them against trees to keep them out of the weather. "Excuse my pits," Bob drawls as we shoulder into a tree trunk, staggering under the weight of a ridgepole. I don't know if he's trying to cheer up himself or me.

I box up the kitchen dishes while Bob packs the food, then we both tackle the leftover cheesecake and pudding pie. "Too bad I can't use both hands," Bob complains as he crams dessert down his craw and licks Cool Whip out of his moustache.

Finally we're ready to load the mules. Bob provides a lot of right-handed muscle, while I do the basket hitches and rope tightening. My elbows get to flying, I'm having so much fun. "Am I in your way?" Bob inquires.

"Not at all," I assure him. By 4 P.M. we're loaded and in the saddle, each pulling a string of three mules. I'm glad Bob is out front so I no longer have to keep stifling the big grin that keeps plastering itself to my face. I'm on a horse with a mule's lead rope in my hand—and I'm home already.

I don't care if we ever get to base camp.

A warm breeze blows up out of the canyon, like some summer twilight miracle in November. Before darkness descends, Bob points out three different groups of elk and I grin and nod, yes, I see them.

Our loads are well balanced and will go the distance. We dismount to walk the steep parts—and it's all steep—so we're walking for miles in the dusk, then in the dark, until all I can see are the sparks from the mule shoes in front of me. And the stars. No moon, no snow. Just blackness, sparks, and galaxies. I could step off a cliff and land in the Big Dipper, which has appeared over the mountains like a skillet to the head.

"There's the Big Dipper," Bob calls out, as if he knows I've been missing it.

"It's beautiful!" I call back over the mule ears. I spread my arms, hum and dance down the old mining road like a fiddler on the roof of the world, and I'm damn glad Bob can't see the lunatic lady packer who is homing in on the hoofbeats and sparks of his mule string.

A five-hour pack out and another hour of unloading, un-saddling, and feeding the stock at base camp, and no one around to squawk at me for "doing the guys' work."

As we unsaddle in the lamplight, on opposite sides of the last mule, Bob says, "I know a lot of young men who would have been whining hours ago."

"Shoot, I'm having a ball," I say, certifying myself as crazy as a coot.

One-armed Bob hasn't done any whining either, and now he's off down the road in his pickup for the seventy-five-mile drive to the Salmon emergency room. I'm all alone at base camp, but too high to sleep. I start hatching a story about how I stabbed Bob for criticizing my home fries. *Yessir,* I like it. Bring on the next hunt. No one will ever gripe about my peanut butter-and-jelly sandwiches again.

Nancy Stevens is a freelance writer and freelance wrangler/packer/cook for various outfitters in Montana and Idaho. She has an M.F.A. in creative writing from the University of Montana. She lives in Corvallis, Montana with several horses and mules and a cat named Drambuie.

JUDY EDWARDS

Orion's Surprise

I WAS LOOKING UP AND DOWN LITTLE BEACH FOR Cheryl but couldn't find her through the sea of undulating skin. Scanning the happily naked multitudes on the beach without looking like I was staring was a challenge, and as my eyes skimmed over the bronzed humans standing, sitting, running about with Frisbees and so forth, my brain registered what my eyes were finding: *penis, penis, umbrella, butt butt butt and penis, boobs, cooler, penis penis beer can*...Shit. Can't find her. It's not a big place but it was crowded on this late Saturday afternoon, and so I gave up the search and slogged up the sand berm to ask a man in a wide-brimmed straw hat and black socks, cradling a beer, the question I knew he'd have the answer to, as news like this tends to spread itself faster than physics or technology can account for.

"Turtle nest?" I asked, already hot and irritated.

He waved his beer at a seething human impressionistic mass under the trees, and as I followed the glint of his can in the sun I finally spied Cheryl's blue hat and long blond hair.

A half-circle of quartz crystals topped what I assumed to be the nest site, fine-tuning the universal good energy just in case. Orion, our grand lady hawksbill sea turtle, had snuck one up on us. This season she'd laid four nests on Big Beach and then, after hanging around Kaho'olawe a while, had swum in a determined-seeming direct line to the north shore of Oahu. We know this because she is fitted with a radio transmitter.

Thinking that Orion was contentedly munching sponges off The Gathering Place island and likely to remain there until her next nesting cycle in two or three years, Cheryl—who is turtle tech, project leader, tireless all-night nest watcher, and enthusiastic advocate extraordinaire—scheduled an end-of-turtle-season party. Cheryl rejoiced at the idea of sleeping in an actual bed again. Well, that was the original plan, anyway.

But on the day before the party, Cheryl got a call that three hawksbill hatchlings had swum up out of the sand on Little Beach, the triumphantly nude bastion of personal expression and interpretive dance, bongo drumming, and Frisbee. A fifth nest. Surprise! The party was canceled and Cheryl went to live on the beach for a couple of days.

Thursday night she watched eight more hatchlings emerge, Friday night was uneventful, and Saturday evening was scheduled for the excavation of the nest and the release of any turtlettes still potentially trapped in it.

Biologists Skippy Hau and Glynnis Nakai were due about half an hour before sunset to dig out the remaining hatchlings which, once found, would be measured and weighed, kept in a bucket of damp sand until dark, then released to make their own way down to the sea. As I said, the mystic underground transmission lines had been humming, Mauians love their turtles, and the beach was packed.

Glynnis and Skippy arrived to a great stir of anticipation and excitement, and Cheryl and I took up station to subtly block the press of humans from the work of excavating the nest. So, what you have to picture is a rough circle of a *lot* of nude people, almost all of them magically armed with digital cameras, leaning way over two biologists who have a bucket and some sterile gloves and very little room to work.

Behind Cheryl there were four or five nice young men on hands and knees, peering over her shoulder and around her body. Glynnis sat to the right of Skippy with her bucket and measuring instruments, and standing to her immediate right was one of the most...*endowed* gentlemen any of us had ever seen, and his bosomy girlfriend. Any sudden turns of Glynnis's head would have resulted in the dreaded Penis in the Eye, and I noted she was meticulous about not turning in that direction as she weighed and measured the hatchlings that Skippy began to rescue from under the packed roof of sand where they'd become smooshed into a hatchling puzzle ball. We'd been told that the nest site, between the fallen weathered trunks or branches of an old Kiawe tree, was a favorite sitting place for the bongo players. Pounded down by bongo butts, it was no wonder that the hatchlings, when detected by Skippy's careful digging, were crammed and wedged just about three inches from the surface of the sand and freedom. Had we not dug them up they'd have expired there while the drumming went on obliviously over their suffocating little heads.

And so, while Skippy eased the hatchlings apart with his fingertips, a man in a tree with a guitar began a catchy version of "Everything's Comin' Up Turtles." Endowment Man kept a steady hand on Bosom Girl's lower back as she leaned *waaaaaay* forward with fascination, nearly filling the hatchling bucket with breast. A helpful round of birth chanting began, and it was nicely alternated with another man supplicating the sun god for long life for the hatchlings. Off through the eye-level pubic hair perimeter I could hear the evening's bongos begin. One woman began to accuse Skippy of "ripping the babies from the womb of the mother earth," but someone eventually calmed her down. A voice from my left suggested that such negative energy was not helpful at a birth.

For her research, Cheryl takes sand samples from different levels of the nest, and so she handed Ziploc bags at intervals to Skippy as he dug. Needing a baggie out of her backpack, she turned around, found herself hemmed in by the nice young men on their hands and knees, and philosophically reached through thighs and testicles to retrieve, in the most sterile manner possible, a Ziploc. She said later that it reminded her of the old game Operation, in which the whole aim is to take bones and organs and things out of an electrified patient without touching the walls of the patient's insides and setting off the obnoxious buzzer.

Eventually and with great care, sixty-nine live hawksbill sea turtle hatchlings were unstuck from the womb of the Mother Earth, weighed and measured, held in the bucket until they were all together and it was dark, and set free on the beach to flipper their way down the sand toward Destiny. Cheryl released them, handful by handful, onto the rumpled beach with a clear shot to the water. The crowd lined up on either side of the "runway" in the purpling evening to chant, sing, and otherwise encourage these little lives into the sea. Every wash of a wave that carried one of the tiny bodies away into the salt mystery that is the ocean triggered a round of cheers. The last hatchling slid into the sea nearly two hours after the first delicate sandy flipper had been found by Skippy's gloved hands. The sun god had gone to bed (or at any rate his priest had given up the effort), the bongos were silent, and there were just a couple of people left giving massages on the beach.

I caught Cheryl's eye, and we both laughed. It had been fun to visit 1969 for a couple of hours—even with the potential hazard of Penis in the Eye.

Judy Edwards is researcher, writer and environmental educator on the island of Maui. Her essays and poems have appeared in small local publications, and she is at work on a collection of poems. She currently lends her time and talents to the Hawai'i Wildlife Fund and Haleakala National Park.

KATHLEEN YALE

✳

The Immaculate Observatory

SOMETIMES WHEN I SEE WILD ANIMALS, NO, TO BE perfectly honest, on every occasion when I spot an animal, I am nearly overcome with an intense desire to touch it. This goes beyond my proclivity for all things soft to the touch—it is something much deeper than that. This feeling is not the result of a desire to tame or use or domesticate. It has more to do with a powerful admiration, a deep fascination that I have had literally as long as I can remember, and also a desire to protect and care for these wild creatures—though I am fully aware that they are in no need of human care.

It's about the way the black-tailed deer can stand facing our backyard fence (which is taller than the tops of her wide ears), and then, in what almost seems like slow-motion, leap over it as if it were no more difficult than stepping over a fallen branch. It is about the deft aerial acrobatics of a raven pair, and the knowledge that they mate for life and can live past sixty years. It's about, too, the piercing howls of a wolf pack, the tremendous prints of a mother grizzly next to her cub's, the impossible flight of the bumble bee, the hare's seasonal color change, and young salamanders surviving a northern winter, deep in pond mud, awakening in spring to swim in rain-water—their small frilled gills like tiny dragons.

Maybe I wish for their energy, for their aura. I want them to recognize me as one of their own—a friend, a guardian, a mother, a subordinate. I want to speak their secret languages. I want to reach out my hand and have a fat robin hop into my open palm.

I dream of animals. I dream we communicate. Sometimes I save them, sometimes they save me, sometimes we fight to the death, and sometimes, I become the animal. The dream may change, but the animals are always there.

I have spent the last few years wandering around Montana, looking for different kinds of animals. During this time, when a form or survey asked my occupation, I could say *wildlife biologist*, and smile to myself. It began in Glacier, where I wove through the woods looking for grizzly hair and scat. Then it was three summers of wading through reedy wetlands and kicking up round river stones, counting the black tadpoles and glistening eggs of the various frogs, toads, and salamanders that live within the park. I spent a winter tagging snowshoe hares, and a spring tracking lynx over Seeley logging roads, and most recently, a few seasons with the Yellowstone wolves.

Last winter I spent many weeks in the Northern Range, watching the Leopold pack through an olive-green spotting scope balanced on spindly black legs that shook in the cold wind. The Leopolds are unique; they were the first pack to form naturally after the 1995 re-introduction of wolves into the park. Our main charge was to observe behavior for as many hours as the day and wolves would allow, and I grew familiar with the cold ache of numb skin. We watched the pack travel and knew many of their routes—we napped when they slept, watched them play and rally, hunt and howl. We

witnessed the rising of a new alpha pair, conflicts with neighboring packs and curious interactions with lone bears, bison,
and scavengers. Every day, clasping my frozen, mittened hands
over a heap of thick woolen layers, I marveled at how lucky I
was to know a small part of all these different creatures, and to
watch fragments of their lives unfold.

There was a raven that I often saw from my wintry perch
on South Butte, the sentinel of Blacktail Plateau. The long,
narrow gap of a missing primary feather made her easy to
identify, soaring in slow circles over my head day after day—
her wing span giving the impression of a missing tooth in a
wide grin. For all of the raven quorks and knocks heard out
on the plateau, never once did I turn my head to a call and
find her at the source. She was quiet like me, and I wondered
what caused her silent observation.

The raven is known by many names—trickster, healer,
messenger, creator, bringer of magic. This was the dark angel
that brought madness to Poe, and symbolized death and decay
to others, making ravens almost as feared as wolves. The Haida
people and other tribes of the Northwest believe that raven is
the god that created all life—sun, moon, stars, earth, and humans alike. The Koyukon often call upon ravens for luck
while hunting. The writer Richard Nelsen lived with this
Alaskan tribe for several seasons, and often heard the cry
"*Tseek'aal, sits'a nohaaltee'ogh*," "Grandfather drop a pack to
me." If the raven calls or rolls, the hunter has been momentar-
ily blessed.

Ravens are clever creatures. They can unzip unattended
backpacks and remove food and other objects from the pockets. The maintenance crews in Yellowstone sometimes place a
small pebble on the outside of garbage cans—a small, simple
signal that tells the driver if the receptacle has been opened,
and that it needs to be emptied. My friend Daniel has watched

ravens fly directly to that small pebble and knock it down, then wait for any scraps to fall when the driver gets out to check the trash. Konrad Lorenz, a famous ethologist, experienced another interesting incident. Once during a routine feeding, his pet bird brought in a damp article of clothing from the line. Lorenz thought little of it, and unconsciously rewarded the raven with food. Many times after that occurrence this same bird would fly off and return with small articles from neighborhood clotheslines—a sock or glove or pair of underwear, in anticipation of a food reward.

It has been documented that Yellowstone ravens follow Yellowstone wolves. They have learned that likely where they find wolves, so too will they find a leftover carcass. Many times I have searched for wolves, scanning the subtle hills and frozen creekbeds laid out ahead, only to catch the stealthy blue–black shadow of a raven—and then followed the bird straight to the pack. Abandoned elk kills are surrounded by hundreds of little trident tracks, peculiar, angular forks, some light blue like the snow, some a deep, wet red. Often at kill sites I would seek out the undisturbed patches of snow, looking for their rare wing prints, little feathered snow angels—the blessing in the wake of their ascent.

Just outside of the park boundary, during the late winter hunt, I've seen over one hundred ravens feeding on elk gut piles, darting between massive bald eagles and chasing magpies. Pairs will feed each other from their black beaks, while the juveniles soar in great parliaments, spiraling up through the air with the thermal patterns, effortlessly floating and dotting the sky.

I soon learned that in order to watch wildlife, you must be in position when they are most active. To find wolves in particular, this means an observer must sacrifice a normal amount of sleep and be outside before dawn. While I have always been a reluctant riser, especially when the stars are still high, it was easy to get used to the coyote choruses, and to the sunrises. They seem to be accentuated by the most bitter of pre-dawn coldness, and I saw more amazing sunrises that winter in Yellowstone than any other. Like the ghost of an old wildfire, an orange glow would burn over the soot-black mountains. Another day the clouds would seem to burst with a magenta flush, spilling wide sunbeams that shot across the plateau. And then the sunsets—beautiful and unapologetic, as they stole away the day's warmth without mercy, leaving us to shiver again until nightfall.

I loved, too, watching the light patterns flow throughout the day, and how they could transform the landscape. To be so constantly aware of how the white sun or day moon hovers, to be able to watch shadows begin, and then follow them through their thin final stretch toward dusk, seems almost novel—a little bit of magic (even if predictable) in a society that has invented numerous ways to prolong light. Things change under different lighting—some become more de- tailed, others less specific in a pleasant haziness. Trees and mountains and animals all pass through these phases of sharp- ness and softness. Some things, like tracks, are even swallowed up in certain light, and seem to reappear in a different hour as if left by invisible hosts.

Tracks are always an exciting discovery. The whole of Yellowstone is divided into a mosaic of animal prints, a thick quilt covered in cross-stitching. The straight lines of lazy- footed ungulates have the appearance of ski trails, clean and direct, dotted with crescent-hoofed prints. They are cut by massive padded wolf prints and the smallest rodent hops. I am reminded of a passage by Tasha Tudor on finding these tiny tracks: "I found some of the most minute mouse tracks this morning, like little necklaces in the snow." I've followed hare tracks for some distance, measuring the length between hops with a long, winding string, getting tangled in the many double-backs and circles of a nervous animal. They call it "tortuosity," a title that seems to rob the joy out of mere wandering.

Now there are even ways to digitally photograph a track and identify a specific individual's paw print, much like a human fingerprint. This technology is taking its place next to DNA hair and scat work, remote sensing cameras, and other non-invasive research methods. These methods are not a substitute for all other kinds of research—certain information cannot be told through movement patterns and heritage alone—but they are pieces of the puzzle. I remember the thrill of finding a soft clump of golden bear hair, swaying from a barbed wire hook, and finding fresh tracks in the mud; but it was through the focused watching that I felt closest to wildlife, where I felt like a secret, but invited spy.

In late November, just before his winter sleep, we watched a fat grizzly slowly amble and follow the Leopolds around for a day. He bedded when they did, and even traveled in a single-file line between wolves that refused to step out and pass him. The different animals would come within several feet of each other, and with no food source to fight over; the bear seemed comfortable, playful even, as if he wanted to briefly break from his own solitary company. This incident was one of the first of its kind to be documented, and was done so only through diligent observation. I never grew tired of watching the wanderings of all of these animals. Though bound by genetic tradition, they are also flexible and adaptable, and they always offered something new to see.

I remember the week that a Hellroaring mother bison stood over the body of her small red calf for a few days. Often a group from her herd lingered in a loose circle around the fallen calf—why I cannot say for sure. Perhaps to protect its cold body? Perhaps to mourn? Elephant herds return to the sun-bleached bones of their companions year after year to stomp and trumpet. There is a certain solidarity there, and I think that the bison share it to a degree. I've seen a group run out to meet a stray and block the wolves in their pursuit. Watching those animals guard the dead calf—it nearly broke my heart to think about what their numbers were like a few hundred years ago, how they are in a sense imprisoned in their surviving ranges and ranches, that the penalty is often death, doled out by the state, to those who follow the call to roam a greater distance.

Perhaps this is what it takes for some people to understand. Maybe they need to sit in the open air and notice the differences in the way ungulates forage in winter—the buffalo nudging the snow from side to side with their tremendous heads, the elk arcing their forelegs to kick it back. Maybe we all need to see the bloody face of a well-fed coyote, follow the sure steps of big horn lamb, and wait with the watchful eagle from her leafless post. Maybe that truly is what it takes for some to realize that the value of wildness is immeasurable.

I entreat us all to look around, just sit down and watch something—the squirrel tossing pinecones from its nest or the robin pulling up earthworms after a storm. There is so much to see, so much beauty and mystery. I could watch these wolves or any other creature on earth, every second for the rest of my life and there would still be secrets hidden from me. The natural world is constructed of the things that are visible and those that are invisible—the line that separates them is seamless, unseen. The open air offers an immaculate observatory for anyone who is eager.

*

I remember that after a few days of nervousness (wanting to see the wolves hunt, not wanting to watch an elk die), we went to retrieve our first kill. In addition to recording all forms of lupine behavior, the Yellowstone Wolf Project also documents ungulate kill rates. Part of my job was to try to find kill sites by direct observation or by reading a variety of signs, such as scavenger activity. Once a kill site is located, crews walk, snowshoe, or ski in to collect data. Bone marrow quality, metatarsus length, tooth wear, gender, and age are the main factors that are examined.

We had waited a few days to pick up this particular kill, as the spotter plane had seen a large, winter-ready grizzly lying over it the day before. Oftentimes, particularly after a bear has been there when you reach a wolf kill, you have to walk a wide radius to retrieve all of the remaining bones that have traveled from the center area. Often, too, you can tell if a bear has scavenged a kill, as they can peel the hide of a metatarsus leg bone down, much like you would a banana. It was a sunny day, and what was left of the carcass was still soft and bloody. At first I shied away from the scene, preferring to watch, rather than participate in the tooth-pulling and bone-sawing. Walking around the perimeter, I counted the wolf beds and put my hands into their melting prints.

Another time we hiked out onto Blacktail Plateau to do a necropsy on a tremendous bull with antlers as tall as my arm span is wide. It took me some time to come to terms with scenes like these, but now I can see the beauty in them—in the red, blood-soaked snow and the branched antlers, a testament to the dual evolution of predator and prey and their cyclical partnership. And of how necessary wolves are to this, their ancestral ecosystem. This bull had a long tapered crack down his mandible, from what we cannot be certain. Nevertheless, such a fracture could have hindered his ability to eat, a theory backed in part by the unhealthy pink-tinged bone marrow, a dangerous sign at the onset of winter. This may have been a weakness that the Leopold pack was quick to exploit. Also, given the great size of this bull's antlers, it is likely that he was a dominant breeder that fall. Bulls are known to become so wholly sex-crazed during the rut that they literally might not eat even a mouthful of grass for two weeks. Two weeks without food. This can be devastating in terms of body fat. I am constantly astounded by these animals—by the fierceness of nature.

I remember, too, collaring lynx up in Seeley Lake one winter. We carefully walked in each other's prints to leave a subtle single track—my padded steps easily fit where the handler Craig's big mukluks trailed. I remember slowly approaching the trap, covered in severed fir boughs, and being received by a low growl and an arched back. We drugged the cat with a ridiculous looking contraption—a pointed needle attached to a long, skinny pole, and then waited for his sleep to come. Then, in the eerie blue glow of a headlamp, I held this lynx. I remember running my bare hands over his soft, banded fur, pausing to see what it looked like rising in little spikes between my frozen fingers; and putting my palm against his tremendous feet, thick with yellowing fur that looked like matted wool slippers, as big as his head. This one was missing a couple of toes—just small, bony nubs poking out of that tangle of fuzz.

I helped to measure his length as Craig drew blood—filling the small vial dark with red, warm to the touch, before fitting a new radio collar. As we worked we talked of grandfathers, canoeing, and the moon; and all the while I could not take my eyes off of the cat, and kept thinking about how lucky I was to have such intimate contact with a wild animal. But in some ways, in many ways really, it saddened me. Because this wasn't true intimacy—not in the sense that you hope for anyway. That was a sense I had while watching the wolves from a distance, where I wasn't interfering with their wildness; or from locking eyes with a mule deer, and then having her continue to graze rather than immediately dart away. Instead I was invading this lynx's space on my terms, not his. And so I felt grateful, so grateful to feel his slow, wild breaths on the back of my hand, to be one of two people to touch this individual, and one of a few people in the entire world to touch any wild lynx; but I also felt guilty, and whispered under my breath continual thanks and apologies.

I know that there are few choices left in how we study wildlife, and although this particular method may be invasive for a short period, it is also a good way to maintain distance in its aftermath. This capture-and-collaring process is what allows researchers to track movements and ranges, follow reproduction and observe behavior, from a distance, without interfering further.

The Yellowstone wolves are darted in mid-winter from a helicopter when the weather is right, and the snow is deep. This gives the capture process a much different feel than trapping. In contrast to the cold, blue night that I held the lynx, I touched my first wolf on a sunny, snow-blinding day, sweating from the rapid hike and surrounded by a team of biologists. Often I saw wolf behavior that reminded me of my own pet dogs, but the similarities ended from this view. You can't imagine how big they are, how wild. Their long, powerful legs stretched out—each hair a slightly different color, their eyes ancient. She was gorgeous, and I hoped to have the chance to watch her run through the icy lens of my spotting scope.

A couple of months later I saw my first dead wolf. We spent a March afternoon hiking up near Tower Falls to retrieve a radio-collared male from the Agate Creek pack in the Northern Range. A tremendous gray male—massive, beautiful head and paws, mysteriously left dead on an open wind-blown slope, lying on his side atop the crusted snow, half buried by the harsh drifts. We searched for hints about what might have caused his demise. His body was still intact—the cold had preserved it well. No tracks were spared, not even his own. In truth, he almost looked like he was sleeping. But a raven had taken his eyes, a final gift to the clever scavengers that faithfully follow packs from the air, feast on their kills, and even pull on pups' tails. So while at first the thought of this eyeless creature disturbed me, on second thought it seemed quite fitting.

Wolves have been killed by prey in the past, as a sharp hoof can easily break bone. This seemed a likely cause of death, but there were few signs to read, and we were forced to bring him back with us for an official necropsy. Therein lies a sad scene. As a biologist I realize and support the need to study these animals—especially a re-introduced species. I also know that his death, whatever the cause, was natural; unlike the two in the walk-in freezer, with fist-sized bullet holes in their sides, shot outside of the park. But still, his departure was not natural. This untamed creature, bound to an absurd neon orange, plastic children's sled—pulled behind alternate people with ropes tied around their waists—lifted over downed trees and frozen creeks by four hands, by backs hunched like pallbearers. It saddened me deeply, this being the end of his body—an orange sled-and-bungee humiliation. When I wasn't pulling him, I walked beside the sled looking down.

After the investigation, perhaps his pelt will join others as educational tools—maybe a child will have the chance to rub her face across the banded fur and realize the importance of wolves, of all things. In this thought I took great comfort. And maybe, years later, the skull will be returned to the land, where short mosses and lichen will find it and turn it green.

Kathleen Yale holds a Bachelor's degree from the University of Wisconsin in Conservation Biology, and a Master's degree in Environmental Studies from the University of Montana. Her essays and poetry have appeared in Camas: Nature of the West, Moon City Review, *and* High Desert Journal. *She is currently living in western Montana, where she has spent the last several years following around wild animals under the guise of a wildlife biologist, swimming in cold water and poking around in the woods.*

* * *

Hurled to the Shark

THIS MORNING, BEFORE I LEAVE OUR LOFT FOR BREAK-
fast, I do not check the calendar. I know what day it is: July
26—put-out day. This is the day we load our nets from the
mending racks on the beach and drop them back into the
water. I am grim. I have done this four times by now in this,
my first season, which makes me still a nervous greenhorn,
since Duncan, my husband, his two brothers, and his father
have been fishing for more than twenty years, yet I know exactly what will happen in the day and night ahead.

Now I stand in the beached skiff as it sits sideways, loading
each of the eight nets into the skiffs. We are clawing the net
with our hands, pulling the green webbing from the racks over
the sand and up and over the skiff sides. Duncan is pulling the
leads, the heaviest weight; Wallace is pulling the corks, the
most awkward job; and I am in the middle pulling the fine
thread of web into a silken pile at my feet. The nets must be
stacked precisely in the skiffs so they will drop clean into the
water, lie where intended, spin out over the stern without a
knot to pull our boot, or all of us after it.

All the nets are loaded now, eight nets in three skiffs. The skiffs with the nets in them have no outboard; they will be pulled by the skiffs powered with the 35-horse outboards. We step out of the last skiff, and I glance behind me as I leave the beach, our little battleships loaded and ready. The opening begins at noon. Though it is only ten, we will put on our gear and head out.

"Leslie!" Duncan yells back as he starts down to the beach and waiting skiffs. Everyone is ready before me. "Get some candy bars!" I am searching frantically for my life vest, hands on every hook, frisking the extra raingear draped around the porch, feel a familiar sponge, grab it. I push into my mother-in-law's cabin, into the tiny kitchen, rummage the cupboard till I find the hidden supply—Unos, Hersheys, and Snickers. I run down the grass yard, onto the sand, leap into the skiff and we are off, the five of us, all looking alike in our raingear, out to skiffs painted red, white, and black. Because of our uniformity, not only our clothes but our gear, the skiffs, the cabins all painted red and white, it feels like an industry, an enterprise so much larger than the facts at hand: a core of three brothers, a father, seven skiffs, and eight nets. For a moment I see us, Weston in the stern running the kicker, eyes squinted in concentration as he maps out the afternoon and evening. Duncan solemn as he watches the water, Wallace, just seventeen, with the same air as his brothers, and their father, DeWitt. And me, my face no different, not because I am strategizing, as they are—*who puts out what nets, in what order, will the NE get worse?*—but because I have taken this world on like a face, except it goes deep already. I am one of them, I think, then no, I am not, but I will be, if I can.

That 6 P.M. minute has enticed us through weeks of scraping and painting skiffs, mending and pulling the hairy weeds out of last year's nets, dropping anchors. It is all for this, now, Duncan standing in the skiff with the 35 kicker, eyes on his watch, DeWitt and I in the skiff with the nets, poised for his word, and then, "Let's go!" as the second hand hits the twelve and it is official, the opening has begun. I have already tied the net in the skiff onto the line in the water. Duncan gasses the kicker now, and his skiff, like a racehorse out of the gate, charges ahead free until the line to my skiff suddenly goes taut. We freeze for a split second, then my skiff jerks forward behind his, the net playing out with a hiss and tumble behind me over the stern. My job—not by my choice—is to clear the net should it catch or snare as it is pulls out behind us. I nearly cringe as the skiffs lunge yet faster. What if the net tangles? I realize I have absolutely no control over this mess, and then a cork snags, the skiff jerks to a stop, begins to swing sideways, the cork creaking threateningly. "Clear the cork!" Duncan shouts, and I lean over, punch the cork jammed in the corner and the released tension yanks out fathoms of net. We are nearing the shore keg and it snags again, the skiff pulling against the locked net—"Leslie! Get it!" I kick it this time, and then just as we come up to the buoy, Duncan shouts, "O.K., get ready to grab it!" and we are over the skiff sides, leaning out as far we can keep our balance, gripping the running line that holds the net in place while Duncan jumps over and leans his full weight on top of us to tie the net without losing any of the tension. "Hold it, hold it!" he warns, as DeWitt and I pant over our balled fists; I screw my eyes up tight, count my breaths, and when I hit eighteen, he says, "Got it!" and we relax, let go, stand up, and then the next is easier as we spell out the net in the hook. Here Duncan kills the kicker and we pull it by hand. *This is fine, this is good*, I say to myself, as we pull—the pressure is off here. When we are done, and the net hangs in the water like a curtain, the row of corks blinking in the waves, I feel good.

"We've got some corks, Leslie. Come on back here and lets get 'em," Duncan says, the tension gone now from his voice. Some of the corks have caught under the net, and need to be freed. This is one of my favorite jobs. So simple, yet some kind of elegance, even poetry to it. I wedge myself in the corner of the stern while Duncan backs down the net, keeping as close as the tide and wind and waves will let him. As we idle down, I lean over and with a quick dunk, palm the submerged cork out from under the net and clear so it bobs up instantly. Lean, dunk, pop, Duncan watching as we go, and if I get every one first try he doesn't need to stop. We just motor down, lean, dunk, pop, all the way down the length of the net, 100 fathoms, until every cork holds its part of the net and it sways and blinks with every wave, graceful.

Then on to the next net and then two more. We will put out four; Weston and Wallace will put out four.

When the nets are in, then it happens, what all of this is for—the fish. Sometimes, as soon as the net is wet behind us, we see silver lifting it back up out of the water, a furious thrash of anger as three, four, a group of salmon hit together. And we stop, no matter what we're doing, smile at one another at the instant logic and mathematics of it—yes, a year of ordering supplies, a month of fourteen-hour work days for this moment, for these salmon behind us and at our feet.

But if it is early in June, or late in August, or in any low year, there may not be much to marvel over. The net may soak for hours and days without a fish, blank. Duncan told me about this, about the early years, how few fish they caught. His family worked off every summer here, and sometimes left four months of work with a slip from the cannery that would pay off their living expenses, but not much more. The risks never lessened over the years. I see that this is a fishery built on faith. There is so little control over so much. Set-netters are not hunter-gatherers who stalk and chase their prey, not even farmers who till and plant and tend what rises. The nets are plunked out here in hope leavened with experience, strung out into the ocean, yet tied to shore, like some kind of giant arm motioning "here, swim in here." There is no way to urge or chase them in. We can only wait for the salmon that choose this place at this depth on the days that the nets are there, and then hope for their blunder into the meshes, and that their blunder gills them fast enough that they hold against the currents and riptides until we come to pull them into the skiffs. But when I have been picking for many hours, so that my back aches and my hands are stiff, they are the enemy, and I don't care if the nets stay blank. But then when I am rested, and Duncan and I look at college bills, when we estimate our living expenses, I know those fish, every one is sent. If God knows the fall of each sparrow, then He knows the path of every salmon. Sometimes I remember this.

If the fish are hitting that night, and they are this night, we pick. I would like to go ashore and be done for the night. What perfect closure, move on from one task to the next, a night's sleep in between. But we don't work that way. The time clock for fishing follows Alaska's summer sun; in May and June, night and day are twins, one a slightly paler version of the other. We nap in the day and work in the night; pick fish in the day, pick fish at night; these nets, these fish, are no respecter of person or sleep or fatigue.

After the fourth net, five hours since we started, we declare it dinnertime, pulling out the candy bars and pop. We sit there, the three of us, our skiff tied to the net, slapping the water gently. This is the only break we will have tonight. Duncan

and I are sitting together as we eat, our rubberized and reptil-
ian legs pressing against each other on the seat. Duncan leans
over and gives me a kiss, leaving a wet spot on my face where
his nose dripped. He's got a couple of scales on his cheek, and
a smudge of fish blood on his forehead. I've got something
dried on my jawline; my gloves are a blend of blood and gurry.
I'm not feeling romantic. He's yelled at me three times already
this put-out. I know later he'll explain that a job's got to be
done no matter who it is, wife or crew or anyone. Then I'll
complain that he treats me like a crewman and he'll say, "Well,
you are." Then I'll say, "No, I'm your wife, and you can't step
in and out of marriage just because you're climbing in and out
of a skiff," and so it will go. I did not expect the skiff to be run
democratically, but neither did I expect such a pronounced hi-
erarchy. I'm not sure what to do about this, how to establish
in this geography the kind of balance and equity we have in
the other.

We were drawn to each other not by physical prowess or
my potential as a fish-picker, but among other things, by a
mutual love of philosophy and theology. After meeting in college on a road trip to Maine, we began a dialogue of impas-
sioned notes and letters when apart and discussions when together about the nature of God, about the puzzles of
predestination and election, about man's free will or is it only
free moral agency? How far does God's sovereignty extend?
How can God hold us responsible if in fact He is the primary
and sufficient cause of all events? How does evil fit into God's
plan, or is evil outside of it? These questions were life and
death to me. Though I had considered some of them before,
at eighteen, I now understood their enormity and could not
proceed with anything until I found some answers. Duncan,
the fisherman from Alaska, who was also class president, cared
as deeply as I did about these concerns. We talked, wrote

notes, studied philosophy together, took classes together, prayed together. The bond ran deep. Where was all of this now? Our most abstract question was likely to be, "How many reds do you think this skiff'll pack?"

For now, though, I'm not wishing myself anywhere else. Not because of supreme contentedness; rather because the world we are floating in is so complete and has wrapped me in its cloak with such strength, I can think of no other place or way to live than what we are doing this moment, and most, what we must do to finish before we can get to bed.

Finally, the nets are judged done for the night. Weston and Wallace come up beside us in their skiff, both looking tired, but wearing the same expression I see on Duncan. They do not even glance at me as they decide the mechanics of who will take what skiff to the tender to deliver, and I am hoping they will not need me. I won't ask to go ashore, though. "You can go in," Duncan finally says to me in my ear. "I know it was a tough one, but you did great. You really worked hard. Thanks, Leslie."

At the beginning of the season I might have protested, but in these weeks I have become grateful for any concessions Duncan makes for me, but at the same time, I feel weak and guilty that I need them. I never needed them before. I could always match my three brothers on most tasks. Why can't I work as hard and long as these men? I was the one out of a hundred ninth-grade girls who could climb the gym rope to the ceiling in six seconds, beating everyone else. In tenth grade, I was the one chosen out of my class to heave the twenty-pound medicine ball in our Winter Carnival Olympics. Here I felt defeated.

I slide out of the skiff, trudge through the black night water up to the beach and the long hill up to Duncan's parents' house. The lights are on. How glorious, like a star! Duncan's mother has hot soup on the stove and grilled sandwiches waiting. I am so grateful as I spoon the soup with numb hands. In five minutes I am done, back outside, walking down to the old warehouse on the beach, to our loft. The wind has not abated any, and though it is sucking sound in the opposite direction, I can hear the skiffs straining under their loads, still going in the dark, just arriving at the tender. I have no energy left to pity them; indeed I do not, for haven't they grown up with this? Doesn't Duncan profess love for this? And is there anything these three brothers cannot do? Then up the ladder and into the tiny room. It is cold in there without heat, about 45 degrees, and the tin roof is banging, and something else is whistling with the wind but I don't care. I notice as I pull off my sweatshirt that I have fish scales stuck to my arms. I leave them there, climb under the three sleeping bags and sleep. It is 1 A.M.

The next morning, the alarm rings at 7, the usual. Duncan is trying to wake beside me. I didn't hear or feel him get into bed last night. I don't want to get up, don't want to put on raingear and face the nets again. But the wind has come down. "Thank you Lord," I whisper.

"Are you awake, Leslie? We've got to get up," Duncan mumbles, rubbing the palms of his hand into his eyes. I won't ask to stay in. How can I? I got in earlier than any of the men last night. But I'm so stiff from trying to harness the ocean last night, I can barely move. We both roll out of the one side of the bed, then fumble for clothes in our wood crates, and in a few minutes we are down the ladder and up to my parents-in-laws'.

Duncan gives the door one rap as he enters.

"Come on in," Wanda calls from around the corner. She is just putting a bowl of hot muffins on the table. DeWitt and

Wallace are already here. DeWitt looks up and smiles kindly at his new daughter-in-law.

"Good mornin' Leslie. How'd you sleep last night, my dear?"

"Oh, it was a little bit noisy with the roof flapping in the wind, but I was so tired I didn't really hear it," I answer as I sit at my place. Then I think, oh, dear, did that sound like I was complaining?

"Yeah, it was blowin' pretty good last night. Wandy, you ready to sit down?"

"Just a minute," she calls as she bustles from kitchen to table, setting down another amazing banquet: fresh blueberry muffins, scrambled eggs, coffee, bacon, canned pears with sprinkled cheese, and juice.

"Where's the fried potatoes?" DeWitt asks, looking around the table as Wanda sits down.

Wanda looks from me to Duncan then to DeWitt. "I didn't make any this morning," she says defensively.

"We haven't had fried potatoes for three days now. You know we need 'em when we're workin' hard. There's nothin' like fried potatoes in the mornin'," DeWitt says, like a slogan.

Wallace and I exchange covert smiles. I nudge Duncan under the table. How will this end? I'm not too worried.

"Well, you can have them for lunch, then. How does that sound?" Wanda cajoles. The cloud has passed. We bow our heads and DeWitt prays, "Heavenly Father, thank you for this good food which has been prepared for our nourishment and enjoyment. Thank you for all your many blessings. Thank you for the fish. Make us grateful in our hearts for these things. Amen."

When our nets weren't working us, we were working the nets. On closures, when Fish and Game closed fishing for a few days to let the salmon up the streams to spawn, we untied the nets and pulled them up, this time using not the kicker to unravel them, but our arms, dragging them up from the ocean floor, heavy with kelp sometimes, sometimes fresh fish just hit. The nets had to be out of the water, not a shred remaining, by 9 P.M. To keep everyone honest, Fish and Game flew over regularly. Take-ups were just as intense as put out, with one ameliorating factor. The speed was our own, not motorized, and so within our control. The take-up of a single net was like the 400-yard dash. Not a sprint, because you couldn't poop out halfway and then just walk the rest. And even if you paced the first net perfectly, so that you made it to the end, there still were three more nets to go.

I was usually the first one in from take-ups, let off on shore by Duncan who knew I had nothing left to give. I knew it as a gift. He and his brothers would go on to the tender to deliver the fish caught before the nets came out. I would trudge up the hill in varying states of emotion, sometimes tearful, sometimes angry, always tired. Often Beverly would be there on the porch, ready to offer sympathy, a hug. She was seven years older than I, and was my sister-in-law, Weston's wife, but we were closer to each other than we were to our own sisters. At the end of one take-up night, near 11, as I pushed my body laboriously up the beach, my limbs like deadwood, she came down to greet me.

"Leslie!" she called. "How did it go?" She peered anxiously into my face and put an arm around my shoulder.

I sighed carefully, trying to quell the emotions I was now allowing myself to feel in the face of such kindness. I couldn't hold it in any longer. The night had been intense. I had made a few mistakes, one running line had broken, the nets had too many fish for us to pull them as quickly as we needed; we had almost gone over the deadline; Duncan had stepped on my back when I had fallen to get to the net. Every loss, every shout, had registered somewhere deep inside my chest, and it was choking me. Until now. I erupted into sobs, heaving, tears blending with saltwater and gurry, my arms over Bev's shoulders. She stood there quietly, letting me cry. When I was done, we walked up together to her house where she made me hot chocolate. Sitting at her table, in a kitchen still unfinished, floors bare plywood, walls unpainted, she handed me a piece of paper, marbleized, with sweeping calligraphied letters.

"Here, Leslie. I thought you might like this." She smiled as my face lit up. It was a verse from the Old Testament, from Isaiah, one we had talked about before. I read the familiar words again: "They that wait upon the lord shall renew their strength. They shall mount up with wings like eagles. They shall run and not be weary; they shall walk and not be faint."

I had memorized it a few years ago while in high school, but had never needed it as much as I did this summer. I wanted to clasp it to my breast, transfer its hope and promise directly through my clothing and skin.

"Thanks, Bev. It's beautiful. I'll put it up next to my mirror, by *the poem*."

Bev laughed, knowing this was the place of honor. "Tell me the poem again. This seems like a good time for it. Do you know it by heart?"

"Only the last stanza." It was a poem I had found early this season in a poetry anthology from college—"The Leg," by Karl Shapiro. The moment I read it the words became my own. In a quiet voice, I recited:

> The body, what is it, Father, but a sign
> To love the force that grows us, to give back
> What in thy palm is senselessness and mud?
> Knead, knead the substance of our understanding

Which must be beautiful in flesh to wake,
That if Thou take me angrily in hand
And hurl me to the shark, I shall not die!

I said the last two lines again, and we fell silent.

"It reminds me of your poem about Job," I said finally, breaking the moment.

"Yes, me too. 'Though He slay me / yet will I trust Him'." We are quiet again. This verse scares me profoundly, and yet it gives comfort too. I don't want to leave, but it is nearing midnight. We hug one more time.

"See you on the nets tomorrow."

"Bring one of your new poems!"

"You bring one, too!" We smiled like conspirators.

One morning, near the end of July, it happened, the run of pink salmon forecast by Fish and Game came running, and so did we. Fifteen million were forecast, and when we stumbled up the hill for breakfast, Duncan looked out in his usual visual check of the nets visible from shore, then, "Hey, where's the hook of the third? We've either got a shark in it or it's sunk with fish!"

It was sunk with fish. And the derby began.

We had fished and caught healthy amounts of salmon up until then, enough to keep us tired and reasonably sure of making our tuition payments that next year, but we hadn't made enough for rent and living expenses. I had hoped for the flood of fish along with everyone else, but now, as my heart fluttered and my stomach turned, as though I were about to go on stage, I wondered, if we haven't been catching many fish yet, what will it be like when we do? And then the answer: what I thought I knew about hard work became a romper room memory. There were pink salmon swarming all over

Kodiak Island, filling the seiners' nets, sinking ours, the ones that got away choking the spawning streams.

We stood in our skiffs in salmon up to our ankles, then our calves, then our knees, walking on them, falling on them as we still bent to pull the net in for more. Three weeks of days and nights nearly indistinguishable from one another, eating and sleeping around the fish, lunch twelve hours after breakfast, my hands so sore and bleeding in the deep cracks between my fingers I tape them before putting on the cotton gloves, a shoulder that hyperextended with any stress at all, Duncan and his brothers' arms going dead-numb at night, their hands locking with carpal tunnel, the dreams—Duncan pulling the covers off me hand over hand shouting, "Coil the line!" Mine— that the net snares my foot while putting out the nets and I go down, drowning over and over because of the fish, the overflow that runneth from our cups, our fish overfloweth, our cups run away, the fish, the fish, and I'm not listening anymore, can't hear anything, I just want to sleep, to hear the sound of sleep curling up into my ears, and only that.

When the season was over, in mid-September, we flew from our island back to Kodiak. The first Sunday back in town, I stood beside Duncan in church, singing hymns, my eyes closed and face uplifted. After four months at fish camp, the congregational voices washed over me like milk. At the end of the service, a family friend strode across the aisle to greet us.

"Duncan! Leslie! How did your season go?" he boomed, his hand extended to Duncan. I knew he was a business executive for a local native corporation. We had been invited over to his house once for a potluck, where I had heard his latest fishing stories—he fished a short subsistence net one day each summer to stock his freezer.

"Oh, we got a few fish." Duncan smiled a bit wanly. We were both still shell-shocked.

"A few fish, I bet!" he grinned knowingly. Then he turned to me. "Leslie, you pick any fish?"

"A few," I said, in the same killer understatement, too tired to care about accuracy or making a good impression.

"Did you? Well, let's see your hands! You know, you can tell a lot by someone's hands," he said, smiling a wink at Duncan.

I held my right hand out, palm up, looking away. He placed one hand beneath to steady it, with the other he pulled lightly on my fingers then brushed his fingertips over what was left of the skin. His smile dimmed. "Yeah, I guess you did pick a few."

"She picked more than that," Duncan said, putting his arm around my shoulder proudly and squeezing.

I smiled blandly at them both, unsure of what to say, only knowing that I had survived, that there were now eight other months before me to return to college and live a different life, and choosing then to believe that though the seasons would circle around again and chase me back to those waters, that island, every summer for the rest of my life, surely I would live, again.

Leslie Leyland Fields lives in Kodiak, Alaska where she has commercial salmon fished for twenty-eight seasons, and where she travels much of the time by foot, boat, and bush plane. Her books are Surprise Child, Surviving the Island of Grace, Out on the Deep Blue, *and* The Entangling Net. *Learn more online at www.leslie-leyland-fields.com.*

ANA MARIA SPAGNA

★ ★ ★

Saw Chips in My Bra

IN A VALLEY OF STEEP TRAILS, MACGREGOR IS THE steepest trail we maintain. We're clearing the trail of wind-blown logs today, Scott and I, and it will be one long walk, with work besides: we will gain 7,000 feet in 7 miles. Then we'll turn around and hike seven miles back down. I'd like to say that it's run-of-the-mill stuff, par-for-the-course, but the truth is that no matter how many times we've done it before, MacGregor mountain is daunting. I slept fitfully last night, and choked down a humongous plate of eggs and cheese this morning. Now we are at the trailhead preparing the gear. Scott will carry two liters of saw gas and a liter of bar oil, a folding saw, a small axe, and some wedges. Since I have worked on this trail crew for the National Park Service longer than Scott has—twelve years instead of two—I will carry the chainsaw. Since Scott is eight inches taller and eighty pounds heavier than me—there's no way around it—the tourists we pass will do a double take.

Sure enough, an hour up the trail we pass a couple of older fellows, experienced old-timey hikers with knickers and wool caps.

"Look at this," one says loudly to the other, gesturing toward Scott and me, "I guess chivalry really is dead."

Several responses come to mind, but because humility is the central code of the work we do, we each give the most generous response.

"She's the boss," Scott says with a grin. He smiles because he is unfailingly polite, not because he is conspiratory. The codgers prefer to take it as a joke, and they laugh heartily.

"He's doing all the hard work," I say.

Here's how it works: I am the sawyer, and Scott is the swamper. When we reach a fallen tree lying across the trail, or lengthwise down the trail, or dangling down into the trail at face-slap height, it is my job to cut it. It's Scott's job to topple the cut logs off the trail. Sometimes the logs are very heavy, a hundred pounds or more, and Scott is wicked strong, so I am not lying when I tell the tourists that he is doing the hard work. But I'm not telling the whole truth either.

We reach a series of steep switchbacks into which several dead willows protrude, effectively blocking travel. A pestilence hit the willows nearly ten years ago and killed them all over the district. Ever since then, these dead willows have been the bane of our trail crew existence. The limbs harden into spearlike points that crisscross and point outward, leafless and barkless, at treacherous angles. And rarely do we encounter a lone willow. Willows grow (or, I should say, *used* to grow) in clumps four or six feet up the steep cutbank. That's where I'll have to cut these today. I remove the saw from my shoulder, put foam plugs in my ears, set the choke, and pull the starter cord a few times. (Sometimes we say that the saw is called an 026 because that's how many times you have to pull it to get it to start: twenty-six.) When it finally starts, I put the chain brake on and balance my way up the precarious bank. Then I set the bar into the jackstraw, release the brake, and begin to saw. The willows release one at a stubborn time, while Scott struggles to yank them free, and tosses them down the hill.

After a while, the codgers catch up with us, and they watch for a while as I slide down the bank, don my pack, and throw the saw back over my shoulder—the saw teeth in the leather glove of my right hand, the power head resting on my pack—and march toward the next switchback.

One fellow whistles through his teeth and shakes his head. Then he turns to Scott, "Can't even keep up with her, can you?"

The remark, well intentioned though it may be, is inappropriate: condescending to me, offensive to Scott. But what's there to say? Scott grins again, shrugs, and shoulders his pack.

On one level, the story ends here. Codgers meet the twenty-first century. One friend, a particularly beautiful blonde, once rolled down the window of the dump truck she drove to announce to a gawker: "Yeah, girls drive big trucks these days." Ditto for chainsaws, you might say. After fifteen years as a girl laborer, I think it's time to admit that the story is not that simple. I'm not sure it ever will be.

The fact that women are intellectually equal to men has been proven. If women are forced to prove it, or worse, prevented from proving it, the injustice is clear as day. The parallel in my world is troublesome: the fact that women are *not* physically as strong as men has been proven. When women attempt to prove otherwise, and worse, are prevented from trying to prove otherwise, the injustice is clear as mud.

This sawing and swamping business is a case in point. I swamped for five seasons before I ever touched a chainsaw. As apprenticeships go, mine was on the long side. Most laborers would snatch up the saw sooner. If my gender played a role (and it did) so did my own uncertainty, my own hesitancy, and a certain perverse obstinance. I swamped to prove that I could. Swamping is pure grunt work. The few tricks—to push with your legs, to pivot rather than lift, to grab from the trunk and not the branch—take a day to learn, not five years, and frankly they don't make much difference when your own weight and that of the log are roughly equal. When you're doing trail work, swamping especially, size matters. Anyone can see it. Don't think it doesn't hurt me to say so. When I was swamping, the sawyer had to cut the logs smaller, which took more time and more gas, not a lot more maybe, but enough to notice, enough to make me humble, and sometimes frustrated.

The flip side is that it's a lot easier to for me to drag my 120-pound self up 7,000 feet than it is for Scott to drag 200. Pure physics. Then there's endurance. Women have more of it, and the lion's share of trail work requires endurance. Endurance alone determines how well you survive the end of the day, or the end of the year, or the end of twelve or fifteen years. And, of course, I'm hardly alone. On this district alone, the mechanic is a woman, the fire crew is more than half women, there's a woman orchardist and a woman arborist. None of these women has gained their position easily, but neither have they complained much. One oft-quoted trail crew maxim is: never show weakness. And we haven't. At least not often. Still there are days when I wish like hell I were as strong as Scott.

Scott is a gentle and capable guy in his late thirties, my age. He's flexible and laid back and clean cut, the son of a banker with a finance degree of his own, who chose the seasonal life of a fly-fishing guide over a suit and tie. A few years ago, his wife's career brought them to this remote valley where the fly-fishing is too lousy to justify guides, so Scott works on trail crew to earn a paycheck, and because he likes to be outside.

That's why I work on trail crew, too, or at least why I started. I like the wind-in-your-hair, sun-on-your-face romanticism, and I like the burn-in-your-calves, achy back physicality. I realized, with increasing dread as college neared an end, and a career—*any* career—beckoned, that it was not enough for me to get to a little exercise on the side. I thought vaguely about coaching PE, or being a travel writer in some adventurous *National Geographic* way. But while those might be outdoor jobs, they are not *physical* jobs. And that's what I wanted. I know this is hard for some people to fathom. I have heard from many people over the years how their parents raised them to be able to live off their "brain instead of their back." I was so removed from any generation that made money from back-breaking labor that surely no one saw it coming to warn me away. Least of all me. They don't tell you about trail crew at Career Day.

About half way up, Scott and I stop for lunch and look out at snow still lingering on the sea of jaggedy peaks on the horizon. The day has blossomed into a gorgeous early summer day, warm enough to sweat. We are tired, but not terribly so. There are logs down, but not terribly many. The season is still young. Avalanche lilies droop at the end of their short run, while paintbrush and lupine grow vibrant and bushy. It is, I have to admit, an awfully nice office.

I shoulder the saw and continue up the switchbacks. Gas is, apparently, leaking from the saw onto my pack, and the smell, against all odds, is familiar enough to make me nostalgic. Once I picked up the chainsaw, more than a decade ago, I never put it down. Not just because it is easier than swamping, but also because it gives you something to think about. The complicated angles, the tension and compression, the movement of the log as you saw, make the straightforward job both challenging and satisfying. I started this work because I liked the setting, but I've continued it for a million reasons. The pleasures and discomforts have melded together—the smell of saw gas and pine needles, the taste of mountain water in a dirty plastic bottle, the too familiar annoyance of saw chips in my bra.

Truth is, these days I do grow weary. I can feel the downslide to forty in the knot between my shoulder blades, in the numbness in my hands in the middle of the night, the sharp pain under my heels after a long hike. For every move that keeps me in shape there is one that tips me farther toward being unable to do this work anymore. I see that possibility on the horizon these days more realistically than I did for many years, and it is daunting, more daunting even than MacGregor mountain. But I know the rule: never show weakness. So I shoulder the saw yet again and continue up the trail.

When, finally, we reach the backcountry camp at 7,000 feet that is our turnaround spot, it is nearly three in the after-noon, just enough time to take the chainsaw apart, shove it into my pack, and hightail it down. The sun has dropped westward, and we head directly into the blinding rays, telling old stories, ones we've told before probably, then drifting into a comfortable silent rhythm, part daydream, part mindless plodding, as we slip past one switchback then the next, through sedgy wildflower meadows and doghair thickets, past the fresh cut logs we've left in our wake, and, at last, to the truck at the trailhead.

As it happens, the codgers sit nearby awaiting a shuttle bus ride. One of them sticks out his thumb gamely and raises an eyebrow, and normally—though it's against government regu-lations—we'd offer the ride, but not today, not to them. Scott

and I each shrug in mock helplessness, then once we're a safe
distance down the road, turn and face each other and shrug
again. And grin.

*Ana Maria Spagna has maintained hiking trails in the North
Cascades for the past fifteen years. Her first book* Now Go Home:
Wilderness, Belonging, and the Crosscut Saw *examines life from
the perspective of the trail and tells the story of making a home on
the fringe of wilderness. She lives and works in Stehekin,
Washington.*

* * *

After the Mountain Men

WITH TEN MILES UNDER MY BOOTS AND TEN DAYS' supplies on my back, I arrived at the brink of a glacier-scoured cirque where lay a chain of granite-clad lakes. Boulders wrapped in black moss garlands lined a lake's outlet stream while above the creek my gaze followed the graceful lines of exfoliating granite and melting snowfields locked in a mutual embrace. Wildflowers—bistort and paintbrush—stood in dabs of white and scarlet in a meadow of tall, lush grass that asked to be laid down in. The ranges north of Yellowstone had enchanted me from the first time the snow clouds lifted the year I moved to Bozeman. Spanish Peaks, the Gallatin Range, the Absaroka-Beartooth Wilderness: mountain names that ran through my mind like those of beaus in a secret black book. On my dance card for this week was a remote quarter of the Beartooth Range.

As I came to know the mountains each chain revealed its singular character, resulting from a unique marriage of geologic history, elevation, and the paths of storms. I assigned each range a signature wildflower and an emblematic stone: Indian paintbrush and volcanic geodes for the Gallatin Range;

mountain heather and garnet gneiss for the Spanish Peaks. My current perch in the Rainbow Lakes cirque basin was a platform of glacier-polished granite, split by frost like a block of firewood. I reached into the crevice, picked a stem of wild chive, and put it between my teeth. In this gesture I found the flower and the stone that spoke to me of the Absaroka-Beartooth Wilderness, and for this place in particular, the Lake Plateau.

Through such private rituals of attention I moved beyond enchantment to call these mountains home. The Spanish Peaks, three ranges and valleys west of the Lake Plateau and a half-hour from my front door near Bozeman, was the wild place I knew best, where I spent sweet summer afternoons wandering in the mountain heather past ancient outcrops of migmatite—a species of gneiss that had endured enough heat and pressure to melt—swirling with blood-drop garnets. The Lake Plateau was as far as I could get from the Spanish Peaks and still be working on my home forest. It was the only place I felt comfortable on a ten-day trip to the backcountry, even in the company of a male colleague. A young woman had recently disappeared from a trail adjacent to the Spanish Peaks, near the Big Sky Resort.

Kari Swensen ran alone on forest paths surrounding Big Sky every afternoon, in training for the U.S. Olympic biathlon team. When she failed to return from a three-miler around Ulerys Lakes a pair of friends scoured her route and were alarmed to see fresh grizzly bear tracks along the trail that Kari had taken. But she hadn't been attacked by a bear; the two men found her the next morning tied to a tree and attended by armed guards. Kari and one of her would-be rescuers were shot in the early morning encounter. The other friend fled. When sheriff's deputies arrived at the scene hours later, the men with the rifle were gone and Kari's friend Richard, shot in the face from close range, lay dead. They found Kari curled in a filthy sleeping bag and bleeding from a chest wound. From her hospital bed in Bozeman she told a harrowing tale.

A grizzled man in late middle-age accompanied by a youth with long, greasy hair had stepped in front of her on the trail and led her to their camp at gunpoint. As evening fell she drew her knees up and accepted the sleeping bag they offered, for all she had against the mountain chill were skimpy jogging shorts and a t-shirt. Time passed and their words became more menacing. *We just want someone to talk to* became *Spend a few days with us*. She slowly learned their purpose—female company for the younger man.

Kari's description of her abductors rang some bells among the sheriff's deputies. Sounds like Dan and Don Nichols, someone said. As word about the fugitives spread, calls poured into the sheriff's office. Every father-son hiking team on every mountain trail in Montana matched their description. They'd been seen in Billings or Ennis or the Cowboy Bar in Jackson Hole. But most likely they were in the Spanish Peaks, keeping to the rough breaks and lonely ridges far from well-traveled trails.

Armed and extremely dangerous, the trailhead posters warned. Backcountry rangers worked in pairs and we kept our radios handy. Some of us were teamed with sheriff's deputies at roadblocks and trailheads to warn backpackers away while helicopters swept low overhead. The Nichols team soon acquired a nickname: The Mountain Men.

Such a title conferred upon these two dirt bags rankled Bozemanites. Until that moment the region's heritage as part of the 1820s fur trade had sat comfortably enough alongside our latter-day pride in local Olympic hopefuls. Our town was named for a mountain man, the trapper and explorer John Bozeman, and there was an annual canoe race on the Madison

River named for Liver-Eatin' Johnson. Though coarse and
ungoverned individuals, the early trappers' violent ways had
long been compressed into benign, if not heroic, legend. I'd
thought of them as various incarnations of the capable and
honorable Dick Summers of A. B. Guthrie's novels. Now the
mountain men of history faded into disreputable myth, and
Summers was replaced by kidnappers, murderers.

Time split like the waters on either side of a divide: before
and after the mountain men. Before, I had hiked alone in the
Spanish Peaks ankle-deep in mountain heather and over ribs
of naked gneiss, rock nearly as old as the earth itself. After the
mountain men, the peaks and meadows no longer welcomed.
While refuge for armed renegades these mountains could no
longer shelter me.

Before, the people I encountered on hiking trails were part
of a clan with nothing to fear from one other. Criminals did
not backpack; they lurked in alleys and city parks. After, a dis-
trustful reticence displaced the natural warmth people felt toward others on the trail. Every group of hikers I met had at
least one large, intimidating dog, a pistol clearly displayed, and
tight smiles that did not come easily. We asked each other as
we passed, "Seen anything?" and when we shook our heads in
reply we left each other with a few moments of relief.

Other than helping with trailhead patrols ("I'm sorry that
you drove all the way from Illinois to hike this trail but I really can't recommend it...") I suspended my trips to the
Spanish Peaks for the rest of the summer, and even in the distant Absaroka-Beartooth Wilderness apprehension dogged my
steps. One night I woke suddenly to the sound of branches
snapping outside my tent. I raised my head and listened hard
but all I could hear was the prattle of the creek and an inter-
mittent wind in the trees. Overcast had moved in behind the
setting near-full moon, and when I peeked out of the tent fly

I saw only dense, inky darkness. Then came another snap—too close. Then a sound like scrambling footsteps—certain, definite, human. Someone was out there.

I felt around for something to use for a weapon and considered shouting for my partner but his tent was pitched beside the creek where even if awake he probably wouldn't hear me. A shout would only alert the intruder to my presence, my femaleness, my fear. Sleeping bag wrapped around me like a shawl, I sat cross-legged with one hand clasped on a flashlight until dawn began to seep through the spruces.

"Looks like you had a rough night," Phil said as he saw me stumbling around camp. He poured water into a bowl of instant oatmeal. "Bear anxiety?"

"I would have been relieved to know it was a bear."

After further questioning he revealed that he'd gotten up in the night to pee and without a flashlight had run straight into a tree. "I was trying to be quiet," he said.

August passed, September passed, and the sheriff's posse, a SWAT team from Billings, the National Guard's low-flying helicopters, and a horde of volunteers were still after the mountain men. Along the rugged crest of the Spanish Peaks, Don Nichols and his son left a cold trail of campsites and hastily emptied caches. The mountain men traveled on foot in terrain no horse or helicopter could penetrate, in mountains that no one knew better. The faces on the trailhead posters faded in the summer sun but they stayed vivid in my mind. The elder man's eyes looked downward with a resignation that said he'd been there before, sitting for a prison mug shot. His son glanced upward and away from between long parted bangs with a sweet, shy smile, a photograph from his high school yearbook.

The searchers brought home stories of food caches, dugout

hideaways, and turnip gardens they'd found in the Spanish Peaks. Hikers counted coup on them, returning from trips with scraps of abandoned gear. Cabin owners reported odd break-ins, the canned peaches missing while stereos and cash went undisturbed. An outfitter claimed to have seen them near his camp and boasted that he'd fed them without mentioning it to the sheriff. Already these mountain men had begun to go the way of their nineteenth-century namesakes, the stuff of legend, tomorrow's heroes.

"I can't believe they've got gardens up there," I said to one of the deputies.

"I've seen 'em," he said.

I raised a skeptical eyebrow. I could barely coax a crop of turnips from the ground in Bozeman before frost. How could these guys farm at 9,000 feet?

"Over by the Beartrap," Bobby said, referring to the ten-mile Beartrap Canyon on the Madison River, nestled against the forests of the Spanish Peaks but thousands of feet lower than the highest crags.

I considered. Beartrap Canyon was low and dry enough for prickly pear cactus and poison ivy, a place where warm winds stirred on December afternoons while the rest of Montana was knee-deep in snow. It was possible that somewhere among the dark metamorphic boulders, abandoned gold prospects, and forests that fanned upward from the Beartrap to the Spanish Peaks and Cowboy Heaven, Don and his nineteen year-old son were holed up, harvesting their turnips and hiding from the law.

The low light of October raked blond-cured grasses on the shoulders of the Spanish Peaks as the search for the mountain men narrowed to Beartrap Canyon. I had assigned graphic granite as the canyon's patron rock—a pinkish mix of clear quartz and interlocking feldspar crystals that resembled chiseled hieroglyphics when the rock was broken on end. Its flower was wild iris, a moisture-loving plant that grew in the gravel soil along the Madison River not far from where the prickly pear bloomed. While hiking along the riverside trail with my litter bag full of beer cans I would wish people a good day as if greeting them in my office. How much more did Don Nichols, born a mile down the road and a lifelong inhabitant of this country, consider the Beartrap his?

In the middle of December the manhunt came to an end. The mountain men were camped in a draw and a rancher checking his cows spotted campfire smoke. It seemed unlike Don Nichols, who had slipped through the forest like a shadow for months, to become careless enough to camp within a mile of the road and let the smoke from his sputtering fire drift into the big Montana sky. But the weather had gathered early into one of the coldest and snowiest winters in years, so perhaps he'd had enough of hiding out, wet and hungry and barely alive. His son must have had more than enough, particularly after the failed quest for female company and no prospect of another. Perhaps the smoke signal was a gesture of surrender.

The sheriff found the mountain men crouched under soaked tarps beside their smoky campfire. He must have wondered how to announce himself as he peered over the edge of an outcrop with a shotgun in his hand, knowing who hunkered there below. He settled for a standard greeting in rural Montana at that time of year.

"You boys seen any coyotes?"

For most of us the story of the mountain men settled into history. Kari Swensen had recovered, mostly, and though she missed the Olympics she was slowly regaining her strength. The following summer, Forest Service rangers hiked the Spanish

Peaks again and rediscovered the art of friendly greetings on the trail. But the legend of Dan and Don did not die quietly, and I found myself in odd sympathy with them. While not excusing what he'd done, I pictured with sadness Don Nichols behind bars for the rest of his life, a wild creature in a cage and forever banished from the mountains he loved. Near the trail where Kari had been kidnapped stood a pine tree carved with these words of defiant claim: *Dan and Don Nichols live in these mountains.*

I was glad they no longer lived there. But I couldn't disagree with what Don had told the sheriff on his way to jail: the white man's world was a mess, and the hills offered freedom and escape. In short, he fled to the mountains for the same reasons I did and the fears, regrets, and paranoia that drove him deeper into the backcountry were only a few shades darker than my own. We shared a love of place and despair over greed and materialism. I had only learned the game of fitting in better than he had. Or I was more willing to play.

Dan and Don belonged to the mountains but their ways, like those of the original mountain men, belonged to an earlier time. It was no longer accepted practice to poach game all summer and leave caches in the wilderness and obtain a girlfriend through abduction. In an age when the wilderness itself was nearly gone, we all helped to perpetuate what was left of it by no longer living there. I lived as close to wild country as I could, and chose a rock and a wildflower to make each range of mountains mine. A superficial gesture, but it tried to say the same thing that was carved into that pine tree. The mountains did not belong to me, but I to them.

On the first anniversary of the kidnapping I camped beside my favorite alpine lake in the Spanish Peaks. That evening I climbed a spur ridge to the high divide where waters spilled south into the Madison River, north into the Gallatin. Pines bronzed by the setting sun cast long shadows down the slope. Rising trout broke the silver surface of the lake below, sending rings across the pale reflections of the sky. I paused at the place where one of the Nichols' food caches had been discovered. A pile of tumbled rocks, no more noteworthy than a fallen-down cairn or the abandoned scour of a mountain goat, marked the spot.

I sat beside the rubble of the cache and gazed across to Cedar Mountain, its solemn face blue with dusk. Between us rose the headwaters of the creeks where Dan and Don hid out, a network of traces that carried snowmelt to the Madison River. Ulerys Lakes lay obscured by trees. Glints of water gleamed dull pewter in the failing light, like shards of a broken mirror.

From the divide each branch of water was a dark crease in the forest, its rushing cascade rendered silent by distance. But the names of the tributaries repeated themselves in my mind, recalling events that took place among them the year before. The young man shot and left to die, the Olympic athlete bleeding in an old sleeping bag, unable to help her friend or herself. The sudden whop of a helicopter, flattening a field of wildflowers in its wash before it disappeared over the next ridge. The faces on the trailhead posters that had disappeared months before, now lingering like campfire smoke among the forests of Hammond, Jack, and Moonlight creeks.

Sundown brought a chilly wind and I started back to camp. Traversing the flowered ramps between spines of stone, I found that mountain heather and garnet gneiss reassuringly cradled my steps. The Spanish Peaks were home again, but it was a different sort of home, a place—like Bozeman—where I no longer left the car keys in the ignition or the front door unlocked.

I'd nearly reached my tent when I spied a man walking along the lakeshore. His hair was long, like Dan's. Streaked with gray, like Don's. But now, on the far side of the divide that had split the world into Before and After, I saw that there had passed a second "After," the one that set me safe again. The man's loose shirttails and unshaven face caused no concern. He carried a fly rod in one hand and a creel in the other. We raised our arms in greeting and made our way back to our snug and separate camps.

Susan Marsh lives in Jackson Hole, Wyoming where she works as recreation and wilderness staff for the Bridger-Teton National Forest. Her essays have appeared in Orion, North American Review, Bugle, *and* Talking River Review, *among others, and have been anthologized in collections including* Ring of Fire, The Leap Years, *and* Going Alone.

✳ ✳ ✳

Near Misses:
Two Seasons at 9°

"EXCUSE ME WHILE I DROP MY TROUSERS," ALEX SAID from a few paces behind me. The sound of Velcro unsticking followed this announcement.

I kept my binoculars trained on the trees above, trying to see if their leaves had "winged rachises," a concept I had only encountered in theory before this job. It was hard to see anything in the midday glare.

After a moment I said, "Want the tape?"

"No," my waggish *jefe* said, apparently pulling his rain pants back on. "No, I think I escaped the invertebrate scourge this time." He walked up to join me and brushed at my shoulder. "You, however, did not. I think you hit a tick bomb."

If you had floated straight up from where Alex and I stood, brushing away the spider webs and Inga branches, the canopy ants and lianas, you would have emerged into the hot blue air of lowland dry season. The sun would have shone, implacably white and fierce, directly into your eyes. Spinning slowly, you would have made out the scalloped extent of our island, leaf-shaped in the sweet lake waters dredged brown with silt. The guayacan trees were flowering then, and their lemon-yellow blossoms starred the canopy and lay across the trails, crumpled like girls' dresses. All around us was green in the dry shades of palms and nameless lime- and aloe-colored leaves.

In that country I had three constants: the island, the earth, and Alex. I worked as his field assistant on Barro Colorado Island, a field station run by the Smithsonian Tropical Research Institute. The island was born when the neighboring river valley was flooded to create Lago Gatun, a feeder supply of fresh water for the Panama Canal. Barro Colorado used to be a hilltop; now it hovers in the constellated midst of dozens of smaller islets. Famous for its research, the island hosts people from all over the globe as well as other luminaries like (once) a harpy eagle, a false vampire bat, and a resident, recurrent crocodile named Gloria. Several crocodiles have held the name over the course of the years.

The Canal channel runs through the lake, straight past the station. Great ships thresh slowly by, dozens a day, stained with black oil or sunk low in the water with huge loads of boxes. Cars, probably, Alex said. I didn't understand how a brisk ocean storm wouldn't just sweep the crates right off the ship's deck. As we drove by the channel, our dinghy bumping over their wake, the ships looked like ruined cities sailing implacably past: desolate places, empty of humans and run by motors and the revolving eye of the sonar beam. At night, their lights were amber and red on the water.

When I consider the four months I spent in Panama, it astonishes me how confused the events become. There remains a distinction between wet and dry seasons, but otherwise everything that happened while I was there—the 2004 elections, Alex's broken toe, adventures with sundry reptiles and flora—merge into a circular tapestry in which everything refers back to itself. Some highlights, mostly avian, stand alone and bright like flares: my first motmot or ibis, my only vampire bat. Unlike flares, though, they do not guide me in any direction, and they light only themselves.

If the events of those times are marked by anything, it is the people I came to know from around the globe. At one point my co-workers represented five continents and ten countries. April, who became a close friend, had come from Australia via Fiji before moving on to Africa. My darling Christoph was German. Two girls from Canada were working for a massive census operation that kept tabs on all the trees in a plateau plot—and so on. Although the months wash together, I recall a sort of pre-Christoph era, and a time when April doesn't figure in my memories. Still, I never know if she was simply away from the island, or if he was asleep, or out netting, or possibly still in Germany and we had not, had never, met.

The fieldwork itself, while it formed the very structure of our days, was a regime I took for granted. Rarely did I devote much time to consider anything beyond its immediate, callusing implication. I knew that each core we took, each air sample we mapped in blue and red lines on the chromatograph, was a step closer to Alex's dissertation. But, increasingly, they were steps closer to the time when I would leave Panama. Or maybe I had trouble remembering what the end goal was. After four months of twelve-hour days, the work took on its own raison d'être.

Alex was writing his doctorate on nitrogen fixation by tropical legumes, and to that end our days went something like this: In the morning, we left the island by boat, or on some occasions hiked up to a plateau of old-growth forest. There, the trees were green leviathans and the forest floor was clear to our trails and spying.

We took random soil cores with mallets and PVC pipe, or spent the time surveying for the right trees, our necks arched backward for hours to gaze up through binoculars. Those plateau days were the worst for ticks; brushing past shrubs and low branches we knocked them onto our shoulders and backs in a silent, steady rain.

In the afternoon, we'd take our packs full of dirt and head home, scorching in the midday heat. There would be lunch, sandwiches usually, and a shower where I peeled off my ticks with masking tape. Then we would spend another five hours or so sorting through the cores with tweezers, looking for the root nodules that signaled nitrogen fixation. These nodules were tiny—the size of rice grains—and glowed a dull white beneath the red and black clay.

If our fieldwork was the skeleton of our time there and other people its pulsing beat, then the island itself was its transcendently gorgeous incarnation. All around us was wonder. We walked past trees with buttress roots ten meters wide, flaring thin and winged to flank the trail. In deluges, land crabs the size of mangoes skittered balefully across the path, regarding us with tiny dark eyes. Cacao trees flowered weirdly, their cauliflorous blooms ballooning straight from their trunks. Lianas fell dozens of meters to coil roughly, thick as my waist, at the tangled floor. And the birds! Jewel-like, spangling the forest's dark veil. Dove-gray tinamous with their marble-sized brains and unearthly calls that sounded like people playing wine glasses. Mealy Amazon parrots flying in raucous pairs above the canopy. Emerald hummingbirds zipping to *Heliconia* flowers; blue-faced antbirds swooping across the trails; a trogon sitting regally in the branches above.

My dreams changed. The howler monkeys woke us at

dawn, with roaring that sounded like a charging steam engine. Just before they started, I'd remember images of red-capped manakins hurrying through the underbrush on little human feet; incongruous spruce grouse beating drums with African rhythms. The cove waters at evening, stained golden and lilac, still appear in my dreams, as do the bats.

When I met Christoph, he was working on his doctorate in ecology, studying how Lago Gatun bat communities had changed in response to a massive fragmentation event ninety years before—the flood that created the lake. He drove a boat out to smaller islands and caught bats all night with transparent mistnets. I went out netting with him three times. With me stumbling through the dark over angled trails and palm leaves, we circled the island's nets and I watched as he disentangled the bats and put them in cloth bags to carry back to camp. Occasionally the nets caught other things. I saw giant cockroaches, glinting copper in our headlamps' light; long, delicate walking sticks tangled high in the canopy nets, twenty meters above the ground. When April was his assistant, they caught a mottled owl and showed me pictures the next day. In one, the owl glares directly at the camera, its furious eyes violet in the flash.

Christoph or April took down each bat's vitals—weight, sex, reproductive status, number of wing mites. She always read the scale numbers out in German, with her Melbourne accent. Then they tagged them with tiny ID necklaces and let them go. The nectar-eaters were fed from a bottle of sugar water to pay them back for the alien-abduction stress of the last few minutes. Sometimes they'd be too tired to fly away immediately, and Christoph hung them head-down from a clothesline stretched over his head. Otherwise, he held them in both hands and let go. They flew right past my face, close enough that the breeze from their wings swept my hair. That is the feeling I remember in dreams.

There are plenty of tiny stories. The time when Alex and I went out to my first off-island site, and when we stopped for water he tossed his pack down in a nest of *Paraponera*: two-centimeter-long bullet ants with an incapacitating sting. When they're roused to fight, they keen a high battle whine and emit a compound that smells like garlic. I have a terrible sense of smell, so the second event did not help me, and Alex's pack muffled the shrill noise of the ants. When he hefted it to swing it cavalierly over his shoulder, they were furiously swarming over the straps and back. Cursing, he dropped it and jumped out of the way, gesturing me back to higher ground.

Once we forgot our randomly selected study plot numbers, and I sat down under a liana tangle in the shade to spin some out with a stopwatch. When I got up, I ducked past the hanging ropes of plant, just missing one with my shoulder, and walked up the slope to where Alex stood taking notes on the tree. He turned to look as I came toward him, blanched, and said loudly, "Oh, Holy Mother of God!"

"What?" I yelled back, a meter from his face.

He pointed. Balanced on the liana tangle that I had so narrowly missed disturbing lay coiled a baby fer-de-lance, its amber eye lit with sunflecks. As we watched, its tongue darted out once, twice, and it turned its head slightly in our direction.

"The babies are worst," Alex explained, "because they don't have any self-control yet. They'll give you all the poison they've got in one go. Older ones look scarier, but they won't hit you with as much."

"Which means?"

"If that had been an adult and it had bitten you, we could have gotten you to the hospital on time...depending on where it bit you."

If I had knocked the liana out of my way, the snake would have fallen directly on my head.

Before they started dredging the lake, it was possible to swim in the island cove. For a while I went out every afternoon, between our fieldwork mornings and the hours spent sorting dirt in lab. A decrepit steel raft floated in the cove, about a hundred meters from shore. I normally dove off the sandpapery dock and swam out, did a few laps around the raft and returned. Slowly. (I should preface this by explaining that I am not a strong swimmer. My earliest memory of trying to swim is of a young instructor holding me under water to make me learn how to hold my breath. At best, I can do a sort of tortoise-like sideways stroke, but mostly it's doggy paddling.) I was twenty meters from the raft one day when I surfaced to see a floating log where none had been a minute before. Treading green water, I eyed Gloria as she glided blithely around. Crocodiles move through the water without seeming to work at all. I made it to the raft and perched there for ten minutes before her surveillance eased and she glided away toward the far side of the cove.

"Hey Lela!" a grad student said at dinner. "Did you know you were swimming with Gloria?"

A tiny anole lizard skittered up a fallen trunk. I watched its movement with one eye as I worked at the soil core jammed intractably in its plastic pipe. Dry season dirt took twice as long to work through, and so we spent even more time crouched in the leaf litter with its armies of chiggers. These

are tiny mites that, horror-movie style, burrow under the skin
and dissolve small quantities of your flesh to consume. They
itch terribly, and people who don't know what they're getting into—like me in October—do not take the right pre-
cautions against these monsters. Even now, I have faint
lavender scars on my stomach from the bites. The ubiquity of
chiggers, and the time it takes people to build up resistance,
means that at any island gathering the bulk of people sat
scratching their ankles and calves, or fidgeting with the attempt not to. I was constantly reminded of some simian re-
lations of ours.

A manakin bird snapped over my head. My fingers were
blistered from breaking up dirt clods with the tweezers.
Unheroic injuries.

It's human tendency, and mine especially, to pick favorites.
But when it comes to the seasons in Panama, they were so differently beautiful that it's hard for me to choose. The wet season, of course, was all about rain. Gray gusts and squalls
sheeting down across the Canal, blinding us as we drove.
Sebastian, another German grad student, gave me a plastic helmet and visor he bought on Halloween to keep my face dry.
The visor part was antifreeze-green, and the helmet read a
convincing POLICE. Midnight downpours woke the howler
monkeys outside my window. And every afternoon, a vertical
green sea: water pouring from the heavens without cease or
restraint. In this climate, paperback books went limp and
curled, leather wallets rotted, and my field clothes started to
smell like mushrooms. I went out netting with Christoph and
the rain slammed down on our blue tarp tent *all night*. No bats
were out, but he had to keep checking the nets anyway, sol-
diering out in a waist-length poncho.

In contrast—clear, glimmering contrast—the dry season was a time of air. By December I noticed a cool, high breeze blowing some nights. "It's like this all the time in the dry season," said Christoph, watching palm leaves flicker. When I came back in February, the rains were over and this breeze blew soft and constant on the water.

My time with him spanned both seasons, yet I don't know what happened when. In January, between stays on the island, I worked briefly in North Carolina and forgot my journal at a Comfort Inn during a surprise snowstorm. When I called later, a woman told me room number 413 didn't exist, and in any case nothing had been turned in. So the first season's thoughts are lost to me, and I have to rely on my sketchy memories to draw it into focus. I remember meeting for the first time, outside the Smithsonian's headquarters in Panama City, sun glaring hazily down and his red hair was bleached almost white in the light. We shook hands, formally. A week later I went out netting with him and Sebastian. That night was when the unreality of my situation finally closed dizzily around me. I climbed out of the boat behind these two boys talking animatedly in their own language and looked behind me. The sun was nearing the lake waters, in plum and scraped-pink, and all the little islands floated calmly Seuss-like in their tufted vegetation. A narrow path led into the forest.

Two nights before I left Panama for the second time, I was in the lab weighing dried litter samples and listening to Brazilian music. Christoph and April were out netting, and I was getting more miserable by the song, thinking about the months—years—ahead without them. I turned off the CD and walked down the hall, into the common room and kitchen. Christoph was standing there in the lowered light. He turned as the door shut behind me, and beamed broadly at my delighted face.

"I'll live," he said cheerfully.

Then I noticed his left hand, held close to his stomach. A gash ran three-quarters of the way around his thumb, and both arms were scraped raw to the elbow.

"Oh my God!" I yelped.

"He'll live," Alex said briskly, appearing back in the room. "I washed out the bite already. You sit down now."

Christoph obediently sat down and held out his arm.

"What happened?" I asked.

"A crazy spider monkey attacked us. Oh, wait," he said as Alex pulled out the iodine. "There is a wonderful herbal tonic up in my room—"

"None of that, mister," Alex said. "We're using Western medicine tonight."

People had started to gather round. "A spider bit you?" the island mammologist asked. "You're going in for a rabies shot tonight, I hope."

"What happened?" I hissed at April, who had materialized next to me.

"Oh, he was amazing," she said, beaming. "This crazy male spider monkey showed up as we were setting up the canopy nets, and started yawping and scent-marking all over the place."

"A lone monkey?" said the mammologist. "That's weird."

"You got the pre-exposure already, but you need the second shot series," Alex said, winding tape around Christoph's wrist. "The game wardens are waiting to take you in."

The ride into Panama City was strangely great. We slid along the lake surface, lit only by the small red lamp of the games wardens' boat. Close to Gamboa dock we passed the dredging operation, lit and humming with machinery, but mostly it was the dark sky and water, and red shadows, and the wardens' murmured conversation behind us as they drove. The wind made it almost too loud to talk.

When we reached the pier, we climbed into a waiting Jeep and started the curving drive down to the city. "*¿Entonces, que pasó?*" one of the wardens, Mario, asked. *What happened?*

"A monkey attacked us as we were setting up our mist-nets," Christoph said in Spanish.

"A monkey?"

"A spider monkey. It jumped onto our nets and started tearing them apart, and then it came after us. We tried to get back to our camp, but it beat us there and started throwing things around."

He had told April to get back to the boat while he followed, but in the melee the monkey lunged and bit him.

"*La rabia,*" Mario said.

"*Si, entonces necesito la vacuna.*"

The private hospital was elegant and empty. Two doctors waited aimlessly in the emergency room, swooping on Christoph as soon as we walked in. Two and a half hours later, he walked out with stitches in his hand and a bottle of antibiotics. "I've never taken these before," he said, bemused.

"Well, you better take them this time," I said, shocked. "You were bitten by some wild primate! Who knows what awful things are swimming around in your blood now!" I paused. "When do you have to come back for the next shot?"

"I didn't get the first one," he said. "They don't have any rabies vaccine here. The Ministry of Health doesn't either."

"What?"

"Well, I don't know, but that's what they said. I have to go to this place in the morning," he said, waving a slip of paper, "so I have to stay in the city tonight."

We checked into the Hotel Lisboa, in a part of town I hadn't seen before.

"If this were Africa, it would be a different story," Christoph said mildly. His elegant hands were crossed over his chest, the stitches lividly visible. "I just read about these people who caught some monkeys carrying Ebola."

I went to the window and looked out. The Lisboa's sign glowed crimson in the open air, casting a faint pink light onto the street below.

This feeling of awful nostalgia in the present, for things still surrounding me, has occurred elsewhere in my life—in the final months of college, for instance—but never as strongly or sadly than at field stations. Even with a place like Barro Colorado, where people reliably turn up again and again, the pang is there. In these field camps of the world, people are thrown together for a brief, intensively scripted moment. They know what they need to do with every instant of their time, down to the last sample; they know the precise hour of their departure.

What no one can count on is the alchemy that crackles to life between people, and that is what makes departure so painful. April, who is in Uganda as I write, e-mails to tell me about her work there, and I read it moments later, so that in a sense she may as well be next door. But, of course, she isn't, and the connection is kept cruelly strong through these artificial means. It is the expectation of separation that makes the moment so dear to us, as with every part of life. In fieldwork, though, the end is known from the outset, as our own deaths are not.

*

Back on the island the next afternoon, the light was a hazy pale pink, equatorial sun glaring through a conch. Playing euchre on the balcony with April and the Canadian girls, I was having trouble paying attention. The sharp lines of diamond and spade seemed to warp and twist in the gauzy light, Rachel's shocking blue eyes, the hiss of the deck itself playing out on the table. The face cards, flipped over, stared straight at the geckos stuck to the ceiling. I imagined a show-down: Jack of Spades versus translucent amphibian. The jack would pull a vicious little knife from his boot; the gecko would wrap him in its cold gluey tongue and pull him in, his feet kicking vainly.

"Pick it up," April said. The king of clubs lay on top, waiting.

Christoph walked out of his office and came up the balcony towards us. "What are you crazy people playing?" he asked.

People at the Smithsonian had finally tracked down rabies vaccine for him late that morning, after I left to catch the early boat. He had had to drive out to some seedy clinic, pick up the vaccine, and drive to another medic to have it injected. His left arm hung loosely at his side as he sat down on the chair behind me. I rested my free hand on the top of his foot, tapping out melodies.

Later they switched to canasta. I didn't know the rules, so I pushed myself back against his knees and watched. Sheelah dealt the cards neatly, her wrist playing out in rhythmic little flicks. Some dreamy house music was playing, drifting up on the rising cool wind of evening. There was a plate of green and orange limes next to me, a violet sky to the west, and I felt the clear thin map of Christoph's bones under my fingers. We could have been anywhere, but we were right there.

Lela Stanley has had the tremendous luck to work outside in four countries, from 44'N to 1'S. Interests she hopes to explore include pelagic seabirds, Latin hip-hop, and cooking with garlic. She lives in southeastern Pennsylvania.

* * *

Firefight

"This, ladies and gents, is an M60, a 7.62mm, light-weight, air-cooled, disintegrating metallic link belt-fed, portable or tripod-mounted machine gun designed for ground operations." A staff sergeant with ropy forearms hefts the gun with both hands, performs two bicep curls. "Eighteen pounds of pure rock and roll."

It's 7 a.m., mid-morning by military reckoning. Two hours ago a drill sergeant played reveille on garbage can lids and since then I've showered, dressed, run two miles in Army boots, wheezed through sit-ups, push-ups, six-count burpies, eaten baking powder biscuits with red-eye gravy and apple pie for breakfast. Now I stand at parade rest at the crest of a hill surrounded by undulating acres of green, heels strictly shoulder width apart, hands in the small of my back, listening to a lecture on firing-range procedure.

I'm eighteen—I have never known guns before Boot Camp. Never tasted red dust, inhaled the resiny note of long-leaf pine, wilted under the oppressive weight of southern mid-day sun. Before eighteen I've known little outside the green, damp borders of the coastal northwest but a month ago, in May 1978, the U.S. Army paid my way to Ft. McClellan, Alabama, where the air swims with the scent of blooming camellia, the heat makes my brain buzz, and the grit on my tongue tastes faintly like blood.

Months before, as a recruiter leafed through the list of available military occupational specialties, I asked for "a job as close to combat as a girl can get." To his credit he didn't laugh; he'd recruited enough bored country kids to know exactly what I meant, even if I didn't. This was 1978. Vietnam was still a wound barely healed, a collection of images and stories that would only gradually be revealed over the next two decades. My naïve wish for something like combat was a knee-jerk response to the cramped and prescribed boundaries of a girl's small-town life. My first airplane flight was two weeks before, Seattle to Alabama, more escape than means to a destination. My enlistment contract reads 95B: Military Police, not because I had any aptitude for it, only because it sounded "exciting."

The gun takes two of us to operate, one to man the trigger, one to feed the linked belts of bullets into the ratcheting chamber. The barrel is wrapped in a perforated metal grid that keeps it cool but also gives it an otherworldly look. The finish is opaque, seems to sop up light and reflect nothing. The stock is heavily padded, presses into the socket of my shoulder. Prone behind the trigger, thigh to thigh with a Detroit boy named Davis, I limber up my index finger. His job is to lightly guide the rattling belt of bullets that whip through the dust while I aim and fire at the large square of white paper downrange.

"Maintain your trajectory at target level," the rangemaster harps. Every sixth round in the belts is a red-tipped tracer. It holds a hot, phosphorescent charge that burns white in daylight, illuminates the normally invisible trajectory of bullets. In a few moments the range will appear strewn with ropes of tiny, white lights strung from barrel to target. The maximum effective range of each round is 3,609.1 feet but at the right moment, on the right day, a bullet might travel over two miles before gravity defeats velocity. "Keep those tracers out of the woods," he warns, "it's been a dry spring."

I grip the heavy handle with slick palms, wait for the command to fire, hear the bark of the loudspeaker, then squeeze. Inches from my face, in a chamber the diameter of my little finger, expellant ignites and explodes 9.17 times per second, 550 times per minute; gas expands with each blast; projectiles rifle through space, 2,800 feet per second. My teeth clatter and my eyeballs jump. I feel unhinged and rearranged—I am pushing every lame-wheeled shopping cart in the universe. The barrel fights to rise; my biceps bunch and burn to hold it level. I breathe once, squeeze again, and watch as the red-hot rain of rounds and tracers arcs through Alabama air and the targets riddle and shred before my eyes.

"Cease fire, cease fire!" The command from the range tower cuts through the chaos. The sun has moved high overhead. Far beyond the targets, out of the rolling green lifts a slender spiral of white, and I imagine I can detect the faint, singed-tinder scent of fire. A buzz travels down the line, *something's burning...someone dropped a tracer in the woods*. Drill sergeants spring like they're bee-stung, clearing the range of weapons, amassing us in formation, gathering in a knot, gesturing among themselves toward the thickening tendril of smoke.

"You, you, you, you," one sergeant prowls down the line. "Line up here." Twelve of us break rank and run, arranging ourselves in two lines. I am swept along with the squad, too dazzled at being chosen to wonder what's in store. "Forward, h'arch." We step out, down a two-wheel dirt track. Our boots drum a dusty cadence on the thick red dust. "Double time, h'arch." We trot downhill, toward the smoke.

In two minutes I am out of breath. I often lag behind the pack during morning runs, but today I will not suffer the small, silent humiliation of one who can't quite keep up. We pound down the dirt track in unison, raising a cloud of fine red grit that rasps the eye, works its way between pursed lips. Around our waists we each wear a woven web belt and an assortment of gear: canteen, rolled plastic poncho, flat folding shovel in a green canvas case. My one-size-fits-all steel helmet jounces painfully as I shuffle in time to the drill sergeant's called cadence.

Then the old musk of road dust shifts, becomes mingled with the fresh-lit-cigarette scent of fire. The blaze is out of sight; it's the aroma of burning resin, incense-like, that shows where to enter the forest. I'm winded from the run, pulse hammering at my ears, but now I become aware of another sensation: a coffee-on-an-empty-stomach fizz of adrenaline that makes me quiver. We follow our noses into the verge, treading carefully, as if we expect the long needles and cones to ignite beneath our feet. These trees have no girth worth mentioning, all spindly second growth, angled half-fallen trunks and bare, tangled limbs. The duff is spiked with clusters of needles and foot-long cones glistening with pitch but nothing green; nothing feels alive in this light-deprived understory. We unsheathe our shovels, unbend the metal handles, and as we move through the undergrowth I wonder if anyone knows what to do once we find the blaze.

Ahead, six-inch flames sprout from the litter in a fifty-foot circle. "Fan out." The drill sergeant waves us away. "Just beat the hell out every flame you find." Within minutes the flames dance themselves high, then higher, climbing the deadfall so that fire flares at eye level. With so little instruction the fire-fighting seems instinctive—some ancient, adaptive response to fire gone out of control. I remember the fire I started as a child when I was supposed to be burning trash, tempted by matches, waste paper, and dry stems of grass. Maybe that was my first real brush with danger: a heart-pounding, boot-stomping frenzy that left me shaking, and curiously happy, even though I knew I'd suffer for the circle of burned pasture as soon as Dad found out. Now, the flat backside of the shovel works to smother small flames, but I have as much success by shuffling my feet and stamping out sparks.

"Make a fire line—like this." In an eerie reversal of authority, one of the trainees has taken over. He seems to know exactly what he's up to, and the rest of the squad follows his lead, turning the shovel blade ninety degrees and locking the collar with a twist. Shoulder to shoulder with the others I stoop and hoe, scraping the duff to bare dirt. Behind us others beat the life out of each glowing point. One section of the fire circle dies, then another springs to life. Laughing and reckless, we hack with more energy than the flames demand. There is a rhythm to our assault, an instinctive choreography of advance, reconnoiter, regroup, that we didn't learn in basic training. One boy trips backward into a bed of glowing cinders, but two more lift him before he knows he's down. Three advance on a new flame, five follow behind, a few patrol the areas we've covered. My original adrenaline-spiked fear has mellowed into fierce confidence and I feel as if I could fight fire forever. When the drill sergeant blows his whistle I check my watch and find that we've been at this for four hours; it seems like a fraction of that time.

The danger is over. The understory is still warm to the touch, still smells charred and resinous. Only now do I realize that my uniform is wringing wet, pocked with holes and singed around the trouser cuffs. My chest aches, my eye sockets seem lined with sandpaper, and my face feels swollen and sore. Our drill sergeant reports in by two-way radio that the blaze is under control and says a C-130 tanker will drench the area as soon as we leave. An olive-drab troop bus pulls up in a gritty billow and we climb on, mute, wrung out. As I lift my boot to the first step I notice my prized spit-shine has dulled to ash.

Evening heat settles around Company E, 12th Battalion like wool. As the bus pulls up our off-duty friends lounge on the concrete steps of the barracks, smoking or learning to smoke. Dinner finished up an hour ago; the mess hall is closed and any leftovers have been discarded or sealed up. All the mess sergeant can offer us is a loaf of white bread, a stick of margarine, and a butter knife. I raise my buttered bread and find a perfect black handprint on white.

Others crowd around, eager to hear about the fire. They spent the day picking up litter; we spent the day on the front lines and have news to report. This is another new sensation in a day of sensory awakenings: being the center of attention for some risky physical feat. Ordinarily I hang in the background, but tonight I describe the flames, the smells, the burns, the boy who tripped, his rescue. Our features are dusky with whorls of soot, like camouflage paint. Someone passes me a cigarette, the first I've ever tried, and instead of declining I lean over the dancing flame for a light. Why not? I feel invincible, as if I've been to war.

Rebecca Goodrich served as an MP in the U.S. Army from 1978 to 1984. She received an M.F.A. from the University of Idaho in 2003 and currently teaches creative writing at Washington State University in Pullman, Washington.

JANE DUNCAN

The Rest of Elvis

My last evening as a guide at Finn Bay, I was sitting with Lance on the deck of the float house savoring a rare moment of late summer sunshine. Finn Bay is located halfway along a temperate rainforest that stretches across the southern coast of Alaska. It is the entrance point to one of the largest pink salmon runs in the state. A half-mile walk inland through a cedar and hemlock forest leads to a rocky waterfall where countless salmon struggle to climb a torrent of water each summer to reach the gravel beds where they spawn. Because the salmon often need several tries to reach the top, they bottleneck below the falls until the creek becomes one writhing mass of fish. With so many salmon it is little wonder that bears congregate in this area.

The U.S. Forest Service built an observatory by the falls where visitors coming by boat or floatplane can hike through the dense vegetation to view the bears. Lance and I spent all season manning the observatory, and now as it was drawing to a close we silently reflected on the summer. Tomorrow morning, I would leave the observatory. I would load my luggage and a week's worth of garbage into a sixteen-foot scow and motor an hour northward to the small coastal town of Sumner, Alaska. I would then catch a plane heading to the Lower 48 and return to school, to the cares of a life that seemed, at that moment, very far away.

I broke the silence. "There's something I want to show you before I leave; something we need to go look for. Come on, we'll take the skiff."

We climbed into a small aluminum boat with a three-horse engine—not a speedboat by any stretch, but it would get us to the opposite shore and back, and that was all we needed. I fired up the engine, and we headed out across the bay. I began, "You know about Elvis, right?" Of course he knew about Elvis. Elvis was a local brown bear who had become something of a local mystery.

The year before at Finn Bay, Elvis was killed by another bear. We found him laying near the trail one morning with his gut slashed open. We didn't regret his demise too much because, as a mischievous juvenile, Elvis had often made trouble around camp, hanging out on our porch and chewing holes in our water tank. He must not have known his place in the bear community either.

The Forest Service decided to remove the dead bear from the area near the observatory, so they boated the carcass down a back channel about a mile from the bay and heaved it onto the bank over the high tide line to keep it from floating away. With so many bears around, we assumed his remains wouldn't last long.

However, a few weeks later some boaters reported seeing a bear carcass floating in the bay without its head. The story made the local newspaper in Sumner: "A Bear Returns, Headless, to Finn Bay." The author of the article suggested that someone had cut off the head and pushed the body into the bay, probably someone with hostility toward the Forest Service (not unlikely) or some kids with too much time.

A couple of local guides lassoed a rope around the floating carcass, pulled it out of the bay, and tied it securely to a tree on the other side of the channel. A few days later, however, some sailors in Finn Bay noticed what looked like the greater part of a bear floating off their starboard side. The local newspaper headline read, "Elvis, Still Alive?"

Lance had heard what had happened to the bear's body, but what I hoped to tell him that night was what had happened to his head.

The previous summer, I worked with a guy named Steven Buckner. He was a handsome, good-natured man who, upon his arrival to Finn, adopted the full beard so common to Alaskans. He had just finished his master's degree, and he'd come north for the same reason I had: a hiatus from the pressures of school. Steven was the one who first spotted the dead bear and alerted Forest Service officials.

One night, a few days later, Steven came back to the cabin with a gleam in his eye and a devious smile.

"What?" I asked him, knowing he had something to tell.

"Oh, I'm just in a good mood," he answered, but I could see he wanted me to press the issue. So I did.

He replied, "I know where Elvis was taken."

"Really?"

"That's why I was late getting here yesterday; I was scoping it out."

Scoping what out? I wondered, but he didn't wait for me to ask.

"I'm going to take his skull home with me as a souvenir."

I looked at him in disbelief, "You are going to row out

there, cut off his rotten, maggoty head, and then what, dig the skull out of it? You're crazy."

"I'll cut off his head, and the crabs will clean it up in a couple of weeks. Imagine how big that thing is!"

"And what do you plan to cut it off with?"

I felt myself being sucked into this morbid scheme, but if he was determined to do it, well, why not join the fun? It wasn't as if I had to do the cutting.

So we looked around the cook cabin for anything that could possibly get through a bear's thick coat and spine. We placed our repertoire of cutting articles on the porch table: the saw from a pocketknife and a pair of pruning shears. They may not have been the perfect implements for the job, but Steven seemed undaunted.

"As much as I would like your help, I will have to do this alone," he asserted. "We need you to stay back at base camp in case someone radios or comes out here in the evening."

I wasn't sure I even wanted to go and *help*, but even if I had, he was right, we couldn't abandon the camp. If our supervisor called and got no answer, she would send a floatplane here in half an hour to see if we were all right. Besides, someone had to be here in case a group of stupid tourists arrived on the scene carrying a picnic basket full of bacon sandwiches intent on luring the bears closer—a scenario that was, surprisingly, not out of the question.

Steven was ready to leave the next evening, which turned out to be a perfect night for it: calm seas, no rain, no one in the nearby tourist cabin, and almost all the visiting boats gone from the bay. Perfect, except that the last group of people still at the observatory showed no sign of leaving.

I was up there with the guests, and Steven was down by the

boats. Dusk was rapidly approaching, and I knew he wanted the whole operation done before it was completely dark. He had two hours at most. With his patience at an end, he called over the radio, "Looks like no one else is coming up for the evening. I'm headed back to the cabin now. Guess I'll see you in *a couple of hours.*"

One of the visitors had just asked me which of us did the cooking. I laughed, as I was pretty certain I would be doing all of the cooking that night and eating it alone, too.

I didn't mind if Steven left while the visitors remained. I could accompany the group down from the observatory alone without a problem. My only concern was that our supervisor Nicole might call from Sumner to see what supplies she needed to bring to us on her next trip out here, but since I knew she wasn't planning to visit for a couple of days, I wasn't too worried...till I heard her voice on the radio.

The guide who was stationed at the trailhead near the boat dock was responsible for answering all calls from Sumner. That's where Steven was supposed to be. I waited to see if he would answer from the rowboat. I heard some repeated static but if it was Steven, he wasn't getting good reception. So, I took over the call, "This is Duncan, go ahead."

"Yeah, I'm planning on coming out tomorrow with some administrative folks—do you guys need anything?"

"Uh, not that I can think of," I replied, hoping she wouldn't try to ask Steven as well.

But she did. "How about you Steven?"

Silence.

"Sumner to Buckner."

Silence.

"Sumner to Buckner, do you read me?"

Nothing, not even static.

"This is Duncan," I broke in. "I think his battery might be dead."

That was my first lie.

Now we were in the adventure together.

I returned to the cabin about the time it was beginning to get dark and saw a note on the table from Steven that read, "Jane, I have a large flashlight, radio with batteries, food and water, bear spray, shotgun, tools, raingear, and rope. I should be fine—don't worry! If the weather gets really bad, I'll turn around. Feel free to give me a call anytime. I'll try to be back before dark, but if not, don't worry; it'll be easy to navigate along the shore. Bringing you back a claw. Wish me luck!"

I radioed him, but as expected, I got no reply. So I waited. It grew darker, and I made dinner. It grew darker still as I ate. I walked down to the shore to see if I could spot his boat, but the sea was empty. In fact, apart from Steven rowing around out there in our only boat, there was no one else for miles— just me standing on the shore with about fifty bears wandering around behind me. I began to worry. I had no way of knowing what was keeping him, and with the radio dispatch closed down for the night, there was no calling for help. Questions paraded through my mind: *What if he'd capsized in the freezing Alaskan waters? What if a bear defending Elvis's carcass as a meal had attacked him? Why was I still standing out here?*

A harbor seal swam close to the shore and snorted at me. I decided to go back to the cabin and make some tea.

Well past dark, my radio startled me out of a half sleep. I heard a smiling voice on the other end ask, "Do you want to come see it?"

I hurried down to the shore feeling tired and relieved. I shined my flashlight on Steven and his prize. They were covered in blood. So was the boat and everything in it. He opened up a garbage sack and showed me the head. It didn't look real.

I smiled and explained, "We've got to do something with that tonight. The admin guys will be here first thing in the morning." I felt like we were cleaning up after a murder.

Luckily, the tide was low. We rowed across the bay to a rocky outcropping which would be submerged when the tide came in, and we buried the head between some curved boulders, keeping it well covered with just enough space for the crabs to enter and clean the skull. Then we set to the task of cleaning up the boat in the dark, and once the worst of it was done, I left Steven to finish up while I went back to the cabin to heat up his food.

"Everything is clean, but I don't know what to do with this rope—I can't get the blood out of it," he said as he approached the cabin.

"Why don't you tie it around a rock in the water and leave it to soak?"

He agreed.

Then I thought about the rest of the bear. "What did you do with the body?" I asked him. "You didn't just leave it on the shore where anybody could see it, did you?"

"I shoved it into the water," he replied, like it was the obvious solution.

"Don't you think it will float?"

He blew off the question. "Nah, maybe for a little while, but it'll eventually sink. I think I'll hide the claws on the roof."

I was glad we weren't accomplices in a real murder.

The next morning when I was up at the observatory, I heard on the radio that Nicole and the others had arrived. Two of the men she brought were speaking to each other by radio. One guy seemed very frustrated, talking about how a random piece of rope floating by the shore had gotten twisted up in their propeller, stalling the motor. I cringed. Nicole would probably ask Steven about that, and I wondered what he would say.

The next thing I heard on the radio was someone talking about a strange object floating in the bay. *A big root wad*, I thought. I'd seen huge ones picked up from the shore on a bull tide. They stuck high out of the water with gnarly roots pointing in every direction. And then I heard, "What do you got over there Steve? Is it a dead bear?" I muffled something between a wheeze and a cough.

So Elvis had returned, as another newspaper article would soon report.

One of the visitors at the observatory was asking me how much the average bear weighed. I thought of returning, "With or without its head?" but sarcasm wouldn't help the situation. I tried to politely answer all of the usual tourist questions, but I really wanted to listen to every word on the radio. I heard Nicole say she would pay one of the local tour guides to get rid of it, and I began to feel very uncomfortable.

As I listened from the observatory, it seemed that every conversation on the radio involved the floating bear. I switched through the marine channels, and even the local boaters were talking about it. I heard one guy offer to shoot a few slugs through it. "That'll sink him. Heh, heh."

I gathered that the unanimous plan was to tie him to a tree on the other side of the channel so the tide couldn't pick him up again. I kept wondering what Steven was doing during all of this. Was he breaking under the pressure?

Then I heard on the radio, "Buckner to Duncan."

"Go ahead," I replied walking to the other side of the observatory.

Casually, Steven began, "I thought I would fill you in on what's going on down here. You remember Elvis, right? Well, his body washed into the bay an hour ago, and get this...he's missing his head! Can you believe it?"

At least I knew we hadn't been found out.

When the time came for us to switch posts, I hurried down to the trail and waited to meet him, smiling anxiously as he approached.

"I kept laughing whenever I thought of you up there listening to everything," he told me. "Get this, the admin guys came to examine the cabin, to see if it was time to build a new one. They looked at *everything*. One guy even climbed up on the roof."

I gasped.

"Good thing I'd decided to put the claws in my sleeping bag instead!"

I punched him.

When I returned to the cabin, Nicole was still there, and she asked me why the pruning shears were on the porch. I told her Steven was using them to clear the way to the outhouse. That was my second lie, and it really bothered me since it came easier than the first.

Anyway, the story made the newspaper, as I said, and it was still a topic of conversation when Elvis showed up in the bay again—this time only a few feet away from where we'd hidden his head.

A couple of weeks later I asked Steven if he had checked on the head yet. I really wanted to know if the crabs had cleaned it off and I didn't think it was my place to go looking without him. He said they had but that it still needed quite a bit of work. I asked him if he thought it would be ready to take with him by the time the season was over, and I was surprised that he didn't seem to want to talk about it anymore. I wondered if he thought the whole thing had become a little creepy.

Right before he left, Steven told me he was worried about smuggling the skull over the border, and so he'd decided not to keep it. I was disappointed. All that adventure for nothing. I toyed with the idea of taking the head home myself, but I still couldn't bring myself to go check on it. It wasn't that I was scared; I just didn't feel like disturbing Elvis anymore.

Steven did not return the next year. He got a job in Nova Scotia as a natural resource specialist. I came back to Finn for another season and thought about going to see the head a number of times, but I kept postponing my visit until that last night with Lance.

I finished relating the story just as we were pulling up to the rocks. A young bald eagle flew out of a moss-covered tree above us. At first I wondered if I would even find the spot again, but when I saw the same curved boulders, I knew exactly which ones to move. They looked like they hadn't been disturbed in all that time. We climbed out of the boat.

"Right under these rocks, huh?" Lance asked.

I paused and looked at him. "Do you think we'll find it?" I was savoring the moment and wondering why I was so nervous. He shrugged. I reached for a stick and pried up the top stone.

There was nothing beneath it. Not a trace of the head Steven and I had left there. I was sure that no one would have found it accidentally, and no animal would have left the stones exactly as we had placed them. Had Steven actually taken it, perhaps deciding it was safer without an accomplice? In the end, had he lied even to me? Lance thought that this was the only plausible answer.

I watched as the young eagle flew back and landed in the tree overhead, and for a moment, I pictured Steven with his devious smile stepping out of the airport with a clean, white bear's skull hidden in his luggage.

Right or wrong, I hoped he had it.

Jane Duncan is currently working on a master's degree in Biology Teaching at the University of Utah. This is her first published work and she dedicates it to her colleague, Steven. (She has yet to get the truth out of him.)

KARLA THEILEN

⋆ ✳ ⋆

Keep Going Up,
Keep Moving On

THE DAY IN LATE SEPTEMBER THAT WAS TO BE MY LAST on Spot Mountain was the very day that autumn crossed the thin and lovely line into winter, drawing the shades down over the sun, slamming the door on Indian summer and her empty promises. No more the sublime days, fierce with life and light, a crescendo of spotless blue, a stroke of burnished gold. Gone were the vanilla notes of sun-warmed ponderosa pine, the cinnamon of buck brush, and the breeze that ruffled yellow leaves of aspen with cool, clean fingers.

On that particular day, morning arrived reluctantly and without pretense; stiff and sore from the cold, dense night. Snow came sideways, carried on a westerly wind, obscuring a bloodless rising sun that spoke frankly of the dim days to come. The season on the lookout tower had wrapped up.

The only fire for miles was the one in my wood stove, crackling and hissing, chasing the cold outside, where it belonged. The spring had slowed to a trickle, just a ghost of its summer self. The ground squirrels had retreated to wherever it was they'd stockpiled the dog food they had pilfered piece by piece from Bandit's bowl all summer long. As snow in the high country crept further down the mountain, so too did the elk in their pursuit of graze, moving incrementally driven by hunger alone.

I was headed to the lowlands, too, but my transition from mountain to valley would take place in just a single day. The Forest Service packer would arrive the next morning with his string of mules to collect my things and deliver them to my pickup truck, waiting patiently next to the Selway River miles below. Bandit and I would walk behind, shuffling through soft pine duff on the trail, milking the last of our summer of solitude.

I'd spent the day cutting firewood for the next season, repairing the screen door, and clearing the area around the lookout of dead limbs and snags to create a defensible space in the event that someday wildfire would decide to make a run for the top. Weary from one day's work that should have been stretched out over the whole season, I propped my feet up in front of the wood stove and settled in to enjoy the fire and the last chapters of my book. Sleet and snow, driven by thirty mph winds rattled the panes of glass that separated me from the raw, ruthless elements.

I poured red wine into a cup from a half-full bottle, no longer to be rationed into thimble-sized portions. The last days of the season are about abundance and frivolity, when precious goods that have been squirreled away become available for unabashed consumption. In addition to the wine, the luxury list contained three cans milk, a half-pound of coffee, a package of fig bars, some Belgian chocolate, and salted peanuts. I had popcorn, tea, and time; a little more precious time.

The first sip of wine was all mine, and so were the moments that followed, filled only with the faint howl of the wind playing bass to the crackling fire. The second sip was cut short, interrupted mid-swallow by the sound of boots on the wooden steps leading to where I was.

Boots. Person. People? I hadn't received a single unannounced visitor all summer. Living at the end of eight miles of trail, and thirty additional miles of sketchy winding dirt road from anywhere does not lend itself to much spontaneous visitation. I'd daydreamed of the unexpected guest, a hiker that would show up one morning for coffee, but this was different, this was night. Bandit sensed my unease and assumed his duties as the assistant manager, barking with authority.

I might have barred the door, crawled into bed with the covers over my head, but one cannot hide in a glass house. Besides, there was something hollow and harmless in the sound of the footsteps; slow and deliberate, each echoing with words like "hungry," "lost," and "desperate." There were a total of fourteen steps the boots had to climb, time enough for me to assume my stance, to don a brave face.

I opened the door for the man attached to the stomping boots. Robed in cold, clean air, he stumbled past me, unfazed by the barking dog, hackles up, teeth bared.

Drunk, I thought. Here was the drunk man I'd been warned about, the only wild animal I truly feared in my mountain home.

"Have you seen him?" he demanded from behind a frosty mustache. The man bore the unmistakable trappings of a hunter; a mix of blaze orange and camouflage, a 30-06 slung over his shoulder.

Before I could speak, he banged the butt of the rifle against the floor and shouted, "Jim!" in reply to a question I didn't ask. "Where is he?" His speech was slow, slurred, insistent.

Out of the corner of my eye I found my bear spray next to the bed where it would be of more use to me in dealing with late-night intruders than to ward off the shy bears that make their living on this mountain.

I assured him no one was there but me.

He scanned the small room in disbelief and stated, "Well, he's got to fucking be here," ripping his cap off to reveal a full head of gray hair, "or we've got trouble," period. He sat down on the edge of the bed and began rocking back and forth, frantically raking fingers through his matted, damp hair which, like a fresh-cut stump, looked conspicuous and raw, as if a ponytail had been amputated from the nape of his neck with a dull bread knife minutes before.

He looked up at me with panic on his brow, fear flashing in his pale eyes. "Oh, we've got trouble, I'm telling you. Trouble...oh, we've got trouble," he chuckled nervously. "Oh, Jesus Lord, we've got some serious trouble," he repeated, shaking his head over and over.

When asked to explain the trouble we were in, he just turned his face to me, silent and hopeless. It was soft and boyish, unsuited for gray hair, age, or trouble. He put his hands to his head and looked back to the floor. After a moment, he looked up again and pleaded, "Listen, we've got serious trouble, and you need to help me out, because I...have got...to go to sleep...goddamnit."

As he stretched onto the bed, visibly shivering, I realized my misdiagnosis: the beginning stages of hypothermia had looked an awful lot like intoxication to my fear-clouded judgment.

I kicked into gear as the resident emergency room nurse. I found my commanding voice.

I ordered wet clothes off. Boots off. Into the sleeping bag you go. There were Army blankets, a dry wool cap, warm drinks to be sipped. Bandit resumed assistant managerial duties by crawling into bed next to him, offering his sixty additional pounds of warmth.

The feet seemed to have taken the brunt of the cold. Pale and waxy, his were refrigerated rubber versions of healthy feet. I mentally referenced my wilderness first aid training, but having worked the previous eight years in the canyons and rivers of the southwest, everything that popped up related to heat exhaustion and dehydration. Scanning the bookshelf for a first aid manual, I found that serendipitously, I had a book on avalanche safety that covered frostbite.

Soaking another person's feet is awkward, especially when the person is a naked stranger, wrapped in every sleeping bag and blanket you own. But as I added hot water to the dish tub, gradually increasing the temperature of the cool water to lukewarm, things began to thaw. His name was Randy. He was from Oregon.

It was the story of a hunting party of two that had become a party of one. One man had made it back to camp at the end of a long day following elk sign, hungry but unscathed. The other, the one with no food, sleeping bag, map, compass, or experience did not return. He quickly became the missing man, the one left alone in the hands of the night.

Randy had been back at camp, stoking a fire, shooting his rifle into the empty black sky to identify his position on the planet, to lead the lost to safety. Still alone at daylight, he had launched a search, an aimless day of wandering, of looking for clues. It led him to my door, the only outpost in this part of the wilderness, where he landed, cold and defeated.

The missing man was Jim, Randy's boss, the owner a sand and gravel company in Oregon. It had been a life's dream of Jim's to hunt elk in the wilderness of Idaho. He'd fancied himself an outdoorsman. He'd gone marlin fishing in Mexico, he'd been on a caribou hunt in Alaska, and now he would shoot biggest bull elk he could find in Idaho, that's what he told Randy.

In lieu of experience, Jim had money. He would hire an outfitter to set up their camp, to pack them in on horseback and leave them to their own devices. Randy had the skills. He knew his place in the woods. This could be seen in the way he carried himself, in the words he used to describe the land-scape, by the knife on his belt, and the eye he kept on the sky. His clothes were made of wool, his boots, leather. He would save Jim the high price of a guide. He was hunter and woods-man, and above all, he was a hard worker. Randy would see to it that Jim got his elk, that's what he told Jim.

"We aren't really even good friends, you now?" Randy said, looking at his feet in the dish tub. "I mean, I've never even spoken to his wife, and now I've got to find a way to tell her about all this; I've got to figure out how to tell her he's gone." He looked at me so intensely I felt I should offer to do it for him. Instead I reached out in a feeble gesture of condo-lence, three fingers on his shoulder, too modest to commit a full hand to the effort.

He sat for a moment, gently pinned by my tentative fin-gers before he shrugged them off and began rocking back and forth again, moaning quietly. I saw a child occupying a man's body, not knowing what to do with the size and weight of it all.

"We really did have a plan," he said finally. "We really did. I showed him everything on the map, I really did."

With the walkie-talkies, Randy had the means to com-municate with Jim through the night and into the day, but the effort was hampered by the fact that the two did not speak the same language. Jim had no map, no compass, no internal bearings. Instead of cardinal directions, Jim would refer to things that were on his right, his left, ahead of him, behind him. He referred to geographic landmarks like, "the rock that looks like a beached whale, a great big fir tree, a steep, burned slope." The information he gave was in reference to the placement of his body on the earth, rendering it all useless, and eventually, communication broke off on Jim's end.

I told Randy that Jim might have been out of range, or maybe just out of batteries.

"Or both," Randy said, shaking his head, "Probably both. The guy doesn't have even a single fucking match."

It was long into dark when I made the call. I left Randy with his feet in the dish tub and went out to the helipad where I could find privacy and hopefully, a signal on the satellite phone.

There was no chance of getting a helicopter on the search until daylight, the dispatcher at the sheriff's department in a town so many miles away told me, but the search party could come in tonight on ATVs.

When they named the said four-wheeled machines "all-terrain vehicles," they were not taking into consideration the terrain of the Selway-Bitterroot Wilderness. The trail to the lookout gains nearly a vertical mile of elevation over the course of eight miles and is no more that two feet wide in places. Steep drop-offs and tight switchbacks make it dangerous for a string of pack mules, impossible for four wheels. Outside of its location on a map, it was clear that the party on the other end of the line knew little of this piece of wilderness, the place where the roads disappear.

Horses, humans, and helicopters: I said those were her only choices. They were the only means by which to access this country. The dispatcher told me to stand by, that she would call me back.

Snow sifted down from the darkness, a soft, glittery dust over the white that remained from the day. I looked north to the lookout where my coworker and nearest neighbor Greg lives. Sometimes through binoculars at night I swear I can see his lantern, but maybe the light I see is just the idea that someone is there. His mountain is only 1,200 feet lower than me, but it is another world. Different plants grow there, different trees; summer comes earlier, winter later. It was hard to believe it could still be autumn only a few miles away, that hope could be that close.

The electronic ring of the satellite phone brought me back to the bitter wind and falling snow in the place where I was.

"We'll have a helicopter up at first light."

Inside, Randy's feet looked like they belonged to a living human being, and complaints of a prickling sensation told me blood was returning to the vessels. In my best hopeful voice I told him about the call I had made and the plans for the early morning search-and-rescue effort. As promising as it sounded though, we both knew that what separated us from daylight was another frigid night.

We tried to call Jim on the two-way radio, to give him the good news to get him through the night, but there was no response. Nothing.

I took the kettle off the stove and made us two cups of tea.

"There was just one little ridge between us," he said, shaking his head in his hands. "I can't believe he got so turned around. You just go up, up, up...you just keep walking up and out of those drainages, you know?"

I did. The Selway-Bitterroot Wilderness is a deep dark

place of secrets. In the parts that haven't been burned by wildfire, its crowded timber is disorienting. It's rare to find a vista,
a clear ridge from which to get your bearings. From the inside looking out, it all looks like trees, but up will eventually
lead you to daylight.

He paced the thirteen-foot length of the lookout, back and
forth, pausing periodically to look at a map on the back of the
door. "Christ, these drainages we were in all lead back up to
the trail," he shouted, thumping the map with the back of his
hand. Randy grabbed at his neck for the phantom ponytail,
then slowly slid his hand forward to rub the stubble on his jaw.
"You have to just keep walking up."

He absently picked up his cup of tea, peering in through
the steam, searching for the reflection of someone he might
recognize as himself. He set it back down again without taking a sip and picked up my Raggedy Ann doll, a thirty-year-
old relic from my childhood. Though I cringed, chagrined to
have been caught with a doll, he was oblivious. He held the
doll up and shook her slightly. He told her, too, that all Jim
would've had to do was to keep going up, keep moving on.

Dinner was a smorgasbord of lentils, dried apricots and
peanuts, a box of macaroni and cheese, canned tuna, some
freeze-dried peas. For desert there were fig bars, more tea, and
the Belgian chocolate I'd been hoarding.

"I'll tell you what, I tried," he said looking over my shoulder and out into the night. "I told him every single thing he'd
need to be prepared. He trusted me," he said to the fork poised
in front of his lips. "And now I've failed him."

He set the fork down, pushed the plate aside and lay back
down on the bed, drawing his knees to his chest.

"Jesus Christ..." he moaned rocking back and forth, "I've
failed him, and now I've got to live with it."

As I cleaned up after dinner, shoving dirty plates under the wood stove, I thought about the times when I'd been driving a car and became irrationally terrified that for some reason, someone would dart out into the road out of nowhere and I would strike and kill them. I'd imagined the police report, the witnesses, the devastated family—how the victim's reckless behavior would result in me living the rest of my life with their blood on my hands.

I put a kettle on for dishwater, and Randy shifted gears, talking about his life in Oregon. He told me he had a piece of property, three acres of land which he had single-handedly eradicated of the dreaded spotted knapweed by pulling it out by hand over a two-year period.

"I would get out there and just pull it, every single day," he said. "You need to get the whole root. Sometimes they're this long," he demonstrated three feet with his hands, "like a god-damn tree root."

I noticed he was missing half of the ring finger on his right hand, usually the sign of someone who has worked harder than most, or someone who was careless.

Looking at the contents of his backpack, fastidiously lined out to dry in front of the woodstove, it was clear he was not a careless man.

We both fell quiet again, two strangers in a fire tower lit by lantern light. Watching snow fall outside, I thought of the man without matches, preparing for another twelve hours of darkness. I looked over to Randy, stretched out on the bed and lied, "I've got a good feeling about this..."

The ensuing silence was significant; a gaping space in which something important was either going to be said or someone was going to fall asleep.

"I don't believe in miracles," he muttered finally from the bed, and rolled over. It was a comforting sound though, the slippery shuffling of a nylon sleeping bag. It spoke of a man, well fed and warm, turning in for the night.

Sleep came fast to him, the snoring heavy. I gathered his clothes from the damp pile on the floor, tenderly hanging them on the line above the woodstove. A strange man's socks, so cold and wet.

My own bed and blankets occupied, I curled up next to the wood stove on my yoga mat, listening to white bark pine popping in the heat. Though warm and comfortable, I found it impossible to sleep. It wasn't for the tea's caffeine, the hard floor, or the lack of blankets. It wasn't for the air of awkward intimacy brought on by a stranger snoring in my bed. It wasn't for the starlight reflecting blue off the snow. It was for the absence of the second pair of boots clomping up the steps, the presence of the burden Randy shouldered, and, most of all, it was for the stillness that I could not sleep. The blanket of new-fallen snow muted the world to a silence so palpable it rang in the ears. It was something I had to witness; it was the loudest sound I'd heard in weeks.

I bundled up and quietly slipped outside, down the stairs, and to the helipad. Pin pricks of light seared through the inky blackness; stars so crisp they were felt in the chest as ice cracking, heard in the ears as glass shattering. It was clear; it was cold. It was winter.

"Jim," I spoke into Randy's walkie-talkie the way a competent rescue worker would on television, "My name is Karla. I'm a fire lookout," I said, pouring out a can of white gas onto the brush pile I'd made earlier in the day. "You're going to be O.K.," tossing a lit match into the center of the pile. "A helicopter is coming in the morning, and all you have to do is walk toward the fire," I said of the explosion of flames. But there was no response: No cheering, no click, no static.

And again, it was quiet. The only sound on the mountain was the roar of fire consuming limbs. Standing next to the five-foot blaze was gratifying; it gave me a sense of purpose. I was doing something, I thought, though I didn't know exactly what, or who I was doing it for. For Jim, the lost and desperate man? For Randy in my bed, snoring loudly as to drown out the scolding voices in his head? And maybe, I thought, I was doing it for myself. I was writing myself into the script.

The hours that followed were occupied by stoking fires. Outside, there were other things to burn; an old hitch rail, the boards of a former outhouse, cardboard, and paper trash. Inside, I added logs to the fire, bringing the temperature of the room to a roast. Tiptoeing to the stove with an armload of firewood I heard Randy shift in the bed he was sharing with Bandit, mumbling the thoughts of the dreaming.

Over the cast iron creak of the wood stove door I distinctly heard the words, "Honestly, it can all be explained with science."

Back outside on the walkie-talkie, I told Jim about life on the mountaintop. As I tended to the brush fire, I told him about the magical water at the spring, about the huckleberries, the mountain lion tracks, the bear that rolled rocks over on the trail looking for grubs to eat. I told him about the sky with its moods and my uninterrupted view of it. I told him about my friend Greg and how one hot, still day earlier in the summer we had gotten involved in a lengthy conversation of mirror flashes back and forth across the fifteen miles of air separating us. I described what the middle of a lightning storm looks like, the veins of the clouds backlit for a split second, an X-ray glimpse at the bones of the sky. I told Jim about water dogs, the white wisps of ground fog, often mistaken for smoke, rising from wet ground as gossamer and into the air like individual souls being called off to heaven. I needed him to know that there was something about the wilderness bigger than his fear.

Though I kept talking and kept stoking the fire, hope got lost somewhere in those desperate hours before daylight, disappearing into the end of the thermometer with the mercury, to the unknown place that marks the infinity of degrees below freezing. Inside the warm lookout though, Randy's disturbed snoring became the even breathing of an ordinary, innocent man's sleep.

Morning came, crystal blue and shocking, and not unlike a slap in the face. Out on the helipad, looking out across miles of white, I reluctantly told the dispatcher that our victim had been missing now for thirty-six hours. She wanted to know what the temperature had been. I cushioned my answer by a few degrees, rationalizing that an embellishment of the truth would somehow increase Jim's chances for survival.

She told me they would do what they could, this woman so many miles away at a desk, looking at a map of where I was.

Inside, over steaming mugs of coffee, Randy's face told the story of the imminent trip back to Oregon.

It was the face of a man returning home, empty-handed.

Sitting near a heart contemplating such weight, I felt guilty for the lightness. I felt guilty for the truth that I had the ability to wander into my own trivial thoughts, to wonder what I would eat when I returned to town that evening.

"There's no way he made it last night," he said with conviction. He, too, had seen the thermometer that morning, the bowl of dog water out on the catwalk frozen solid.

Speechless, I looked up at the ceiling then out to the blue sky, but found no answers there either.

The day was otherwise still on. There was a helicopter on the way. There was a man riding up a quiet trail on a creaky leather saddle leading a string of mules, naive to the goings on just a few miles away. He would expect me to be waiting, my things packed, ready to load onto his mules for the trip down the mountain.

As I chipped ice off the steps with a rusty ax, Randy stood with his coffee in a nervous way that gave me the impression he had never watched another person work before. He told me more about the sand and gravel business in Oregon, how he got started in it, his goals for the future. He told me he didn't really believe in luck, that the only thing that ever brought him what he wanted was hard work.

I told him I thought that luck was what kicked in when you had worked hard enough.

Slurping the last of his coffee he said, "I just want to go home." He swirled the grounds in the bottom of his cup around and tossed them over the railing with a flick of the wrist. They landed below, a spray of black against the otherwise undisturbed white of new snow.

I walked back inside to grab the coffee pot from the stove, that's what I could do—keep clothes dry, fires hot, cups filled. As I did, the two-way radio, the one my words had disappeared into all night, crackled to life. Static, and a man's voice. "Randy," it said unmistakably, then, "Randy," again. That was it.

Shots fired from the rifle of the lost man were so close I felt them in my teeth. A piece of orange flagging on a knoll less than a mile away gave away Jim's location. This would be a live rescue, I assured the dispatcher, not a recovery effort.

Randy was gone in no time, headed down the mountain

to where Jim was, wearing warm, dry clothes, pockets stuffed with peanuts and fig bars. Every trace of him was packed up and on his back, save for the coffee cup perched on the railing of the catwalk, the impression of a sleeping man left on the unmade bed, some coffee grounds in the snow. We'd shared a tearful embrace punctuated with sincere thank-yous and vows to keep in touch. As he walked away though, I knew it would be the last I'd see of him.

We would not get together to talk about what had happened; though in our own words, in our own lives, we would keep each other alive by telling our own renditions of the same story in the voice of the character we had played.

What we had belonged only to that space and time. Back in the other world we would not know one another, but in the wilderness, stripped clean of our societal markings, we recognized one another as friend, as ally.

It was a scene in wide angle: the distant sound of a helicopter rotor, an insect in the distance, then a bird entering the frame. The shot tightened as the bird became a machine, flying so low over the lookout I could read its tail number. As it flew on, the blizzard of snow it churned-up in its wake died down, settling back into a silent blanket, covering up any mistakes, any evidence. It flew to the spot where orange flagging, visible with the naked eye, marked the place where a man stood waiting for a ride out of his nightmare.

What happened from there was not unlike the end of a movie where the war is won, the dog comes home. And at the end of our movie, everyone lived, miraculously, keeping all of their limbs, even their toes.

I thought about the ride, and how sometimes with a happy ending in sight, even the most harrowing experience is over too soon. The space between raw terror and comfort becomes a small crack where once was a chasm. A helicopter flight, a horseback ride, an eight-mile walk to the rest of the world is never long enough to process what actually happened in the space of two nights, three months: a lifetime in the wilderness. Too soon the introduction of people who were not there, of people who haven't visited the outskirts of their lives. On the other side of the buffering spine of the Bitterroot Range, people were waking up to alarm clocks, driving to work with mugs of coffee sloshing between their legs. Over there were people who would never know the heart of a wild place.

A sinister gang of stratocumulus, thick-bottomed and heavy, approached from the southwest, coming in so low it appeared they would shear off the top of the lookout. Judging from the distance, it had already traveled through the pale sky, it was clear the sun would slow its trip to the western horizon for no one. The packer would arrive soon and there were duffle bags to be packed, floors to be swept and shutters to be put up until next season. And as quickly as it had begun, the adventure was over.

In the end, it was just another day on top of a perfectly good mountain, and there was work left to be done.

Karla Theilen spent years in the Grand Canyon at the working end of a shovel before migrating north to watch for forest fires and roam the hills in the presence of animals much larger than herself.

⁺

Caught for Sure

IN THE '70S, WHEN I WAS WORKING FOR THE FOREST Service, I was catching and eating fish every day. I was alone all summer and had some time on my hands. With my bare hands, I decided to challenge my fishing instincts and lay down my pole. I knew of a cold stream above timberline just below a 300-acre cobalt-blue lake where some pretty big trout hung out. I discovered that I could nestle among the boulders, hiding my shadow, and hold one of my hands in the creek waiting for a fish to swim by. Quickly, my hand would turn numb from the cold water. Patiently, I would "tickle the tummy" of a fish, grab it, and harvest dinner and breakfast.

One day, I remember watching for hours as a man on horseback slowly worked his way from the top of a mountain down the rocky trail to where I was. When he finally pulled up next to me, I held up my line of fish and proclaimed with pride, "I caught them all with my bare hands!"

Well, as it turns out, he was a Fish and Game officer, and it's illegal to catch a trout with your hands. According to the law, a trout has to willingly bite a hook. Pleading "ignorance of the law" didn't fly either. He confiscated my fish, set up his camp for the night, and ate them all himself. I never heard anything more, so I decided he must have taken heart and dropped the matter.

. A year or so later, a Fish and Game officer was featured in a local newspaper. The story was something like, "A Day in the Life of a Fish and Game Officer." Among his duties, he told the reporter, he was trying to find a young woman who once worked for the Forest Service and "serve a warrant for her arrest for a Fish and Game violation." I figured it was me. I turned myself in and was driven several hours to a small Wyoming town where the local judge held court in a laundromat on Main Street. I was fined thirty-five dollars. "Fishy" somehow. "Caught" for sure.

MaryJane Butters, former Utah wilderness ranger turned Idaho organic farmer, is the author of MaryJane's Ideabook, Cookbook, Lifebook: For the Farmgirl in All of Us. *She publishes the self-titled magazine* MaryJanesFarm *and created the successful Farmgirl Connection at www.maryjanesfarm.org.*

✦

First Watch

MY TRUCK'S HEADLIGHTS GIVE ME AWAY. AHEAD, TWENTY Labradors bounce up from their sleep, backlit by the glare off their stainless water buckets. Their racket threatens to drown out the whine of the struggling heater. I park the truck at the end of the kennel row and stuff the training collar into the pocket of my camouflage jacket. Opening the door to the commotion, I shake my head in amazement and mutter, "Who needs caffeine?"

Halfway down the row of barking dogs, I kneel and pull off my glove to stick my hand through the wire fencing. "Sorry girl, not today," I apologize to the eager-eyed black Lab. I scratch the silver-flecked muzzle and am thanked with a warm lick. "I think it's time we gave that son of yours a try."

I move two runs down to a still-frenzied younger dog. "Get down, Rebel," I admonish as I open the gate. "Let's try to remember our manners."

Squirming, he manages to sit just long enough for me to snug the training collar around his neck, before releasing him out into the yard. He races off and disappears into the darkness, marking his territory.

"Here!" I call him to the back of the truck where I've loaded a bag of decoys and a dog crate. "Load up, Rebel. Let's go get some ducks."

The drive to the duck hole provides a welcome time to indulge my daydreams. Glancing up at the rearview mirror, I can see Rebel's restless outline in the crate behind me. I smile, reminded of how quickly he grew from a tottering puppy to the muscled-up adolescent that sneaked training dummies out of my handler's bag. I remembered my husband John's parting words over breakfast: "Just like we tell our clients, the first hunt should teach the dog that birds come from the sky. And don't get him into situations above his training level."

The truck bounces over a rut, snapping my attention back to the road. I see the orange-flagged tree marking my turn and head toward the faintly glowing horizon. Stopping the truck under a towering cottonwood, I take the lanyard of duck calls hanging from the rear view mirror and drape them around my neck. Sounds of Rebel's thumping tail greet me at the tailgate.

"Settle down, boy," I whisper, tugging up my waders. "You're going to wake the entire neighborhood." I unlatch the crate door and catch his collar just in time to soften his landing as he leaps to the ground. He circles me, jumping in a fit of exuberance.

The weight of my shotgun and decoys slows my way to the jutting edge of the pond. After finding a safe place for my gun, I begin tossing the decoys out into a pattern I hope is inviting to the migrating ducks. The plastic bodies *thunk* as they hit the water. Rebel splashes around me, rearranging some of my handiwork.

"Hey, cut that out," I tell him.

Scolded, he follows me obediently back to the bank. I lay the now-empty decoy bag on the ground and settle back beside it under a small thicket of willows, pulling some loose brush up in front of me.

"Kennel," I say, motioning toward the bag. Rebel takes his place by my side. "Now all we have to do is wait for the ducks to come in."

His eyes, eager for understanding, glimmer in the growing light.

Soon the sun begins to warm our backs and I hear the familiar sounds of approaching ducks. I grasp the curved wood of my favorite duck call and begin imitating their language. Rebel's panting skips a beat and his rump starts to rise up off the decoy bag.

"Sit," I hiss, dropping the call from my mouth.

I raise my gun toward the incoming pair of drake mallards, keeping the dog in my peripheral vision.

"Sit *down*," I command again. His hindquarters lower to the ground, only to spring him forward at the sudden blast of the shotgun.

"Here!" I yell.

Reluctantly, he returns to sit by my side. I pause for a moment to make sure he locks onto the sight of the duck floating out amongst the decoys. With only a sharp call of his name, he bounds out into the water, snatches up the fallen bird and wheels back toward me.

"Here," I encourage as he reaches the bank.

Then, true to his training, Rebel comes and sits sharply at my feet. I reach out and put my hand around the duck's body.

"Now hold," I firmly remind the dripping dog, giving him a chance to settle. I can hardly contain my excitement at Rebel's first duck. "Drop," I tell him and he pulls his mouth back, gently releasing the bird into my hand. I quickly remind him to sit as I take a step backward.

"Rebel, shake!" I barely get the words out before he lets loose a wild spray of water. I toss the duck behind me and turn back toward my dog.

"What a dog, Rebel! Good boy!" Praising him, I pat his heaving shoulder. "That's what you were bred to do," giving him another pat on his broad head. Then feigning sternness, I shake my finger at him. "But now let's see if we can do that again without you breaking."

Within a few minutes, another small flock of ducks begins to circle our decoy spread. Keeping my head down, I slowly lean toward Rebel to whisper mark, cueing him to watch the sky. I mount the gun to my shoulder, swing through the duck and pull the trigger. This time, Rebel holds firm before I send him after the bird floating belly-up in the water. A clean return and a hearty slap on his shoulder reward his effort. Looking fondly over at my hunting companion, I start to read his growing understanding of where the ducks are coming from.

The morning progresses with a flyby of whistling widgeons. I miss the shot and swear I can sense Rebel's disappointment in a lost retrieving opportunity.

"We all need practice, boy," I reassure him with a quick scratch along his neck. "That's why we're both here."

Suddenly Rebel's ears prick up. The brush rustles behind me and I ease around to look over my shoulder. Just on the other side of my willowy nook, I see a man in a uniform approaching with a glint of a nameplate on his breast pocket. This can only mean one thing—game warden. He rounds the edge of my blind and Rebel stands, watchful of our visitor.

"Morning...ma'am." He stammers out the last word only as I pull my camouflage facemask over my head. His face reddens slightly.

I chuckle to myself, but try not to show my amusement at his near gaffe. I nod. "Good morning, sir."

"Nice looking retriever you've got there," he says appreciatively. Rebel breaks away from my side and frisks the warden with his nose.

"Thanks," I respond proudly. "Today's his first hunt and I think he's beginning to get the hang of it all."

"How many ducks have you shot this morning?" He straightens from petting Rebel and peers over my shoulder at the small pile lying beneath my shotgun.

"Just two. Haven't seen that many." I shake my head. "I thought with that Alberta Clipper we had, it would have moved larger groups through here, but since it's warmed up, I'm beginning to think they're just scattered." Frowning slightly, I survey the sky. "I'd sure like to shoot one more for my dog today." Rebel nudges my hand and I stroke his head.

The warden glances approvingly at the nodding decoys. "Looks like you're set up pretty good here."

"Yes, sir," I answer. "I've really set it up this way for my dog. It's best to work a green dog off a point of land like this. Everything's just a straight line, out and back. And I just shoot the short-range birds. Basically, I'm being careful not to get him in over his head, training-wise."

"Well, I'm glad to see trainers like you take the time to turn dogs into true conservation tools," the warden says. He starts to continue his thought but is interrupted by the sound of approaching ducks. Three sets of eyes turn in unison and begin to track their flight. "Looks like you're going to get your wish for one more duck." The game warden tips his hat. "You and your dog have a good day, ma'am," and he disappears back into the brush.

"All right, Rebel, this is our last group of the day. Show me what you've got, boy!" I pull my facemask back down over my head and crouch back into the willows. I pick up my duck call and begin with a hail call, mimicking a hen's invitation for all drakes to join her. The group's circle tightens, but they do not commit to landing. As they head away from me, I hit the call again, this time louder, more insistently. It works and the ducks bank into the wind, cupping their wings over the decoys. "Mark," I urge. Rebel's head swings with the barrel of my shotgun and I pull the trigger. Feathers explode—it's a longer shot than I expected and I squint to follow the fall. I take a quick glance at the waiting dog as I lay my gun down, but his intense look assures me that he's seen the bird. The crippled duck struggles out in the water and Rebel whines deep in his throat. All it takes is a quick utterance of his name, and he's off. He charges into the water, leaving a bubbly wake. With powerful strokes, he reaches the edge of the farthest decoys, pauses, and lifts his head to look around. I suck in my breath and hold it as he makes a small circle, seemingly unsure of his next move. But heart, training, and frantic flapping of the crippled duck renew his confidence and he moves out into the open water. He grabs the bird and I cup my hands to my mouth to yell, "Here!"

One wing of the bird obscures his left eye and he shifts his grip on the bird's body for the long swim back.

"Good boy, Rebel, here."

Soon the green-headed prize is delivered to my waiting hand.

"Have you had enough ducks for today?" I ask the panting dog. "Well, you sit here on the bank while I pick up the dekes and then we'll go home."

He obligingly watches me as I wade back out into the water to retrieve the decoys, wrapping their weights around the keels. We hike back to the truck, where I heave the sodden decoy bag into the back.

"Load up boy. Your education is paying off—you did a good job today."

As I drive back home, I hardly notice the sputtering heater. Instead, I'm warmed by thoughts of the day and the stories I look forward to telling my husband. My latest protégé showed all the drive and desire that his pedigree promised. As we create more memories afield together, I know he'll become one of my favorite hunting buddies. I tell myself, "You did a good job today, too."

Beth Ann Amico is a professional retriever trainer and owner of Deep Fork Retrievers in Choctaw, Oklahoma. She is a national award-winning gun dog writer and is a member of the Professional Retriever Trainers Association, Dog Writers Association of America, Professional Outdoor Media Association and the Outdoor Writers Association of America. Her other interests include promoting various outdoor women programs, big game hunting and music. Visit Beth Ann at www.deepforkretrievers.com.

CHRISTINE BYL

* * *

Dirt

FIVE MINUTES BEFORE I AM TO GET MARRIED, MY FRIEND Rachael kneels at my feet, painting my toenails. It's a hasty ritual; we are running late. Three days ago, I was hiking out of an eight-day hitch in filthy Carhartts with a chainsaw on my shoulder. Half an hour ago, I was cruising the washboard road in my pickup, attending to the last details of a rural wedding—generator, weed whacker, extra gas. I thought I was to be the only bride this century who didn't get to take a shower. But now, clean, I sit in my chair, trying not to fidget—the guests are waiting, sitting in a half circle down in the cottonwood grove by the river. My sister braids my damp hair with wildflowers from the meadow in front of the cabin—a daisy, a sprig of valerian. I twist in my seat and Rachael slaps my knee.

"Stop wiggling," she says, poking the air with the wet brush. "I'll get it on your dress." I hike the skirt up above my knees and close my eyes, feel the strokes on my nails, her strong fingers separating my toes, moving gently over the bruised big toenail, the calluses. By the time Gabe and I walk to the wedding circle, ushered within the cluster of our families, the polish is almost dry and we are ten minutes late. We ran out of time to paint my fingernails. They are pale, unpolished. My hands are not the soft, gloved hands of the magazine weddings. Veins push up against the skin. A sliver in my thumb. Creases in my knuckles faintly brown.

There, in a meadow on the North Fork of the Flathead, beneath the faces of the mountains we've labored and played in, Gabe says his vows to me. I look down at our feet; I can't watch his face without crying. My toes are already dusty, the nails pink. I wiggle them, enjoying their ceremonial shimmer.

You can trust dirty fingernails. Generalizations don't usually fit so well as this one, but it's true. I am drawn toward people with a darkened half moon atop their fingers. I can guess they've been transplanting flowers from pots into beds, protecting the wispy roots until they are buried safely in the ground. Maybe they work in the field, in a dirty truck, with hand tools. They could be teachers, the ones who kneel on the ground next to the kids, examining earthworms in wet mud. Potters, naturalists, firefighters, farmers. Dirt is like a secret code, the special knock of a fraternal order. You glance at each other's hands, and you know. I trust this little sign; it implies a tangible investment. To get dirt under your fingernails, you have to touch the world.

Dirt is an old word, an earthy word. It inhabits its meaning in the way it sits on your tongue when you speak it. "Dirt" never came out of Caesar's mouth; it can't be declined in a lyrical list. There is nothing fancy or trilling about the sound of dirt. It's not like "excrement," or "detritus," not "organic matter," or even "humus." From Old Norse, it made its way into Middle English as "drit"—the filth that collected in the treads of Chaucer's travelers' shoes. Dirt stands alone, humble and round, underneath everything, hidden in the creases of our skin, blowing in the air. It's solid and unglamorous. *Old.*

When I was five, I announced to my mother that I wished I were a boy. I had her cut my pigtailed hair into a shiny bowl whose edge rimmed my eyebrows. I wore t-shirts with numbers on them, ragged shorts with wide leather belts, striped socks pulled up to my knees. For church, or when dresses were forced, I had a denim Oshkosh jumper, under which I wore no shirt. My nipples peeked out from the gap between the buckles. My parents were unfazed. My mother fondly remembers that I told her, when asked if I wanted to wear a dress to a birthday party, "Oh Mom, don't you know, I'm the casual type?"

Until I was twelve, my obsession with boyhood continued. I loved my androgynous nickname, which allowed me, in a navy sweatshirt, with a wicked arm, to play undetected on the boy's baseball team. My grandfather took me fishing at the shore of Lake Michigan, and when we met a friend out on the pier who asked, "Is this your grandson?" my happiness lit my face and wet my armpits in a ringing rush. My knees were permanently tanned from sliding into bases and crawling in the yard. I kept frogs and bits of string in my pockets, went a whole week at camp refusing to take a shower. I dreamed of a career in archaeology, where I would travel to distant lands and uncover deep mysteries with a shovel. Did I know anything about gender then? Had someone told me that boys would grow up to be men with more power, that the carefulness required of panty hose would never suit me? Not at five, eight, even ten, really. But I knew that a girl could never pitch for the Tigers, that jump rope was boring, that mud felt good between my toes.

✳

Why shouldn't dirt be reassuring? Dirt is nothing if not permanent. It comes from the oldest, purest things—rain, rock, ice, wind. Glaciers form and move slowly, carving rock and mineral thrust up from earth's core; ice melts into rivers, coursing through weak spots in the firmament, forcing tiny, incremental change. When rivers and air meet, condensation forms. Weather results, and weather makes dirt. Water from the sky—snow, sleet, downpours, sprinkles—hits the surface of the earth in small drops and in wide puddles and in rushing currents. Wind blows across it all, urging dirt and water onward, to drift and move and finally come to rest in some other distant place. There are molecules of dirt in this room that blew in from the clothes of a slave on the Egyptian pyramids; the mud on the tires of my bike may have once cradled the perfect bones of some delicate, gossamer wing.

In fifth grade, my treasured teacher took me aside after class when the other students went out for recess. She was the girl's soccer coach; small and wiry, she said what she thought and I admired her desperately. I had turned in a writing exercise for her, a paragraph about what we wished for. I wrote, "I wish we had a color television, I wish no kids were ever hungry, I wish I were a boy." That day, she told me what no one had ever thought to say to me before. "Don't wish you were a boy, Chris," she said. "Boys are fine and good, but guess what we can be? We can be strong, dirty, feisty *women*." She clenched her fists at her sides while she talked, her eyes wide and wild. I believed her.

Dirt, loam, clay, dust, grime, loess, fill, mud, soil. Language seems most perfect when it is this elemental. When beneath the single syllable, there is bedrock.

★

Eight seasons I've worked in the woods, building, repairing, and clearing trails. I have dug borrow pits to find fill dirt
for projects, holes so deep that when it's time to get out, I
need a hand and could just as easily lie down in it like a grave.
I have hauled dirt in bags and buckets, used it to fill turnpikes,
make ramps, patch holes. Once I calculated, and at thirty-five
pounds per bag, two bags per person, working all day, our
four-person crew moved more than three and a half tons of dirt
by hand. The weight of work makes my elbow joints ache; the
outsides of my thighs are bruised from the rhythmic banging
of the buckets against my legs. My pants are filthy, the hems so
caked in mud that when I look down, I can't see where my
boots begin. My roughened hands, thick-heeled feet, the
wrinkles around my eyes from squinting into sun and wind—
by work and dirt, my body has been made.

Trail work has taken me from the mountains of northwest
Montana to the lush woods on Prince William Sound to the
open tundra of interior Alaska. I have cut down trees with a
saw, chopped them out of the trail with an axe, swinging until
my back is as hard and tight as brick and at bedtime, I groan
when I lift my toothbrush. I have dragged rotten logs a hundred yards through wet brush, cleaned culverts of leaves and
debris by hand, built walls six tiers thick made of rock. I've
sharpened chain, oiled blades, sanded handles, hiked miles
with these tools on my back. I have pumped the gallon and a
half of water I will drink from the creek, and wiped myself in
the morning with the leaves of a thimbleberry, wide and
rough. I've worked days without seeing people, in places no
humans have been for years. I've learned from strong and dirty
women, and labored side by side with competent men. I've
gone ten days without a shower, and come home for a cold

beer on the front porch of the local bar, my t-shirt brown, my eyebrows matted, my nails black.

In return for these labors I have received many things: perfectly broken-in work clothes; calloused hands and feet; dollars per hour, plus per diem; a raging metabolism; patience and foresight; a premonition about weather; muscles like small animals, twitching beneath my skin.

But most of all, this: every day, I have received my lunch hour—mountain pass or sand bar, pouring rain, gentle sun. After a morning of manual erosion, I sit on the ground and open my Tupperware lunch box. I shift my weight until I find a space between rocks and stumps and roots for my small backside, and I settle in. My crewmates around me, I lean back against my faded red pack and look at the sky. The air in my nose, my tendons relaxing from their constant contracting, the sound of the wind in larch needles or water flowing over rock. My stomach in a growling tangle, I remove my sandwich from its wrap. Holding it in my filthy hands, I look down at the chipped polish, the dark half moons, the sign. I trust myself.

Christine Byl lives just north of Denali National Park in Healy, Alaska with her husband and their furry sled dog, Campion. Her fiction, non-fiction and poems have appeared in GlimmerTrain Stories, The Sun, *and* Bellingham Review, *among others. She is currently at work on a book about backcountry trail work in Western Montana, and a collection of short fiction entitled,* Deep Enough for Drowning.

COLLEEN O'BRIEN

⋆ ⋆ ⋆

A Hole Worth Digging

I LOVE BREAKING OPEN THE CRUST OF EARTH, THE BLADE of my Pulaski sinking deep, cutting through sod, slicing roots, releasing smells—licorice and sage and a rich scent that has no name but causes me to breathe it in, draw it deep. I once threw a shovel of dirt, and as it flew I caught a glimpse of a Calypso orchid—a ladyslipper. I sifted through the rich blackness. The delicate, perfectly pink spires still radiated above the soft white and pink spotted tongue which held its yellow center like a jewel box presents its jewel. The soil I'd hurled had broken the stem. I felt bad, bad enough to cry. You can do a lot of things on this job—cuss, throw tools, lie, smoke, laugh till you just about wet your pants, moon passing trains, mock tourists, and pee wherever you please—but you'd best not cry. And while you're at it, don't whine or complain or grouse around either because everyone on your crew is doing the exact same thing and experiencing the exact same discomfort. I pressed the blossom between the pages of a small notebook and headed down the trail to my next drain.

I love the saw, love to ferry it across my shoulder, love when it starts, love when the chain's so sharp it shoots chips that curl like package ribbon. I love the smell of the gas mix, the viscosity of bar oil, the word "scrinch." I love sharpening the teeth, taking down the rakers. I love reading tension, dropping trees, pounding wedges. I love its heft and how it wears me to the bone like a contentious toddler you want to pull close, draw to your center because that's where you're strongest. And when I notice myself holding the motor head below my belly, that's when it's time to turn the chaps over to my buddy. I love the saw but I also fear it, much like the pack string.

I love mantying the loads, pulling the ropes taut, fastening sure knots that give way with a single tug. I love the mules, their power and burliness. I love that despite their surliness and neuroses, we all love them. This gives me hope for myself and my friends who possess our share of idiosyncrasies. I love holding the mules while the packer loads them, their dusty animal smell, their hot breath, the astonishing reality of their height, ears higher than I can reach. I love it even when they rodeo, busting their pigtails and tearing off, bucking free of their loads. That sting of adrenaline as I hold on and then surrender to the inevitable and let go so they can all kick and scream as only mules scream. That sting reminds me that I am alive, alive and in a beautiful place rife with forces larger than I. Those mules make for a comfy camp complete with a full-sized pillow, three novels, and more warm clothes than even I can manage to wear at once.

I love working with men and not seeing myself in a mirror for ten days at a stretch, and for the first time in my life not caring what I look like because it truly does not matter. I love the mountains, my mountains, how they change with the light, the way their moodiness buoys my spirit. I love that even when it's 38 degrees and pouring down rain and I'm so cold I eat as quickly as possible so I can work again and get warm, I know it won't last and eventually I'll be in a dry tent, layered up, curled in a sleeping bag and all the more grateful for it because I've been chilled. I love the meals we cook for one another and eat together—pasta, soup and sandwiches, burritos, stir-fry, and for international flavor, falafel. I have never eaten better, never enjoyed the experience more. I love watching a griz with three cubs across the lake from our work site. I love the way the little ones race and tumble and glissade down snowfields while mama feeds. I love waking to the hush of snow in July. I love that first shower after ten days and putting on a dress and drinking a cold beer on my back stoop and listening to the rumble of the train.

I love the guys I work with—Jeremy, Tony, Chris, Quinn, and Glenn. I love being in perpetual awe of what they can physically do. I love that four of us can haul a quarter-ton section of bridge down a trail using nothing more than a wheelbarrow, timber tongs, and our backs. I love that with a mean age of thirty-six, the other districts refer to us as "the old crew." I love these guys' humor and language (sick with a hard "k" is supercalifragilistically good), the fact that they have oodles of positive adjectives and no negative ones, their lack of pretense, their frailties, and the soft side they reveal only in rare moments of honesty. I love that when they send me for nails I now know an eight from a sixteen. I love that they taught me to hammer one-handed. I love this exercise in humility, for there is so much about this job I don't know. I love that with these guys I can just be myself.

Then there are the times I am frustrated and fatigued to the point of tears, knee deep in a snow melt swollen stream attempting to bank enough large rocks to crib our bridge and it's raining and still the mosquitoes are biting. And I could cry. But I don't because you can do a lot of things on this job—fling snow balls, eat chips and bread and candy bars, sing "*The Monkeys*" theme song off-key to get it out of your head and into someone else's, build bridges, lay culverts, crest passes that afford heart pounding views into the next valley, make ruthless fun of everyone and everything including yourself—but you do not whine or complain or bitch, and you certainly do not cry.

Colleen O'Brien lives within spitting distance of Glacier National Park on the Blackfeet Indian Reservation. She works trail crew in the park during the summer and teaches English at Blackfeet Community College during the school year. She's addicted to mountains, wind, and bite-sized powdered donuts.

⋆ ⋆ ⋆

Trail Guard

IT RAINED OFF AND ON FOR MOST OF LAST NIGHT. Before I went to bed I stood outside my tent and watched trees sway and the occasional electric flash of lightning brighten the granite canyon walls, although I never actually saw the white, jagged lines shooting down from the sky. Thunder ripped overhead and I thought something inside me had split open. I could feel the place where the sky breaks and falls, like God re-arranging heavy furniture across a hardwood floor.

I have been here eight days now. I think I will be here five more. As a wilderness ranger, I am accustomed to sleeping in leaky tents for ten days at a time, seasoned to solitary work, tired feet, and a sore back. I'm used to digging through fire rings looking for trash that doesn't burn, hauling out garbage on my back, and answering questions like, Where's the prettiest place to go? Or, What's *your* favorite spot? I am familiar with the surprised looks on hikers' faces when they see a Forest Service ranger backpacking alone, twenty miles from the nearest trailhead. I know what it's like to set down my sixty-pound pack not to rest, but to chop a fallen tree out of the trail with a dull Pulaski. I know how to hike long days and sleep solid nights.

Usually, I'm on the move. I never have any reason to stay in one place for more than a night or two in this vast, rugged wilderness we call "The Winds." But this time, circumstances are different. I am stationed at the junction of the Continental Divide Trail and Clark Creek Pass—a good fourteen miles or so from the trailhead. I was instructed not to move. I spend all day within sight of the weathered sign, usually within twenty feet. I was even told to camp, contrary to our own wilderness regulations, right next to the trail. The only time I leave the junction sign itself is to fetch water from the confluence of Clark and Trail creeks—a mere fifty feet away.

My job? To keep unwary hikers and horsepackers from continuing down the trail into the danger zone of a wildfire. It's a difficult selling point when every night is drenched with buckets of rain, there is no visible smoke, and—worse yet— after they make an exclamation like, "Boy, I sure do hope they get it out!" I have to tell them, "Well actually it's *wildfire use.*" Upon seeing their befuddled looks, I explain further, "The fire was a natural, lightning-start and we're letting it burn, but keeping an eye on it."

"So there's nobody up there fighting it?" they'll ask.

"There are two people up there, but no, they're not fighting it," I'll answer.

The folks who have seen National Geographic specials on the Yellowstone fires of '88 will nod in understanding. The folks who haven't will exclaim, "*What?* I have to hike eight miles out of the way because there's a fire that nobody's fighting?" And then, I go into my spiel about forest ecology and opening up the unnaturally thick timber to support bighorn sheep and so on and so forth. Then, whether they like it or not, I send them up and over Clark Creek Pass to my counterpart at the trail junction on the other side, eight miles away, who sends them out a different trailhead.

On a given day, I'll meet between zero and three groups of people. Needless to say, some of my co-workers, who had already spent ten to fourteen days up here in turn, complained of hearing voices. Some also mentioned insanity, boredom, and memory loss. Scott, an aspiring fourth-grade teacher, spent ten days going over multiplication tables in his head. Another spent his days contemplating the green fungus growing on his big toe.

My beloved junction is in a high, broken meadow stitched together with rows of whitebark pine and Englemann spruce. Granite walls rise in nearly every direction, some concealed by forest, some open to reflect the light of sun and moon and lightning.

This morning when I awoke, the meadow grasses were damp and covered in a fine dew, even the air was filled with moisture—light and unable to land—although the sky was clear and bluing. I stood out in the middle of it. The mist seeped into my colorful wool hat, into my fleece sweater, my wool gloves, dampening my silk scarf. I was loving it: the cool, damp darkness. The mystery. But I realized, too, that I reveled in this morning dew knowing one thing: in two and a half short hours, it would be gone. The sun would work her way down the canyon walls and paint her glory over the meadow grasses and outstretching pine boughs. Only the deepest darkest places, the places tucked between two thick spruce trunks, would be saved from her overwhelming power to dry. And it was knowing this—that soon I would be dry and warm, and even hot—that I could stand there and enjoy the dark dampness, the bluish gray of dawn.

On my first day, as I was hiking in, I had spotted a small, lightning-strike fire that was barely burning in the duff.

Yesterday I was allowed to leave my post to check on it again. The fire was cold, but as I toiled my way back up the switchbacks to the junction, I had one singular and specific desire: to bathe in the creek.

As I wound up the last half of switchbacks, dark clouds and a tree-swaying breeze took over the sky. I knew I would not dunk into icy water without the sun overhead, cheering me on. By the time I got my things together to pump water and wash clothes, the sky was opening up again and only a few puffy white cumulous clouds were visible. I walked the trail down to the creek. The deep pools were seductive and I thought to myself: all I need to do is get on the other side of that bend, and no one coming down the trail would see me.

I stood on the rocky bank and wondered which chore I should do first. I looked up at the small slice of sky and knew I should dunk first, before more clouds rolled in.

Shy and feeling scandalous about bathing mid-day while technically on duty, I was still afraid of getting "caught." I kept my bright yellow Nomex shirt on while I washed my legs. But then I realized nudity would be the best camouflage of all. So I took off the Nomex and my sports bra and sat on a white granite stone as I bathed with a bandana and splashed cool, fresh water onto myself. With my feet and hands bridged over two rocks, I dunked my torso into the creek—the rush of it hit me and sent a wave of cold shock up to my collarbone.

The sun felt warm and comforting on my nakedness and I could feel my skin tighten and dry. I laced up my boots, but continued to air-dry as I rinsed and scrubbed my socks, underwear and bandanas. Afterwards, I put my sun-dried clothes back on but decided, spur of the moment, to let my hair down and wash it, too.

I dropped to my knees and dunked my hair into a pool, making sure that every inch got wet. Then, I pulled my head up and wrung the creek out until my red hair hung in front of my downturned head in loose curls. I pulled it all back into a thick, loose braid, knowing full well that it would be full of knots. I liked the feeling, the way wet hair, heavy with the green smell of creek water tugged at my scalp. I felt wild, primitive, as though by bathing in the creek and letting my hair down, I'd resigned myself to the rhythms of this place and adopted it as my own. Like a captive who finally resigns to eating the food offered by her captors.

My food is getting stocked by a local outfitter. Since the entire area that he outfits has been shut down to visitors, the Forest Service has kindly employed him to re-supply the fire monitors and trail guards so he doesn't go completely bankrupt. This morning he dropped off enough bagels, cheese, instant coffee and fresh batteries for the satellite phone to last a month. I helped him unload the mules and offered him a cup of cold, instant coffee, as I had no way of heating it with a broken stove and an official ban on campfires.

"So," Todd asked, "what the hell are you doing up here all day anyway?" I told him I was knitting socks. "What? Are you pregnant? That's a bad sign, Gretchen, when you start knitting."

Besides knitting, I have been walking around barefoot for the last six days with this self-imposed idea that I will toughen up my feet. Ah, if only the safety officers could see me now, I think to myself. Sure, I've got my fireproof Nomex clothing on, but my eight-inch leather boots are tucked neatly away under a spruce tree.

Barefoot is nothing compared to what I imagine my counterpart—Sarah—is up to. She is stationed at the trail junction on the other side of Clark Creek Pass. Sarah is new to wilderness work and a devout Mormon who is rediscovering that the divine rests in the natural state of things. Needless to say, fourteen days alone in the wilderness in one place and I can imagine her dancing circles around her junction sign wearing only her wedding ring and a silver necklace. I try to check on her sanity by questioning every hiker that passes through from her direction. I have no radio contact with Sarah. And she has no radio contact *with anyone* unless she climbs to the top of the pass.

The elk in this park have been dancing circles around my imagination. Sometimes I try to look for them, but I don't really want to see them. I am content with learning their noises, the pulses they send through the air and underground, to my feet.

Last night, before I bedded down, I heard rumbles like a stampede, or distant thunder, or a rockslide some thousand feet above me, or stones shifting in the river. But it was a dry, heavy sound: hooves beating the drums of a hollow meadow.

I could feel their presence, like wild Indians, tantalizing me with sounds so faint I'd wonder if I really heard them. And just as soon as I would get to doubting it—thinking maybe it was just the way blood was pulsing through my jugulars—then they would give me a definite sign: a loud, defiant snort just outside my tent. Or this morning, when I was deciding between elk hooves and shifting river stones, I caught a glimpse of a long, tan back and rounded rear end just on the bench above me, not even a hundred feet away.

I crept up to the edge of the bench, peeked over and saw, of course, nothing. But I could feel them just behind the spruces and pines. I wondered if I had a sixth sense for elk. I thought it impossible that I could be hearing something so faint. I found it more likely that I was feeling it reverberating through the ground. Almost as though the air got thicker, crowded with such large bodies, when they were nearby.

Now, I am basking in the sun and watching a fly on my foot. I can't feel him except when he walks over certain, sensitive places—like the thin skin where my toe meets the bulk of my foot—or my arches, or the tops of my ankles. It feels good today, this fine tickling.

Plans changed three times this morning. I called out on the satellite phone to learn that I'll be hiking out tomorrow morning. At first, I was going to hike out everything I could and leave the rest to be packed out by Todd in a day or two. Then my supervisor called back saying Todd would pack me *and* the accumulation of stuff out in the morning. Finally, it was decided that I would hike out behind Todd who would pack the bear panniers, satellite phone, and other assortment of things left by the string of trail guards.

I have to hide my disappointment at leaving. I'm not sure if I should be embarrassed or proud of my enjoyment at doing almost nothing. I have settled here in such a way that I no longer measure time. As John Muir wrote, "Life seems neither long nor short, and we take no more heed to save time or make haste than do the trees and stars. This is true freedom, a good practical sort of immortality."

I never knew I could find such freedom and peace while practically tethered to a trail junction post. I never knew I could lose my usual backcountry cravings of pizza, beer, and apple pie and be content with cold instant coffee. I told my supervisor I could stay up here forever. Never before had I spent so long in the wilderness in one place. And I wonder if I will ever do it again—if such a situation would arise that I would remain still, dawn 'til dusk, in a wild place. It's phenomenal to me, what the closing down of certain freedoms does to open the body and mind to experience a place wholly and on its own terms.

They came around again last night. I tried sneaking up on them. But I think they caught me right away. I heard clamoring in the trees, probably just out of sight. I heard them this morning, too. Faint sounds of hoof and hide, almost like a memory or a dream.

It's starting early today. The sky is arranging itself for another afternoon and evening of rock-splitting thunder and rain.

Gretchen Dawn Yost lives and writes in western Wyoming. She spent four years working for the Forest Service as a wilderness ranger in the Wind River Range, which she still calls home. Her work has appeared in numerous anthologies including Heart Shots: Women Write about Hunting *edited by Mary Zeiss Stange, and the annual* American Nature Writing *series edited by John A. Murray.*

JENNIFER ESTERL

Alyeska Invert

I START THE DAY LIKE MANY OTHERS, WALKING THE three-block distance to Alyeska Resort over varying combinations of slush, ice, and mud. I ruminate on recent events, town politics, the shenanigans of the local ski instructors association, my struggles with my own ski technique, certification, and career issues, et cetera, et cetera, until I have worked my morning breakfast into a churning acidic stew.

Meanwhile Mount Alyeska and the rest of the Chugach Range loom over me with their powdery slopes, barely skiable ravines, and hanging glaciers. The mountains here look as if they surged out of the earth sometime yesterday. Unlike me, they don't seem at all timeworn or world-weary. They are rugged, craggy, as sharp as brand new chefs' knives, and look like they are poised to raise a ruckus with the heavens, to show the sky what's really up.

Me, on the other hand, I can feel myself growing older by the day, as if a part of me had been waiting to settle here and start slowly mossing over. After twelve years in Alaska, I feel like some kind of Chinese elm, blown in on a trade wind and now rooting myself tenaciously into the soil. Though it is my second year in Girdwood teaching skiing, I worry whether I really belong here, and then I realize that the question of belonging is rather a moot point for Dutch elms.

Later that day I look at my struggling ski student—four years old, as of last week. Katy's age group is one of the most challenging for me, and I often wonder if I have the foggiest idea what I'm doing. Sometimes I feel like I'm just waiting for the landscape, my students, or my co-workers to completely humble me, once again. It's a big part of what I either love or hate about the business; I'm never sure which.

Katy and I have spent the last forty-five minutes going up and down the same fifty yards of barely sloping beginner's hill. I have been trying to teach her how to stop by making a wedge shape like a pizza slice with her two skis. I have said, "Bigger piece of pizza, Katy! Bigger, bigger, bigger!" a hundred and fifty-seven times. At least. I have been hunched over helping her up the pony tow, hunched over holding her as we ski down the hill, hunched over helping her back up, over and over.

Katy is now starfished in the snow, gazing up at me with watery eyes. I am saying in my very cheeriest voice, "That's O.K., Katy! Let's just get up and try it again!"

Nothing happens.

Katy stays motionless in her lavender cocoon of a snowsuit, her two-foot-long skis splayed in the air. Her eyelashes are clumped together with barely repressed tears. Finally her lips poke out a little farther and her chin starts to quiver.

Silently I am wondering if my back will ever recover or if I'll be stooped and a full foot shorter before I'm even old enough to join AARP.

"Come on, Katy, I'll help you up!"

I stay cheery, at least vocally.

We're not supposed to just lift students, and I am waiting for some recognition of what I'm saying, or eye contact, or anything, really, at this point.

I say, "Katy, if you don't get up, we can't ski!"

Then I realize, as if Katy actually tells me in so many words, *that's the whole point, you crazy fool.*

I lie down next to her in the snow. It's fairly warm out, and the snow is soft enough to mold around us, making customized beds. My back feels supported, and comfortably iced. We are cradled in the snow.

Katy slowly begins to acknowledge my existence again.

We make up stories about what the clouds look like (every single one of them reminds Katy of some creature or another from *Finding Nemo*, but whatever. At least she's enjoying nature, right?).

Looking to one side, I notice for the first time that the brown snow-covered day lodge is the same color as hot chocolate with marshmallows on top. I point this out to Katy, and she actually laughs. Together we crane our necks backwards to look at Mount Alyeska, upside down.

From here we can't see the top, or any of the expert runs at all. Skiers funnel towards the lodge like colorful ants. The spruce trees stand along the sides, sheltering us from the road and the houses beyond, framing an expansive sky. The Chugach Range looks like little more than a series of stunted stalactites. Alyeska is a completely different mountain from this point of view.

Lying there on the snow, I remember reading about vocalists singing while standing on their heads to stretch their range and about artists painting things upside down to challenge their assumptions and perspectives, and I wonder when I forgot what a fantastic thing it is to turn things topsy-turvy, at least every once in a while. Local politics, professional organizations, careers, personal ruts and routines—ah, the wealth of mountainous things to be shaken up and reexamined.

I am humbled again, to be sure, but also inspired.

Jennifer Esterl has gone from being a professional musician with a passion for the outdoors to a professional outdoors woman with a serious music habit. Whether this is progress she can't say. She currently lives in Girdwood, a small Alaskan town, and has an addiction to skiing.

* * *

San Pedro Mártir

THE ENTIRE WALL OF MY SON'S BEDROOM IS A MAP OF the world. At not quite a year old, he probably notices little detail beyond the swirls of blues, greens, and browns. I, on the other hand, change his diaper just inches from the places I've been, the places I haven't, and the places so small, so off the beaten track, that they don't show.

Isla San Pedro Mártir isn't even a speck on our wall map, where only three of the hundred-plus islands in the Gulf of California archipelago actually appear. But a quick glance to that spot on the wall and I'm back: to soaring heat, to the frenzy of thousands of seabirds, to the muffled barks of sea lions sounding like a stadium of people mumbling through hand-covered mouths.

A single square mile of rocky basalt, San Pedro Mártir is isolated mid-Gulf about twenty miles from the nearest point of land, another rocky outcrop. With mainland Mexico thirty miles to the east and the Baja peninsula about twenty-seven miles due west, San Pedro Mártir is not the lush and inviting tropical paradise of popular cinema but a desert island in the true sense of the word.

I stumbled onto San Pedro Mártir. Having just finished a field stint monitoring desert-nesting bald eagles in central Arizona, I was at loose ends when a flyer caught my eye on a biology department bulletin board at a local university: "Doctoral candidate needs volunteers to document territorial behavior of endemic lizard *Uta palmeri*. Six weeks on remote desert island. Primitive living conditions. No pay. Opportunity of a lifetime." I removed the piece of paper, replaced the thumbtack, and called the long-distance number from a pay phone six feet away.

The five of us converged on the fishing village of Kino late on a sparkling April afternoon. Bougainvillea burst against a blue sky and ocotillo fences bloomed around small adobe houses, indicating a recent rain. Only Diana, our post-doc candidate, was in academia. We were simply her crew, twenty-somethings with a background in biology and a thirst for field experience. In four separate states we'd seen four identical flyers; I hopped aboard, the latecomer, because of my familiarity with coastal Sonora and because I spoke Spanish.

The next morning, still dark, we rousted ourselves from our sleeping bags on the beach, scratching bites left behind by sand fleas that had kept us from a decent rest. Our panga driver, Fermín, was already loading his twenty-foot skiff with the supplies Diana had boxed up earlier. I paused, eating my breakfast banana, to consider the panga's seaworthiness. I'd been in worse, in places even farther from home. The outboard had four blades. Good. There were only two lifejackets. Less good. I made out a lone oar under the wooden benches just before it was buried beneath gallon jugs of fresh drinking water.

It was barely dawn when we set out. Ours was the last functioning boat to leave the beach that morning, the local fishermen having launched an hour earlier. Six or eight boys splashed alongside in ankle-deep water. Outwardly curious, they teased our lone male, Kent. "Four women and just *one* macho?" The youngest among us, Kent knew enough Spanish to toss back a quick retort that I missed in all the commotion. The boys yowled with delight.

It was two hours before we caught our first glimpse of the island, and another two before we arrived. The water was choppy, the outboard motor noisy, and the wind relentless. We didn't talk much but did a lot of pointing as seabirds flapped past, our heads swiveling to keep up with cormorants, swifts, pelicans, boobies, gulls, and grebes. An occasional dolphin left its school to play hooky in our wake.

San Pedro Mártir sits smack dab above the southern stretch of the San Andreas fault, a fault famous for its shifts, groans, and terrestrial mischief. Local lore, passed down from generation to generation in both the Mexican and indigenous Seri villages, says that the island is haunted. People I spoke to on the mainland seemed so certain. Who was I to doubt them?

But this reputation more likely grew from stories told by fishermen over the years. With offshore trenches reaching 9,000 feet, the sea around San Pedro Mártir is deeper than Lake Biakal. Powerful currents ring the island, churning nutrient-rich waters. The plankton feed the fish that in turn provide a choice cuisine for thousands of pelagic birds. Recognizing this, the Mexican government declared the island a *refugio federale*, or migratory bird sanctuary, in 1978.

Approaching from the sea, we see a massive pyramid-shaped rock rise from a base of mist and haze. A soft whiteness blankets the lower two-thirds of the island, dripping down the thousand-foot cliffs like the glaze on the sides of a steep puff pastry—the guano build-up from seabirds over millennia.

In the late 1800s a government penal colony mined the island's guano for nitrates for gunpowder and fertilizer production. Exactly how much guano was extracted, or how many prisoners were condemned to this dismal fate, I don't know. Most likely, guano was scraped from the rocks and piled on to rock ledges for transfer to a ship. These ledges are still visible over parts of the island and it was on to one of them that we leapt from our panga for our "opportunity of a lifetime."

We unloaded the panga in record-setting time to Fermín's shouts of "*¡Apuraté!*" (Hurry!) as he kept the motor revving slowly in reverse to avoid smashing against the rocks. Our human chain was still tossing supplies to higher, drier ground when I glanced back just in time to see Fermín rounding the corner from view. I was still staring at the spot where the panga disappeared when, in a matter of seconds, the tiny harbor was filled with the shiny, bobbing heads of a dozen curious sea lions. Ebony-eyed, with lashes nearly as long as their whiskers, they must have slid beneath the surf when we'd arrived a short time earlier. We barked back our thanks for their warm welcome, smacking together our hands in a poor imitation of their flippers, equally excited to make their acquaintance. All thoughts of Fermín, the panga, and our lifeline to the mainland left me.

With our supplies securely situated above the intertidal, the four of us followed Diana up over the white rocks along a path more felt, underfoot, than actually seen. This was the second of Diana's three-year commitment to study her beloved *Uta palmeri* and being back on the island, away from her cubicle and colleagues, ignited her playfulness. And it was infectious. We were all enchanted by the fantastic feeling of otherworldliness that comes from being so removed from a peopled world.

A short walk led us to a saddle across the lowest part of the island, to an area that was relatively flat, or as flat as a boulder field can be. It was clearly man-made, with three-foot-high walls cordoning off small rooms and doorways, and I wondered how many hours some nineteenth-century prisoners spent stacking rocks, never suspecting that a group of gringos in synthetic sleeping bags would bunk here a hundred years later.

In my experience, the first day of arriving at any base camp anywhere is virtually the same. After hauling supplies from the drop-off point to the actual site, my senses begin to relax and absorb my new surroundings: smells, sounds, the lighting; what's soft, hard, growing, moving. From the moment I locked eyes with the wildness of San Pedro Mártir, I felt like a privileged visitor, honored to be there. I never wanted to leave.

With our supplies shuttled from the cove to camp, we unpacked. Amongst rooms that once defined the penal colony, we established our temporary home: a kitchen, a pantry, a cache of equipment; and off to one side, in an area of larger rocks for privacy, a very airy privy. Large white plastic buckets held our food and gear and doubled as our chairs. Our personal quarters popped up: my small dome tent, Diana's pup tent, and a mesh tent designed to house a picnic table in a suburban back yard, where the others slept. This transformation took less than an hour.

With a half day of light still ahead of us it was time to explore the island. It was just past noon, hot and cloudless, but we were on autopilot now. Negotiating another hint of a trail, we followed Diana up to a rocky plateau and slope of cardon cactus, the spindly candelabra-shaped cousin of the Organ Pipe cactus up north. Around us the sounds were changing. The roar of the crashing surf was replaced by the squawks of nesting birds perturbed by our presence.

Walking through this dense thicket of statuesque cardon felt like being in a house of mirrors. I knew that this disorientation would eventually subside, but for now one towering cactus or guano-bleached boulder mimicked the next. The locals were right; there was an eeriness here. Not a spooky eeriness, but an *ancient* eeriness. A people-don't-belong-here eeriness.

By now Diana was prancing around, waving her arms, describing the layout of our field site, or grids. She assured us that the birds would soon grow accustomed to our clumping about, but the longer we lingered, the more visibly annoyed they became. I carefully side-stepped blue-footed Booby nests and brown booby nests, the parents on their eggs as furious at me as the sea lions had been curious. Later I learned to distinguish between male and female boobies by their pupil size, which differed greatly, but for now I felt enormous and clumsy, the biggest-footed booby of all.

While nobody said anything, we were all harboring the same thought: Where were the lizards? Weren't we here to study the infamous *Uta palmeri*? Except for a fleeting glimpse of what *may* have been a lizard back at camp, we hadn't seen any sign of reptiles here. So when Ann, the calm, quiet Texan in our group, bellowed a deep, Fat Alberty "Hey, Hey, Hey" we were quick to follow her stare. And there it was—our raison d'être. Five inches long and mottled gray, only the slightest tilt of its head kept me from thinking this lizard was dead. Diana, biologist to the core, noted the swollen gonads at the base of the tail: male.

Lizards began to spring up everywhere, as though one had bugled "ollie-ollie-oxen-free!" They dashed from rock to rock like miniature wind-up cars. They were smarter than we were; they sought shade. After the initial thrill of watching them wore off, someone suggested we return to camp for an early supper and bed. Like an infectious yawn spreading from one person to the next we noticed our hunger and exhaustion and wove our way back down the slope in complete silence.

All field biologists know the joy of those first few days when the fruit is still fresh and the cheese mold-free. Diana had snuck a dozen eggs into the rations and, miraculously, they'd survived the panga ride unscathed. We feasted that first night on cheese omelets with avocado, onion, and salsa.

From then on, the menu returned to the same basic fare I'd come to expect and accept: granola with powdered milk for breakfast; peanut butter and jelly or aging cheese on tortillas for lunch; beans, rice, potatoes, or pasta for dinner. Five bowls, five spoons, and five cups were rinsed off and tucked away until the next meal. Our kitchen looked like the three bears had company.

Tired and content, we were lulled by the sunset. It was twilight and the Baja Peninsula lay on the horizon to the west. The jagged mountains had turned purple and softened. Above them layers of orange shimmied into the night sky, the sea's swirling currents reflecting the glow.

Against this canvas, thousands of seabirds enjoyed a last-light flight. The sound was deafening. We learned, that first evening, to always wear bandanas or hats. We learned never to leave our bowls uncovered. And we learned that for every incoming bird, a thousand maddening gnats swarm at sundown. We revisited these three truths every dawn and dusk of our entire stay.

After dark, phosphorescence sparkled in the water below the cliffs of base camp. We traced the sea lions as they zipped about like tiny torpedoes, trailed by a fairy dusting of bioluminescence. Later on, we discovered that if you threw a rock over the cliff, the phosphorescence would explode in concentric circles upon impact. But we decided not to delight in this fanfare further when our rock-chucking startled some pelicans too dark for us to see. Frightened into flight, their webbed feet smacked against the surface of the water, leaving brilliantly glowing "tracks" to linger for a few seconds in their wake.

The morning exodus of birds from their nests to their feeding grounds was as deafening as their Happy Hour had been the evening before. We woke at first light, catapulted into the day by the cacophony overhead. After surveying the damage in the kitchen and pantry areas, thanks to a few resident rats, descendants from the convict ship days, we realized we'd have to be more vigilant about stowing our supplies. The utensils we'd left out were boiled in water on the propane stove. Then just to be sure, they were sterilized again. Soon after sunrise, we were hiking back up the slope to the cardon forest, nesting boobies, and our elusive lizard friends where, for the next two days, we painstakingly mapped our project's grids.

Plotting a grid required a lot of tape measuring and anchoring down of little yellow, plastic flags with rocks. It required recording slope and exposure and upsetting boobies as we stumbled through their nursery with the grace of five blind elephants. Despite our early departure from camp, the heat had drained us by late morning. In the shade of a tarp tied between four tall cardon, tired and hungry, I was torn between dozing and devouring my lunch. As cheap aluminum chairs don't invite much rest I settled into a slouch to eat, surrounded by my four equally tired and hungry companions.

Diana now put on her herpetologist hat. We were here to determine the ratio of males to females in each grid and to document their behavior. That much I knew. What I *didn't* know was that we'd be capturing these little guys with dental floss nooses tied to bamboo poles. We had our first lesson then and there, stomachs full and feeling more ready for a nap than a jag as the hangman's apprentice.

Ann tied the best nooses by far. Ann was a piano player, as

was Diana, and I'm certain their fingers were the more agile for it. Karen, Kent, and I struggled and eventually mastered the basics. The loop must be large enough to slip over a lizard's head but small enough that the lizard cannot escape before it is cinched. Diana assured us we'd all get the gist of it and sent us out into the sun and the rocks to practice.

Midday was a ridiculous time of day to practice capturing lizards, as most lizards were flat beneath a rock seeking shade. But we gave it a go, finding a few sun worshippers to practice on. In less than an hour, the wax on my floss was sticky from the heat and the slide mechanism dragged just long enough for my quarry to look me in the eye and slip away. I suggested we try using non-waxed floss but Diana assured me it was even *less* effective, having no slide at all. I thought of all the crazy things I'd done in my life and knew that this, Noosing 101, was near the top.

We practiced noosing those first few evenings, around base camp, and by the third day on the island, grids mapped and noosing like old pros, we began our work in earnest. First we needed to identify individual lizards. It was then and there that I determined I was destined to become a "soft" scientist, more of a naturalist/field biologist than a focused-on–the-minutest-detail hard researcher. Here's why.

After documenting where a lizard was caught, we would settle into the shade beneath the tarp to record its weight, length, and head size. Then, with dollar-store nail clippers, we removed individual toes for identification purposes. Thus, lizard #25 would lose its second and fifth digits. These toes were then dropped into a small vial of formaldehyde for later observation under a microscope back in Diana's stateside lab.

From the toe rings, or cell growth, the lizard's age would be determined. It's not unlike reading the rings on a tree stump or the fine growth lines of a fish scale. The bagged and bewildered lizard was then returned to the exact spot of capture, but not before a bright yellow #25 was painted onto its back with a fingernail brush for easy identification on the grid. I whispered an apology to each lizard I released.

Noosing lizards under a hot sun grows old fast. With the grids mapped and the lizard population satisfactorily numbered, we were ready to begin data collection in earnest. Each morning, after a granola breakfast, four of us took off for the day's work. Hauling lunch and water, bedecked in cotton and sunscreen, we made our way to the grids just as the chatter overhead quieted down and the gnats went wherever gnats go all day.

For the next eight hours we worked around the birds: nests, eggs, irate adults, and, as the season progressed, their anything-but-cute chicks. I discovered that blue-footed boobies might have dazzling feet but that the tuxedo-clad brown booby has a temperament I prefer. I heard the sound a frantic parent makes when a gull successfully steals an egg. At first I considered flapping my arms to intervene, but the chick was doomed whether it was eaten or dropped. Besides, I wasn't *that* soft a field biologist.

Clipboard, pencil, and binoculars in hand, we worked independently on the grid. At twenty-minute intervals I waited and watched for yellow numbers to scamper by. This became easier with time, as different lizards assumed different behaviors once I got to know them and their territory. There was Stubby, who was short and squat, and Zippo, with his onomatopoeic name. Hot-to-Trot never left the ladies alone, and Delilah was his nemesis.

Then the day came when I realized I was screwing up my eyes to read the yellow numbers that had begun to fleck and fade like a manicure past its prime. The lizards were molting! We began again, recapturing them, relabeling, and I wondered if Zippo, Stubby, and friends might not feel their worst night-mare had returned in the form of a mint-scented noose. Happily for all concerned, we did not have to remove any more toes. The clippers had grown terribly dull.

Working on San Pedro Mártir made for one surprise after another. Just when the days became seemingly predictable, something extraordinary would happen. There was the day, late in the first week, when a terrific *KABOOM!* sent us rac-ing toward the cliff. Hundreds of feet below in crystal clear water, a fin whale was surfacing for air, about to blow again. The crash we'd heard was the smack of her immense body against the tossing waves. As if that weren't breathtaking enough, a calf swam alongside. I was speechless. The world's second-largest cetacean *and* her baby, casually swimming by.

Like counting the distance of an approaching storm, "one one-hundred, two one-hundred" I mapped her dive se-quence. Five, six, seven blows—more magnificent than any human-made fountain—approximately seventy seconds apart before she submerged again. Her flukes rounded out one continuous arc as she dove down, down, down and out of sight, calf close by.

Even now, years later, the memory is crisp but the words elude me. For five weeks the whales circumnavigated the is-land, dancing their slow-motion duet and feasting on plank-ton soup. I heard them daily from the grid, from base camp, even in the middle of the night when I woke to pee. Then they were gone. While the occasional gray whale passed by, we never saw the mother fin or her baby again.

Smaller moments also left their impression, like the day I lost Stubby. Male *Uta palmeri* lizards are aggressive when they want to mate, and Stubby was no exception. I was not overly surprised when I saw him tackle a female on his turf, But when the two of them locked together, vent to vent (use your imagination), only to tussle and roll twenty feet over and around rocks toward the edge of the cliff, I was horrified. In what I'd like to think of as an embrace, they plummeted over the ledge like a barrel over Niagara Falls. By the time I looked over, they were lost from sight. If it wasn't so tragic, it would have been comical.

After five weeks of data collecting, Diana was curious to see how male lizards would respond to intruder *Uta palmeri* being lured onto their territory. As bait, we needed the moist, semi-digested fish, or *regurge,* coughed up by sea birds for their chicks. This protein-packed slime was a favorite food of the lizards. So at the end of our workdays, before returning to camp, we would hike above the grids to where pelicans nested and fed their young.

An invisible line divided our work site, commonly known as "Booby Central," from the pelican nursery just a few hundred feet further up island. While the booby nests were essentially depressions in the guano-covered ground between the rocks, the pelicans had hundreds of stick nests, the woody remnants of ancient cardon, some three or four feet wide. Pelican chicks were everywhere. Kent and I discovered a nest with a newborn, still soggy and looking more like a dinosaur than a bird, with another chick on the way. A half-inch hole had been pecked through the baked potato-size egg's shell and chirping could be heard from within. We moved away quickly so the mother could return.

Pelicans excite easily and it was hard not to feel bad for disturbing them, especially the fluffy white juveniles with large wings but underdeveloped flight muscles. Not designed for overland travel, the young pelicans were both hilarious and disconcerting to watch as they stumbled away on webbed feet, squawking so loudly we could look right down their throat to their vibrating voice box.

Scooping slimy *regurge* from nests, careful to borrow just a small amount from any single source, we tried not to gag as we packed it into plastic peanut butter containers with a spoon. While Diana insisted this was *not* vomit in the true sense of the word, we were not convinced. The next day we smeared tempting globs here and there on the lizard's rocks to watch and record the outcome. The entire maneuver joined noosing reptiles on my life's short list of things never to repeat.

One afternoon, we went beyond the pelicans and above the guano to where the rocks were the distinctive brick-red color of basalt. Enjoying the top-of-the-world feeling that comes with first ascents anywhere, I was aware of how calm things were, an almost complete silence I'd never experienced on the island. The sea was so far below that I couldn't hear it. No birds were in the vicinity, on the ground or overhead. In fact, even the cardon had thinned out. The contrast with the raucous, blindingly white world below was stunning.

I paused to rest, straddling two large rocks, when I heard a loud "*tik-tik-tik*" directly below me. The largest rattlesnake I've ever seen (and I've seen many) filled the entire space between the rocks I was balanced on. Its tongue, flicking wildly, was a black ribbon dwarfed by a head nearly the size of my hand.

In an instant I was airborne. Like the *Road Runner* of Saturday morning cartoon fame, I traveled so fast across the basalt plateau that my feet seemed to be moving in circles. It wasn't until I was safely surrounded by bright white guano again that I paused to consider how lucky I was. No wonder the pelicans were so jumpy; their closest neighbor was the deadly, thick-bodied, western diamondback.

Every fifth day we were entitled to a "camp day"—time to ourselves away from the grids with no obligations beyond writing in the group journal, making that night's supper, and preparing tortillas for the next day's lunch. We're talking real tortillas: ground *masa*, a little water and salt, and a sizzling hot, cast-iron skillet. I prepared the tortillas soon after breakfast, mixing, patting, and grilling them before the air temperature soared even higher. Then after washing a few clothes in salt-water suds I would head down to the cool intertidal and splashing surf.

For safety reasons, we never swam alone, but at least a part of my free days was spent down by the little cove where Fermín delivered supplies and mail every other week. With binoculars, books, and my personal journal, I would sit within a stone's throw of fifty brown pelicans and a harem of sun-bathing sea lions on the rocks across the way. Dolphins played just offshore and beyond them, gray whales fed.

After the others returned from work, we would swim there. Forty, maybe fifty feet from shore, enormous bull sea lions, with their tiny excuses for ears and shiny excuses for noses, would spin circles around me. Just when I'd think an eight-hundred-pound pinniped was too close for comfort, he'd pirouette and glide off in the other direction. The shyer females kept their distance. I knew some of them were new mothers. One night we heard primordial groans from the surf below camp and I lay in my bag, certain that one sea lion was destroying another. But peering over the ledge at daybreak, we discovered a newborn pup tucked beneath its mother's flipper on a rock hundreds of feet below.

At the end of a sweaty day on the grids, the long after-noons back at camp were luxurious. We were a compatible quintet, balancing togetherness and solitude effortlessly. Discussions ranged widely: over dinner, beside the cliff at sunset, in the mesh tent where I had joined the group for fear of blowing away with my own tent on a windy night. We talked of food and the books we were reading—then food again and the state of the environment and the world. From Kent, destined for med school, we learned that "giddy' comes from *gid*, a loss of equilibrium in sheep caused by a parasitic white worm that burrows into its brain. Some evenings, we read Whitman out loud or pooled our celestial knowledge as we stared up at the stars.

Leaving San Pedro behind wasn't easy. I spent my free time leading up to our departure torn between taking pictures and simply sitting still, taking in the smells and sounds, coming full circle from my initial impressions. What had seemed hauntingly mysterious was now comfortably familiar. Each cardon now stood apart, separated by shapes and scars, just like the lizards. The beat of bird wings, the pounding surf, even the background barking of sea lions, now felt the norm. How could I possibly leave?

As we cleaned up the grids and closed camp, I made my quiet goodbyes: to the boobies, the pelicans, and the lizards. Some looked me in the eye, others squawked, most ignored me. I found myself returning rocks to where I thought they'd been before we disturbed them. I stood in one place and turned a few degrees at a time, clicking my Minolta in a vain effort to capture a feeling on film. Then I pointed the lens straight up at the sky and snapped my final photo.

We had worked together so well for so long that, before I knew it, our entire camp had been shuttled in reverse back to the cove. I never heard the panga's approach, but saw the sea lions dive for cover seconds before Fermín rounded the point. It wasn't until everything was stowed away and we were heading into open water that I glanced back. There the shiny heads bobbed, eyes wide, noses pointing in our direction. Our sea lion friends were completely silent. None of us could speak.

＊

When my son is older, he may ask about specific places on his room's wall map. By the time he notices the smudge about where San Pedro Mártir should be, he will be the height of a six- or a seven-year-old. He'll be old enough to hear this story and appreciate the photographs, though he may wonder about the one that looks like a messy splotch of random specks. I'll tell him how his mother felt when she turned her face to the sky and saw thousands of sea birds coming home to roost.

Maggie Webster McManus had the great good fortune to cross the Atlantic four times, by boat, before she was two years old. After a childhood abroad, and years spent as a biologist in the field and overseas, she has landed in north central Washington where she and her husband have a pear orchard, two young children, and maps on half the walls of their house.

JENNIFER BOVÉ

* * *

First Night at Field Camp

I GLANCED UP AT THE CAMP TRAILER WINDOW TO SEE Lissa draping a wet dishtowel over a chair, her mouth stitched in a tight seam across her face. I knew it wasn't dish duty she was upset about—she was probably glad for the excuse to get away from us. Lissa's problem, as far as I could tell, was that she was having second thoughts about committing herself to a summer of in the sweaty, tangled wilds of Ozark hill country. Suddenly she seemed to realize that she'd gotten herself stranded a good hour from civilization with a group of people she'd avoid like a swarm of mosquitoes back on campus at Mizzou, and it had her spooked. She just didn't fit in with the crew, and she wouldn't even loosen up enough to try. So, of course, the guys had already started cracking jokes behind her back.

Secretly, I couldn't help but feel a little sorry for Lissa. Even though I had a few more calluses than she did, I understood what she was going through out there. It was the first time I'd ever been away from home, too—alone and unsure if everybody else on the job knew more than me, afraid I'd screw something up and look like a fool. The difference between

Lissa and me was that I'd decided to *act* my way to cool, and so far, it was working; the guys on the crew were duped. But Lissa wouldn't follow my lead. In fact, I think she was just as scared of me as she was of them. That day was our first in the field, and she'd cringed every time somebody had cussed or stepped into the bushes to take a pee. She hadn't dropped trow all day, I noticed, and we'd worked an hour longer than planned.

Lissa shut off the propane lantern and stepped quietly from the trailer with her head bowed, undoubtedly hoping she wouldn't get noticed.

Will, the resident bigmouth, couldn't resist; he was compelled to prod her. I swear it was like survival of the fittest, and Lissa had a broken wing.

"Hey," he yelled at her from his lawn chair, "you want a beer?" He opened the cooler beside him and pulled a can from the cold creek water within. "This one's got your name on it."

"No," she said, "I don't drink beer."

She scurried past the campfire toward her tent with the timid desperation of a mouse in a coyote den; she wouldn't look at any of us.

"Come on," Jaysen from Colorado piped in. "We made it through the first day. We gotta celebrate."

She hesitated for only a second, then Will had to add, "Yeah, come sit by me. I promise I won't bite, unless you like that kind of thing."

Oscar, a reticent young Cherokee from Oklahoma who was sitting next to me, shook his head, and everybody else laughed—even me.

If Lissa could have just cracked a smile she might have gotten some footing in the crew, but apparently she couldn't even fake a sense of humor. She stormed off in disgust to her tent, and I lost a little bit of sympathy for her. She was going to have a miserable summer, that much was obvious, and I sensed she'd try to hover over the rest of us like a dark cloud, too.

"Man, she's a bitch," Will said.

"What's her deal?" Jaysen asked. "Nobody did anything to her."

I shrugged and swatted a bug from my face. "She's just a little uptight."

"How about you, Jen, you want a beer?" Will asked me.

"Thanks, but I'm not much for beer either," I said, holding up my glass of cold orange pulp. "Juice. Carrot-apple. You ought to try it."

"Shit. Talk about a pussy drink."

Jaysen snickered.

"Last I checked, Will, I didn't have a dick."

A chorus of "oooh" rose from the other two as if I'd really gotten Will good with a simple statement of fact.

Will glanced at my crossed legs, and I looked at his hands resting on his thighs, and maybe it was the carrot juice, but I felt pretty sure he and I might have some things to sort out inside a sleeping bag before the summer was over.

"Seriously, though," I said, "You guys had better mellow out around Lissa."

"Screw her, man," Jaysen griped. "She's not my problem."

"She could be. If she wanted to, she could get any one of you in real trouble."

"She's right," Oscar agreed.

"What do mean, like sexual harassment shit?" Will asked.

"Yep. I heard a crew boss got fired one time just for saying fuck."

"Fuck that," Will said.

"I'm not kidding."

Oscar said, "Yeah. Did you know you're supposed to go, like, fifty yards from a girl to take a piss in the field?"

Will shook his head and took a swig off his beer. "That is seriously uncool."

"At least you're not like that, Jen," Jaysen said.

"Yep. Lucky for you goons."

A twinge in my belly reminded me that my period was due to start the following day. I drew a sip of sweet liquid from my mug and managed a smile despite an internal rush of panic. The thought struck me right then that I might have forgotten to pack tampons.

My brain reeled. *What would I do?*

I pictured myself trying to rinse out a bloody sock in the river, and that image very nearly melted my cool into a puddle beneath my chair.

Take it easy, I breathed. *Of course you packed them.*

Right, of course I had. I recalled putting them in the side pouch of my pack under a box of matches.

Hallelujah.

Picking up the conversation again in the middle of a lousy joke that Jaysen was telling, I felt certain that those guys had no clue how tough adaptability could be on a girl.

"So, the boss man Dan is supposed to be down here tomorrow, huh?" Jaysen asked.

"Yeah," Will said. "He's bringing the electroshocking equipment. He thought I should run the backpack shocker since I know what I'm doing, and you guys can net 'em and take measurements. We'll be catching a shitload of fish, and a few cottonmouths, too," he added, giving me a wink.

"Big deal," I said. "I doubt you have any more snake charming experience than I do."

He grabbed his crotch and raised an eyebrow at Jaysen. I could've kicked my own ass for walking into that one.

Will *had* actually worked on the project the year before, documenting the species composition of fish in the Jack's Fork

River, so he knew more about shocking fish than the rest of us. As far as I was concerned, though, he had a lot of work to do to live up to his ego.

"I heard Dan say that three of us would be shocking and the other two would have to do sediment collection like we were doing today," Jaysen said. "That kinda sucks."

"Yeah, well, we're just going to have to take turns. Nobody wants to get stuck digging up rocks all the time," I said.

Sediment duty was just as important as the fish work. It would provide critical data about the morphology of the stream channel and the available invertebrate habitat, which indicated the overall health of the watershed. But it wasn't nearly as glamorous as handling nets full of shimmering fish, every species of the rainbow.

Will set his beer down and buttoned his flannel shirt. "And nobody wants to get stuck working with *Lissa* every day either."

I was sure I heard her shift around in her tent, and maybe Will did, too, because he shut up before the hole he was in got any deeper.

Just then Oscar flicked a cigarette butt toward the fire, and Jaysen leaped forward in his chair, startling everybody.

"Watch it, man!" he barked at Oscar. "Make sure you don't drop those things outside the fire ring!"

From what I understood, Jaysen came from a long line of wildland firefighters who traveled around the country battling yearly blazes and bringing in big bucks, compared to being a fish tech anyway. Like a spaniel on point, he was known to get a hard-on when anybody so much as mentioned the word "smoke." I wondered why he was here instead of out in Montana somewhere.

Oscar didn't say a thing. He simply leaned toward Jaysen and glared at him, eyes gleaming like obsidian.

Jaysen shrank back in his seat a bit and dragged his fingers through his hair. "I'm just saying, dude, you can start a fire doing shit like that."

"There's bare dirt for thirty yards," Will said. "Take it easy, man."

"I'm telling you guys, it ain't funny. How do think all those fires started out West last year, huh? You gotta be careful where you put out your smokes."

Oscar grunted and sat back again, and I stayed out of it altogether, observing the males' bristled display. Jane Goodall among the chimps.

It was late, and I was starting to get a little chilly, and the thought of getting up at sunrise made my head hurt, but Will pulled another beer from the cooler, and there was no way I'd be the first to give in to exhaustion.

"Aw, who am I kidding?" he yawned. "I'm beat. Anybody else want this beer?"

We all shook our heads in a unanimous "no way in hell." Somehow, Will's surrender was the cue to break we'd all been waiting for. Jaysen got up and immediately started rummaging around for a bucket to dowse the fire. Oscar, who had driven his own truck down to the site, opened the camper shell and unrolled his sleeping bag. Will walked twenty feet away from the fire to relieve himself on the trunk of a white oak beside the cook trailer.

All things considered, I was awfully glad I wasn't Lissa. I was looking forward to hanging with these guys, spending long days out in hot sun and clear water and getting into a groove that Lissa would fight tooth and nail. It didn't make sense to me why somebody would teeter out onto such a brittle limb as she had by taking this job, terrified to fail. But maybe that was just it. Maybe some deep, driving instinct in Lissa told her she should push herself beyond the bounds of safe and orderly college classrooms. Maybe only then would she grow up a little, start to bend, and even learn to fly. As much as it irritated me to see women like Lissa in the field—with their perfect grades, soft hands, and even softer sensibilities—I thought that if she'd let me, I might try and help her come around. If it didn't work out, I figured we could all keep our fingers crossed that she'd give up and slink back to some dark campus lab and stay there.

"It's gonna be an early morning, boys," I sighed, heading for my tent. "Whichever one of you gets up first had better make some coffee."

Jennifer Bové worked in the wild for five years as a field biologist before heading into the uncharted territory of fulltime motherhood. She now devotes her time to her family, writing, small business ideas, and all sorts of art projects. Her first anthology, The Back Road to Crazy: Stories From the Field, *was published by the University of Utah Press. Visit Jennifer online at www.bovesboots.blogspot.com.*

* * *

Tracking Hope

I IGNORE THE SWEAT BEADING ON MY FOREHEAD AND remain focused on the ground in front of me. My breath is labored from the grade of the slope and weight of my pack. My legs feel heavy. As I climb, I keep count of the number of plants I know to distract myself from my burning calves. I've counted thirty-two thus far, a low number, I think, for this lush westside forest of the Cascades. My focus on the ground is interrupted by a solitary snowflake falling through the afternoon light. I blink, not believing that it is beginning to snow, but when I open my eyes again the flake is still in front of me, dancing in its battle between the buoyancy of the air and the pull of the earth.

Looking up, I see more flakes following this one and soon I am in the first snowfall of the season. I smile at the craggy peaks heading the valley as they absorb the white crystals into their hard skin, baked from summers spanning geologic time. Wiping the sweat from my brow, I take off my pack to dance with the snow. This yearly welcoming ceremony is a reprieve from the day's disappointments. The snowfall surrounds me, flakes the size of nickels, wet and heavy, turning the large trees into ghostly silhouettes and swirling the landscape into obscurity. I follow the movement of the snow, spinning around and around, feeling the flakes land and melt, one at a time, against my warm cheeks. Dizzy, I stop my revelry and, face turned skyward, and let them soak into my skin.

It is October and I am three days into the backcountry, and well into my second summer of looking for the grizzly bears of the North Cascades. Many believe the bears are gone from these wild mountains, that their populations became too small to survive after extensive hunting and the subsequent human encroachment into their essential lowland habitats. But there are many others who believe the bears still exist. I am one of these believers. Inspired by stories of grizzly sightings we tend to highlight the occasional and questionable evidence of expansive digging and large boulder moving that is more characteristic of a grizzly bear than of a black bear. In habitat teeming with grizzly food and roaming space larger than Yellowstone or Glacier National parks, how can there not be grizzlies? Between the believers and the disbelievers, the grizzly of the North Cascades has taken on the elusiveness of Bigfoot. It is a creature that exists so quietly and carefully removed from the human world that it is shrouded in myth and legend.

Regaining my balance, I shoulder my pack and sigh. My hair-snare site yielded no bear hair today. Even amongst its remote peaks and wild loneliness, I feel I have wasted my time in this valley, and in the last year of the project, with a scant three weeks left to the field season, time is precious. Far from any trails, nestled between huckleberry bushes under the canopy of an older forest and an avalanche chute filled with mountain-ash berries, the site looked like bear heaven. I was sure bears would be roaming through this area searching for the calorie-laden fruit to prepare them for hibernation.

Two weeks ago, when the berries were just beginning to ripen, I set up what is called a "non-invasive" hair-snare site with a field partner. These sites all look the same: a single strand of barbed wire placed a few feet off the ground and pulled taut around a ring of trees. A bait tree in the middle of the circle—oozing with the lure of decayed fish juice, deer blood, and skunk scent—is meant to attract the bears. To get to the yummy bait tree, the bears either have to step over the barbed wire or crawl under it, losing some hairs on the barbs in the process. We then collect and test the hairs to determine if they belong to a grizzly bear or a black bear.

The last official sighting of a grizzly in the Cascades was ten years ago, in 1996—a bear by the Canadian border. That particular grizzly was thought to be a transient, not part of a resident population. The sighting was rare at the time and there has not been any concrete evidence of a grizzly bear in these mountains since. If the university project with which I was working found a bear, two bears, a family, we might have a card to play in the highly political game of carnivore conservation. The evidence would be a leverage point for more education, more protection, and possibly more land to ensure the survival of this great bear.

Without irrefutable proof that grizzlies still live in the Cascades, their tenuous situation will only worsen, driving the few that might be left to extinction. Ignoring the bears is far less controversial than dealing with the public sentiment that would inevitably arise if the grizzlies were to re-establish themselves here. With a scientific name of *Ursus horribilis,* the human-attacking, livestock-eating stigma surrounding this particular bruin is hard to dispel. Currently, we are powerless in asking for more measures for the benefit of the bears when the response of politicians, park officials, and wildlife biologists is always, "Grizzlies, what grizzlies?" The Endangered Species Act makes no provisions for ghosts.

I continue my ascent toward tree line where my dry tent and warm sleeping bag wait. Snow is quickly covering the plants whose names I was hoping to remember. The rhythmic and familiar sound of my boots drops away with the new-fallen snow; the normally dripping green forest has been muted to stillness—a hush so audible I feel as if I can hear silence settle over the landscape. The transformation seems magical in that something as small as one snowflake can, with its family, recast the landscape.

I find myself envious of the power of snow, wishing I could harness it to bring the grizzly back to the Cascades. I have traversed over a thousand miles through these wildlands and my fellow project members have traversed thousands more. The lack of sign and consistently negative results from the hair sample tests are beginning to wear on me. At the outset of the search, I believed we would find something, some definite sign of a grizzly bear. I had to believe we would find one because I did not know if I could endure the loneliness of humanity if the bears were gone from this place. To me, the presence of the grizzly means that wildness is not lost, that the place I call home is not tamed by man, that it is not too late to stop the loss of species and the destruction of ecosystems. If the grizzlies are here, there is hope that the ecosystem and the piece of my soul that depends upon it will survive.

But now, at the end of the search, after collecting over eight hundred bear hair samples, not a single strand of which belonged to a grizzly, my belief in their existence is wavering. My body is tired from hiking difficult terrain with the weight of ten days of supplies, smelly bait, and barbed wire on my back, my mind is tired from organizing, planning, packing, and convincing my body to go on. But most of all, my heart is weary of holding out the hope that the turning of the next corner will bring a grizzly track, or that at the next site, a bunch of thin silver hair glistening like tinsel on the wire will, for once, not belong to a light-colored black bear.

Lost in thought, wading through a new world unified by whiteness, I am surprised by a depression in the snow. Two summers of searching have tuned my mind to recognize this size and shape—it's a bear track. I continue past it. Why bother stopping, I think, when every track I examine inevitably belongs to a black bear? But, stubborn desire makes me stop and turn back. Squatting over the quickly disappearing depression in the snow I wonder if my eyes are tricking me, playing on a final thread of hope to create the mirage of a grizzly track in the snow.

I look harder, trying to make out the details in the ever-increasing snowfall. The toes are arranged in such a way that they make more of a straight line than a curve, all far above the depression of the paw pad. I lay my pencil across the top of the pad and cannot believe what I see. This time, all the toes lie above the line of my pencil—a grizzly track! I quickly drop my pack and search for the camera and plaster of Paris to record the evidence, necessary documentation for this to count as an official sighting. I extract these, a ruler, my field notebook, and turn only to see the toe marks covered in snow.

Awestruck, not wanting to believe the terrible irony, I watch the track as it continues to disappear beneath the falling snow, until even the depression no longer remains. After some moments where time seemed to hover weightlessly, I find myself staring at nothing but smooth snow, and I cannot help but smile in spite of my disappointment, realizing the secret the bear has just shared with me. That grizzly must have been here only moments before my arrival, but now there is no hope of following its trail. I wonder if it consciously decided to get so close because it knew the snow would cover the evidence of its travels, if it was a gesture of thanks acknowledging my belief in its existence, if its mother had taught it how to live in a human world. I imagined it moving up to the mountains, appearing illusory through the snowfall. Would it den near here? Would it choose a spot on the other side of the crest? Is it a male, a female? I even dreamed of its siblings crossing high ridges, or in valleys like this one—devoid of trails and mostly of people. I pictured the Cascades from above, the landscape dotted with the beautiful hulk of grizzlies, and warmth returned to my soul—*they are out there.*

In order for the bears to have survived, to still be here under our seeking eyes, I believe they have learned to keep their distance from us noisy and often intrusive humans. Living away from people and their structures, altering their travels and home ranges to avoid us, must have become instinctual. This bear's mother must have taught it to move through the forest like an 800-pound phantom. The grizzly bears that remain in the North Cascades have learned over the years, from errors and a careful awareness, to persevere in our altering, alarming, and overwhelming presence. Maybe it started with one bear, maybe a momma and her cub, maybe a few that were already in the most remote places learned not to venture far. Maybe it was a collective action. However it happened, this learned elusiveness must have sprung from a need to survive, an instinctual obligation to persist, a duty to ancestors and future generations to keep their subspecies of the grizzly alive.

That track was evidence for me that there are grizzlies that have adapted and learned to live within the limits we have placed upon them. In that, I find hope. Not because species might be expected to adapt to the world we are continually altering and degrading, but because humans are an animal species with similar capabilities of adapting, surviving, and learning to live in a world with limits.

The snow continues to fall as I crawl into my sleeping bag. Peace blankets me this evening, the hand of Mother Earth on my shoulder assuring me that my work is not merely a gesture of an impossible desire for her salvation. The grizzlies are still here, still enduring, and by doing so they are giving us the gift of time, time to learn from our errors, time to become more aware of the effects of our actions on the earth, and time to realize that survival—ours and the bear's—requires living within the earth's bounds. I lie down beside the bear's secret, adding myself to the family of flakes that gently, but surely, re-casts the landscape.

Kathy Marieb is currently working with the Wildlife Conservation Society's Jaguar Conservation Program determining priority areas for jaguar conservation across the range of this great cat. She also teaches field-based courses for college students throughout the West. In her spare time, she can be found scaling rocks, running mountains, or writing prose.

SUZANNE WADE

Precautionary Landing

WILDERNESS ADVENTURES WEREN'T EXACTLY COMMON in my line of work with the military. As a helicopter pilot, I flew over many miles of pristine country, but rarely was I able to spend time enjoying it. Oh, there was the occasional raccoon that would wake me up while scratching at my head during a field exercise because I'd erroneously used my MRE (Meal Ready-to-Eat) as a pillow. Or the wild boars that were quite prolific in the backwoods of Bavaria, chasing and treeing one of my fellow pilots as he went to "take care of business" in the middle of the night. Or even the unexpected visit of a turkey vulture slamming through the helicopter's cockpit window onto my lap—have you ever seen (or smelled) a turkey vulture in close proximity? Not exactly the type of natural encounters to dream about, but wilderness experiences come in many forms.

Flying around Alabama did provide me with the occasional, if unexpected, foray in the woods. I spent three years as a helicopter instructor pilot in UCLA (Ugly Corner of Lower Alabama), teaching basic and advanced combat skills to new aviators. In basic skills class, the emphasis was learning how to navigate without the use of instruments. I'd teach the students how to understand terrain and relate it to a map. Streams that looked wide open on the map were most likely obscured by deciduous trees and therefore harder to recognize on the ground. If a river happened to be wide enough to see from the air, it wasn't the fast flowing variety I was used to growing up in western Washington. Alabama rivers seemed to ooze along at a leisurely pace, much like the southern lifestyle that I was beginning to embrace. Also in distinct contrast to the waters where I grew up, these slow moving rivers and adjacent ponds were home to quite a few alligators.

Two of my students and I were flying over this swampy terrain when a caution light came on that indicated a possible problem with the engine oil. A few weeks prior, the helicopter I was flying suffered a compressor stall. Loud bangs from the engine can get your heart beating much faster than a caution light, but the signal still needed to be taken seriously.

"What's the emergency procedure for an engine chip light?" I quizzed my students as I looked around for the closest open field.

"Land as soon as possible!" answered the student in the jump seat.

During our approach, I scanned the area to determine which direction we should go for help once we landed. Just east of us was some very marshy territory, which, in alligator country, did not seem to be the best choice. We were flying near the western boundary of our training area, and traveling any farther west would put us in a "no-fly" region, deemed hazardous because other pilots had observed a shooter in the area. It seemed the local people were either tired of helicopter noise or just liked shooting at them for sport, so I reasoned that they wouldn't be all that happy to help me out of my current situation.

"This is Charlie 06, 4 K's (kilometers) west of RT222, making a precautionary landing." The radio crackled static back at me, and I realized that we probably wouldn't reach anyone since we were so close to the ground at the outer edge of the training area.

I spotted a small meadow where we could land. On the ground, I quickly shut down the engine, and we all crawled out into the oppressive midday heat. Southern Alabama in August is something that just can't be described adequately. I've heard some say it is like a hot, wet washcloth draped around your body, making it difficult to breathe and causing you to wonder why you bothered to take a morning shower. As soon as we exited the aircraft, that washcloth enveloped me, sapping my energy in seconds. I certainly did not want to have to traipse too far through the woods.

In the air, I thought I'd seen some sort of a building not too far to the north, but I couldn't be sure if that was just wishful thinking. We hadn't received a response on the radio, and even though I knew someone would eventually come looking for us, our training area was large, and it could take some time. I decided that we might as well start walking and try to find some help.

For security purposes, I left one of my students with the aircraft and set off northward with the other. I was glad I had ample water in my bottle because by the time we had reached the edge of the clearing, I was already soaked with perspiration. My student was quiet, probably wishing he'd been left with the helicopter but knowing better than to complain. Nearing the end of his nine-month flight training, I'm sure he wasn't inclined to do anything that might jeopardize his graduation.

Don't think about alligators, I thought to myself. But I couldn't help it. Should I make noise to try and scare them, or would that just alert them to our presence? I recalled reading that there were approximately fifty times more alligator attacks in Florida than in Alabama. Looking around at the dense foliage we were hacking our way through, however, I doubted this was as popular a destination as Florida, hence the lower numbers. I could only wonder what the statistic looked like for those few who were brave (or desperate) enough trek across this swampy southern wilderness.

After trudging along without a word between us for a half-mile that felt more like five miles, I caught sight of a house. Actually, what I first spotted was the outhouse that belonged to the house, complete with a half-moon cutout. The tune "Dueling Banjos" played in my head as I stepped past the outhouse toward the main structure with my student in tow. The door was wide open, and I could hear voices. I knocked and slowly peered through the doorway to find three people lying around a large television. No air-conditioning or indoor plumbing, but the house was equipped with a state-of-the-art satellite TV. Just as odd, the couple and their teenage son were home mid-week watching TV in the sweltering afternoon heat. I hadn't noticed a road nearby, or even a driveway. I couldn't get the movie *Deliverance* and those damned banjos out of my head, but I suppressed the urge to run in the opposite direction. Suddenly, the father figure exclaimed, "Look—it's Fergie!"

Sarah Ferguson, the Duchess of York at the time, *had* taken helicopter flying lessons a few years earlier, so I guess the fact that I was a woman with strawberry blonde hair wearing a flight suit convinced this man that royalty had dropped from the sky onto his backwoods Alabama doorstep. Tempted to speak in an English accent, I explained our predicament. Luckily, in addition to a satellite dish, they also had a phone and were pleased to help out "Fergie in distress."

*

As we followed our trail back to the helicopter, I couldn't help but shake my head at the experience. Making a mental note to add swamp survival training to our curriculum, I heard the sound of a helicopter on final approach. One of the pilots in my company had received the message and was coming to pick us up.

Laughing at our story, the pilot took off and headed south out of the clearing, away from the cabin in the woods. I looked down just in time to see the rotor wash hit a nearby pond, causing a fifteen-foot alligator to slide off its sunning log into the water. There was no question about it; I had definitely picked the right direction to go for help.

Suzanne Wade flew Army helicopters for nine years. After a short stint in Seoul, South Korea as a Public Affairs Officer where she honed her journalistic abilities, she went on to complete her Master's in Resource Management. Currently she is a Geographic Information Systems (GIS) specialist and spends her work hours producing computerized maps and analyzing spatial data related to conservation. Off hours, she, her husband Randy, and their dog Solstice explore many of the areas that she has mapped throughout the Northwest.

ANGELA CANNON

⋆ ⋆ ⋆

Collecting Clouds

A CLOUD COLLECTOR. THE TITLE INVOKES IMAGES OF someone running across mountain ridge tops with a butterfly net, or a vacuum. It's far from that, and yet not so different. As a gatherer of clouds I have spent countless hours, blind to the world beyond a mountain research station, harvesting water from their ethereal mists. The ghostliness of the clouds atop Esther Mountain, a flank of Whiteface Mountain in the Adirondacks of New York, is intensified by the specters of the trees. Acres upon acres of red spruce skeletons and other dying trees spread across the mountainsides. Their eerie presence in these thickly forested mountains is a testament to some deadly impact. Something human this way comes.

Acid rain is the prime suspect in the deaths of the trees in this forest as well as similar die-offs in the Appalachian Mountains and in several northern forests of Europe. But in order to affect significant changes in our society that will reduce the destruction caused by acid rain, we need *proof*. That's why I'm on Whiteface Mountain this summer, working for the Atmospheric Sciences Research Center at all hours of the day and night. I'm gathering evidence in the form of cloud water.

Today, cloud cover settled over the top of Whiteface Mountain by late afternoon. Saucer-shaped lenticular clouds and sweeping cirrus strokes created a heavy, pale sky that grew darker and thicker, forming a vast cumulonimbus cloud—otherwise known as overcast with the threat of rain.

The weather came out of the west, from areas whose air masses are known to contain high concentrations of acidic ions, which means I will probably be up all night, on the mountain, collecting clouds. With work imminent, I snooze lightly from nine to eleven P.M., never completely able to sleep, and then the phone rings.

"Esther's in cloud, 2300 hours. Time for a hike, lady." Scott's voice sounds like he's talking through a tin can. He works at the Summit Station on Whiteface, a seat of luxury compared with the dripping tarp that is the base station for the Esther Meteorological Tower where I'm headed.

"Thanks, Scott. I'll get going and check in as soon as I'm set up."

"It's a date."

"O.K. Llama, out."

My full field radio name is Dali Llama, but it's based on a joke with far less lofty connotations than one might think. I was baptized with the title one day while my boss, Jeanne Panek, and I were lugging car batteries to power our equipment up the mountain trail. Panting, I suggested we check into using llamas for pack purposes. She looked at me, smiled, and said, "What do you think I got you for?"

I reach the Atmospheric Sciences Research Center, where I have to stop and collect my gear, a little before midnight.

The Center is housed in an enormous log building that served as a ski lodge in the 1940s. Sometimes I think I can still smell wool knickers, cocoa, and hotdogs emanating from the pine walls.

My preparatory ritual begins. I fill a large sprayer bottle with de-ionized water and set about collecting a bag of small Nalgene bottles, a rainproof field notebook, markers, and pencils, and then I load these things into my muddy backpack, which already contains a headlamp, batteries, walkie-talkie radio, a thermos of tea, a bag of popcorn, and a book to read. Before leaving the center I sign out, noting my time and destination, and grab the keys to a work truck that will take me up the foggy, dark, and desolate Whiteface Memorial Highway.

People often ask me if I'm scared to go up on the mountain at night. My usual shift is graveyard, from midnight until dawn. I have to admit my fears sometimes get the best of me while driving up the road to the Esther Mountain trailhead. Even though the road is blocked by a spruce-beam gate that I open with a key and lock behind me, I can't seem to shake the fear of another person out there, and it gets my heart pounding. Once I reach the trailhead, I dodge into the woods with a small headlamp to light my way. The trail is narrow and winding, soft with dark rich humus and sporadically strung with a web of spruce roots. The mountainside forest is a place I know intimately. Here, I feel safe.

I make my way a quarter-mile uphill, across the slippery roots and rocks, to the base of the thirty-foot tower. The base is sheltered under a tarp, and a small data logger computer is encased in a box there. I dig the notebook out of my pack and record the time, wind speed, direction, temperature, and barometric pressure from the glowing numbers on the data machine. Then, I strap on a blue harness belt, secure the harness to the cable on the side of the tower scaffolding, and begin to scale the cold metal rungs of the tower ladder. The veil of cloud around me is so dense that I can barely see the rungs even with my headlamp, so I feel my way up.

The Met Tower rises just above the trees. From the top on a clear day, I can see distant fields, winding roads, and the small towns of Bloomingdale and Gabriels below. I can see a couple of the High Peaks, as well as St. Regis Mountain lying in the distance like a voluptuous woman on her side. I often spend time at the top of the tower, relishing this view that hikers must climb all the way to the summits to see.

The top of the tower holds an assortment of meteorological recording equipment, an open-precipitation bucket, and a cloud collector covered in a plastic bag. The collector is basically a wide plastic tube, about two feet high. It's strung with several yards of plastic wire that "catch" cloud water. I had to restring one once myself, after an unfortunate incident with a black fly. My co-worker Carrie was tied into the tower with me, and we were working carefully together to reattach a new collector when a tiny black fly landed on my nose. I leaned toward Carrie to have her swat the biting little bugger, and the collector, which was balanced precariously on my back, slipped from my pack and fell thirty feet to the forest floor. Needless to say, the spruce needle carpet wasn't soft enough to fully cushion the impact.

After spending many overtime hours restringing the instrument, it reminded me of a tubular violin, I noticed with greater appreciation the humming sounds of wind passing through its strings. Strung by my own hands, it now seemed to sing.

Cloud water moves through these strings of the collector, condenses into hundreds of tiny drops on each line, and drips steadily down a long plastic tube. The hose-like tube winds its way down the scaffolding to the base of the tower. This is where I will hook up each small plastic bottle that I brought from the Research Center, filling one at a time, over the next several hours.

Atop the tower, still sitting balanced in the harness, I remove the collector's plastic bag cover. I take my pack off one shoulder and retrieve the sprayer bottle from inside. Hanging in the dark above the spruce treetops, I feel the wind moving the cloud past me, through all the many delicate needles of spruce and balsam fir. Vapors from the cloud wet everything they touch with tiny droplets. I take out my sprayer and give the collector one good rinse to make sure it is clean, and then I descend from the breezy treetops toward the dark, misty forest floor below.

Once I'm set up, with bottles ready and a permanent marker in my pocket, there isn't much more to do but stay awake and wait. Not usually too difficult a task, considering the mountain's so cool at night, and the collection site is by no means cozy. My only real comforts are my warm clothes, rain gear, and thin knit gloves—the polypropylene kind that not only help keep my fingers warm, but also keep book pages dry while I read the night away.

"WK263, ASRC Esther to Summit Station. Do you read?" I call into the hand-held radio.

In a moment there's a crackling reply from Scott, "WK263 Summit to Esther, I read you, Llama. You set for the rest of the night?"

"Affirmative. You snoozing or having a jam up there?"

"Oh yeah, gang's all here. Robot collectors are making appetizers and playing tapes. I think one of 'em is a dancer."

I have to snicker. We can't chat long; the FCC has regulations about using airtime for anything other than professional encounters.

"I've got my tools in order. I'm set for the duration. You got any results yet?"

"Yeah. I've got readings as low as 2.78 up here. I think that's just about lemon juice. It's a wonder we don't all pucker up."

I cringe. The numbers are really low. Rain is naturally acidic—around 5.5 on the pH scale, which ranges from 0 to 14 and measures how acidic or basic a substance is. A pH of 7 is neutral; less than 7 is acidic, and greater than 7 is basic. It doesn't seem like a reading of 2.78 would be that much lower than rain's natural acidity, but the scale is logarithmic, which means that each whole pH value below 7 is *ten times* more acidic than the next higher value. Scott is right; readings that low mean the rain samples are as bitterly acidic as lemons.

"Send your results to the EPA tomorrow, will ya? Or just send them directly to the White House."

"Affirmative," Scott replies with a sardonic chuckle.

I sigh, "Llama signing off."

"Summit King, over and out."

Sometimes I lose sight of why I am doing this work. I look out over dead trees in disbelief. It seems so obvious that air pollution is the culprit. Even stone monuments and buildings are crumbling—dissolving—under the strain and burn of acid precipitation. It's an established fact that smoke and fumes from burning fossil fuels are destroying significant parts of the environment by combining with moisture in the air and falling as acid rain. We all know it's time for more stringent air emission controls and new sources of cleaner energy—don't we?

The misty damp night clamps down. Silence booms in my ears. After a long period of meditative quiet, I begin to hear trees drip randomly from the collected moisture. Below my site, I hear the rambling of the distant stream that tumbles through the deep crease of the Esther Mountain watershed. Occasionally, a gust of wind rolls up the side of the mountain, passing through the trees above and moving on, as if it were a being of its own, large and alive. Stillness takes on its own tone amid the fragrant breath of the forest. Before long, I notice the stream no longer rambles, but sounds like the many voices of forest sprites in laughter. As night passes, and bottles fill, my body grows stiff and weary. My entire world, stretched taut in sound, becomes visually as small as the reaching fingers of light from the small bulb at the tower base. The forest is my tent.

The water voices continue to whisper to me all night long. I ponder the way clouds live between the worlds. They are vapor, and yet they rain down in solid form. They are part sky, part earth. I am part of this, and like a cloud, part of two worlds. I am part of the technological society that causes environmental problems, and like all humans, I am part of nature too.

By the wee hours of morning, the world is becoming pretty surreal. Not a star or distant light to be found. Why am I here again? Oh yeah, I'm here to change water bottles. Stay awake. Change water bottles. Stay awake. I can't see the trees dying, can't taste the acidity of the rain. I change another bottle and label it. It's damp and cold, and I do some jumping jacks to keep warm, to stay awake.

At dawn, the chickadees are barely visible, silhouetted upon the spruce branches. In the grainy light, I recognize them by their flittering movements and low-sung songs informing the world that the sun is on its way up. Orb weaver spider webs, intricate discs radiant with droplets, begin to appear throughout the forest. Finally, a radio call comes in to let me know I am relieved of my post. I can come back down, out of the forest.

I must acknowledge that I have heard the call. But how do I find the words to answer when I have spent all night listening to the language of the mountain?

My voice seems lost in whispers from the cloud water passing overhead, calls from the stream, and echoes reverberating from the ghost trees, the forest floor, and the soil. The mountain's voice is a mantra foaming along the edge of my thoughts. "Feel my discomfort," it sighs. "Know my disease."

I glance at my pile of sample bottles full of cloud water, the proof we need in order to begin healing. I have faith that someone other than me will hear the mountain beg for hope. I believe humankind is listening.

I hit the speaker button on the radio.

"Coming," I answer. "All clear. Over and out."

Angela Cannon is a writer, naturalist, and teacher who has worked for such organizations as the U.S. Forest Service, Trees for Tomorrow in Wisconsin, and Merck Forest and Farmland Center in Vermont. Her research work and wilderness experiences have led her from Alaskan glaciers to the High Peaks of New York. She currently resides in the hills within the beautiful Finger Lakes region of New York with her children and many animals.

⋆ ⋆ ⋆

Take the "C" Train

DESPITE MY BEST EFFORTS TO STAY OUT OF TEEPEE Hole, we're being sucked toward it like logs to a timber chute. My raft with its sole passenger is lined up perfectly for the brown, crashing current that's fast approaching and less than one hundred yards downstream. We're going to have to run the frothing mess, a reversal of flow that collapses back on itself in the middle of the rapid's main wave train. Accepting our fate, I'm pushing on the oars to move us into Teepee, building momentum. In fact, a spectator happening on the scene at this instant might guess that I'd intended to run the hole all along. Forget that it's a brisk morning when no one wants to get wet, half an hour before the sun will light the water and warm the canyon. Forget that a monster boulder lurks just beneath the hole. And never mind that for all the awake I feel, I should still be wrapped in my sleeping bag back in camp. We're committed.

From experience, I know that Teepee is a keeper, a watery trap to be avoided anytime. The river dances in it like droplets in a hot pan, shaken and imprisoned. Boats that enter the hole share the fate of the water, becoming one with it. How will my passenger react when we drop into it? Will his head spin and eyes pop? Will he register anger, joy, surprise? He has the bulk of two men—can his weight carry us through if we land dead center in it? What if we flip and he has to swim?

We charge over the brink of the hole and bump down with a jolt. For a moment we continue to track and it seems we'll continue downriver with no problem. Praying we won't be stopped, I keep working the oars to move us forward, dipping the blades quickly like the paddles of a windmill. A brief time passes in which I seem to be effective, until the boat gives a telltale shudder and abruptly halts. For one awful moment we hover, then we're drawn backward toward the heart of the hole. There's where the nasty business can occur—we may get sucked down, engage in endless spins, or overturn in a sudden, breathless flip.

My passenger remains relaxed and facing downstream, as motionless as a mannequin. He seems to be unaware of our upstream creep, or he may consider it just part of the show. Or he, too, is still waking up, or he's too petrified to move. I figure he'll be alarmed, though, when I climb over the gear and walk past him to the nose of the boat. But no—when I do, he doesn't react, as he doesn't react visibly when I grab the front D-ring and step off the bow into the water. Quickly I lower myself into the cauldron of churning current. Submerged except for my head and forearms, I hold tight to the D-ring with both hands. No way I'm letting go of it. My body and legs catch a tendril of current that's streaming downriver, and the boat with passenger intact follows me out of the hole.

I climb back into the raft, wet but feeling heroic, finally awake.

That evening in camp, my fellow guides congratulate me for the neat trick in Teepee. One guide especially is intrigued—Michael, an inquisitive person with an intense van

Gogh gaze. "Throwing out a human anchor," he says. "Where'd you learn to do that?"

I could reply, "At spring training, where the senior guides told me, 'When you're stuck in a hole, take the "C" train.'" Because they did tell me that.

"Meaning?" I'd asked my trainers.

"The current! Get something—anything—into that downstream current. It'll pull you out."

My answer to Michael has to be more complex than that—it wasn't enough for someone to simply instruct me. Rather, I had to give credit to a litany of killer holes that have claimed me or others before me: "Skull, Crystal, Phil's Folly, Clavey, Warm Springs, Lava Falls, Satan's Gut, Widowmaker—"

"Right," Michael says. "Well, those places must've been in your nightmares. You looked asleep when you jumped off the front."

"Maybe I was asleep." My move to the bow may have been instinctive, an unplanned response contained within my cells, more destiny than decision. How else to explain a move smooth as a dream, slow as a waltz?

Practice, practice, practice. Al, my jazz ensemble teacher at the University of Utah, ended every improvisation session with that advice. I took in his words, my face burning at how poorly I played the guitar in my lap. Determined to do as he said, I still floundered each time my turn came to solo. His words reminded me that all the talent and teaching in the world come to nothing if not cultivated. Practice and intentional experience are key.

Every night I took home my instrument and played the standards Al had set before us—"So What," "Autumn Leaves," "Satin Doll." Fingers to strings, I deconstructed chords and strung their notes together into chains of rudimentary

improvisational melodies that I prayed would grow more so-
phisticated with time. Faithfully I mapped out each solo in my
head and practiced, practiced, practiced. Starting slowly, I'd
build a line of music, then set the metronome faster and faster
to see how much speed I could handle. Often the flow of the
metronome's ticking would sweep by me, leaving me behind.

During jogging breaks in the neighborhoods at the base of
the Wasatch Mountains, I tried again to find a rhythm I could
catch. Humming the chord changes to "Green Dolphin
Street" and "All the Things You Are," I pounded the sidewalks
and streets of Salt Lake City to forty-year-old melodic pro-
gressions. Today the music is still linked in my mind to the
mountains' snowy couloirs flushed with alpenglow, brick
houses with white shutters and in-law basements, barren ter-
races rimming the mountains.

But in the harsh fluorescent light of the practice room the
next day, my little melodies would crumble under the un-
yielding beat of the ensemble's momentum. Al would stroll
among us and listen without emotion as we struggled with
our instruments. A suave man in polo shirt and slacks, he stood
with arms folded over his chest, his concentration a spotlight
on each soloist in turn. As I hammered out mush, day after
day, his expression never changed. I gave him credit for not
cringing, at least not within my sight. And I pledged myself to
even greater amounts of practice time, as my face still burned.

At the end of a day of boating on the Yampa River, I sit
near the water, contemplating reversals. Otherwise known as
holes, reversals are places in the river—like Teepee Hole—
where the current stalls on the downstream side of a barely
submerged boulder or rock ledge. The water hovers a while
in the hole, crashing back and upstream. In the clear mountain streams where I learned to boat, the boulders gleamed

underwater like submerged faces—the shining white of granite, the dusky red of chert. On the dun-brown Yampa, though, which brims with silt and fine sand, the holes show up only as mounds at the river's surface. They look a lot like the smooth, rolling shoulders of water marking the tops of innocent wave trains.

A raven crosses from our camp to the far shore, and my eye is drawn to the opposite bank. Shadow chases sunlight up the buff-colored sandstone cliff while the pink glow of sunset grows in the canyon. After the direct light leaves the rock walls, colors still shine off the river's surface in a lustrous rainbow. Then the many colors on the water give way to reflected salmon pink, then crimson. Soon night settles over the river, and the midstream holes become only dim humps. I strain to study them anyway, until I believe I could find them in the dark.

Practice, practice, practice. Al continued to end every ensemble rehearsal with those words. My fingertips developed thick, impenetrable pads of callous that allowed longer and longer practice time at home. In the evenings I jogged through the neighborhoods to the rhythms and melodies flowing through my mind and heart. At night I played my guitar until I fell asleep with it in my arms. Then every morning under fire in the ensemble room, I'd painfully trip through an improvised solo, unable to get into the stream of music rushing past me.

Practice, practice, practice. I'm sure the words apply to other artistic endeavors as well. To meet the muse, we must show up for it on blind faith, as Romeo showed up in Juliet's garden. But unlike Romeo, we must be there time after time to see what will happen. We have to be ready to be swept away, or the courtship is doomed to fail. Why shouldn't it? Even if we stumble upon the great treasure we seek, without experience and readiness we may not even recognize it, and it will pass us by.

My favorite rivers are full of holes that have stopped me or my friends abruptly in our paths—Clavey Hole on the Tuolumne, Crystal Hole and Satan's Gut on the Colorado, Warm Springs Hole on the Yampa. We've watched each other go awash in these holes—recirculating in Clavey, flipping in Crystal, dropping backwards into the Gut. We've skirted Warm Springs Hole with no room to spare, in fact dangling our bows over the gaping maw of churning water while praying we wouldn't get sucked in. Lava Falls in the Grand Canyon finishes with some monumental tail waves that sometimes collapse back upstream as rough reversals, and my colleagues and I have run those, too, countless times. Usually a raft running the falls can't miss Lava's tail waves—a boater just has to punch through them as straight as possible and hang on for the ride. Sometimes they break on you; sometimes they don't.

One time I hit the tail waves just as they decided to crash, and they stopped my six-passenger, two-ton snout boat midstream. We surfed as if we weighed nothing. The river screamed on downstream all around us, eager to reach the bottom of its thirty-seven-foot drop, while the boat skimmed in place, made weightless as a beach ball. Snatching the oars from my hands, the current pinned them to the sides of the boat. There was nothing to do but ride it out, and we hung for many moments in the reversal, water mounding and towering past the nose of the boat. The sun backlit the water purling above us. A seven-person excursion on the Banzai Pipeline of the Desert Southwest, it was also a first-class river surf.

Just when we seemed to be lingering in the wave hole forever, we twisted a notch sideways. Someone yelled, "Hang on! We're going over!" and the boat tipped up on a back tube.

Rubber hovered over us, blacking out the view we'd had of wave and sky.

Wondering why I'd want to hang on if we were going over, I fell off the rowing seat into the boiling water below us. I had to swim the rest of the tail waves, Himalayas of water though they were. Only after my passengers had pulled me back into the boat farther downstream did the events of the incident become clear. It seemed that I was the only one the river had wanted. Having exacted its human sacrifice, it righted the raft and finally let it go into the downstream current.

Skull Rapids in Westwater Canyon, Colorado, has a hole to be reckoned with, too, and I had the honor of plunging into it my first run through. A boatman's plan entering Skull usually involves avoiding the hole, which comes up fast near the bottom of the rapids. Despite my following the traditional strategy of starting midstream and cranking left, I crabbed an oar at the entrance and tracked directly into the hole's open mouth. My passengers and I dropped quickly into it like children tripping at a dead run. I was mortified—an army of boatmen watched from shore, and I knew I'd be the talk of the town that night when we all got off the river. *If* we got off the river.

We stayed in that bad reversal for entire minutes, not the usual three seconds exaggerated by disaster, but two or three full minutes, as the raft twirled, filled with water, spun, and pitched like a demon in the hole. My passengers screamed and staggered around the lurching boat, characters stuck in a B-movie nightmare. Advising them all to jump, I resisted my own powerful urge to abandon ship. But no one did. Instead we all sloshed around interminably, holding dearly to something—a D-ring, a line, each other—until one of the passengers finally fell into the river. He grabbed onto the downstream side of the raft, pulling on it as the river tugged him downstream, and the raft popped up and out of the reversal like a beast set free.

So, after Lava, I vowed never to be stuck in a reversal again.

Weeks at the University of Utah turned to months. Months grew to semesters. Classes ended, summer passed on the river, and the school year began again. I showed up again for ensemble despite my discouragement, not sure I could stay committed much longer. This Romeo was looking like a no-show. Once again leading our jazz ensemble, Al continued to watch without expression as he strolled among us. Sometimes he applauded those for whom things seemed to be working; the rest of us he listened to carefully but tight lipped. And he always sent us home with the advice, "Practice, practice, practice."

Then one morning in the middle of "Green Dolphin Street," Al spoke to me over the music. "Try this," he said, as my solo approached. "Play just one note per beat for sixteen bars. Keep it really simple, really sharp."

I closed my eyes. The music that had grown so familiar flowed on. I waited for my cue, then plunged in, playing as Al had told me, one note per beat. I didn't so much sound the notes as place them on the stream moving past me, a quick four-beat of musical waves carrying the pieces of the song's chords. It wasn't easy, letting my fingers hammer out this unheard, unplanned tune, but I forced myself to stay with it. Allowing the rapid key changes to pull the melody from within me felt like a plunge down a very steep slope. But I'd already leapt, so I fell, finding somewhere in my soul the lost advice that said "*get something—anything—into that downstream current.*"

Sixteen bars passed in a moment that not only lasted forever but also ended in an instant. I opened my eyes. The ensemble had frozen in place, instruments still to fingers and lips, but with music silenced. Coming out of my musical sleepwalk, I was surprised to see Al standing before me, a huge grin on his face.

"Congratulations, kid," he said. "You pulled it off."

Finally awake, I looked around for confirmation. It was true. The other musicians set down their instruments and applauded.

A few weeks following my early morning encounter with Teepee Hole, I'm back at the boathouse, writing out food orders for an upcoming trip. Michael of the van Gogh eyes is just returning from a trip on the Yampa. He pulls a trailer load of muddy river gear into our boat yard and parks near the warehouse, where he can offload equipment. Before he moves a single item, though, he crosses the yard to say hello. I'm resting on an old bus seat under a tamarisk verandah in front of our boatman's trailer. Many miles distant, thunderheads shift above the bare rock of mountains, and the light changes dramatically.

Michael stands before me, the shadows dancing far behind him. He focuses his blue-eyed stare on me. "I landed in Teepee Hole this time," he says, then quickly adds, "actually it was intentional."

"Why do a thing like that?" I ask.

"To try the human anchor trick."

"What? You're nuts."

"Maybe. But it worked like a charm." He appraises me as if he's a rookie pilot reporting in to Chuck Yeager.

I'm not sure how to react. After all, I'm a pretty conservative boater, not one to drop into reversals for thrills. "Wouldn't it be better to just stay out of the darn thing altogether?"

"What?" Michael looks scornful.

"Row around it."

"I could've, I suppose." In a rare break in intensity, a grin crosses his face like a light. "But it was fun," he adds. "And I needed the practice." Then he turns to unload the gear from one more river trip.

Rebecca Lawton went to the river at age seventeen and never left, becoming one of the first women guides in California, Arizona, Utah, and Idaho. Today she works as a geologist in watershed research in her home valley in northern California and leads workshops on writing about the natural world. You can visit her at www.beccalawton.com.

ERIN C. ALTEMUS

The Mushing Life

As I release the rope holding my sled to a pole, the six dogs lunge forward, pulling me, my two passengers, and our sled up and over the boathouse dock and out onto the frozen bay. They round right, and I lean into the turn, my legs nearly flying off the runners. I grip the handlebars with a steady resolve not to fall off.

"Gee, Little Bear, gee!" I yell to my lead dog.

Little Bear veers right where the trails in front of her diverge and heads west around Chapel Point. "Good girl, Little Bear, that's it!"

Little Bear and William are my lead dogs today. They work well together, hardly pausing when I give them a direction. We will head toward Daniels Lake, then across the Baby Grand Portage to clear some downed trees on the trail, turn around on Rose Lake, and follow our trail home. This is a ten-mile trip, but we aren't sure how long it will take. The trail out to Rose will be untracked, which means we will be breaking trail. My team is followed by my co-worker Elissa and her team of five dogs in chase.

I never dreamed before I started this job that mushing

could be such hard work. I have had my share of challenging jobs, from milking cows to guiding teenagers on canoe trips to several waitressing jobs that have often been the most challenging of all. When someone wants a double vodka martini—with two olives, on the rocks, extra-dry—and there are ten orders to take and dinners waiting to be served, it's enough to make you want to cry. Sometimes I did cry. But this job, dog mushing, may be my biggest challenge to date.

My friend Elissa and I run the mushing program for YMCA Camp Menogyn, located on West Bearskin Lake adjacent to the Boundary Waters Canoe Area in northern Minnesota. The camp sees most of its activity in the summers when teenagers come to the camp to go on wilderness trips. But the winter is a quiet time, quiet except for the chorus of howling dogs echoing some far-off wolf pack and the groups of visitors that arrive in a chaotic bustle on Friday afternoons. This is our third week mushing dogs for the camp.

On weekends we take groups of students, families, women, and even disabled visitors on dog-sled rides. Our aim with these groups is to introduce them to a new way of experiencing the wilderness while challenging them to do something not entirely within their comfort zone.

During the week, though, we usually just take the dogs out on our own to keep them in shape, learn the terrain, and maintain trails. Today we are taking some Americorps workers with us on a maintenance run. Several large trees are down on the Baby Grand portage trail, obstructing passage, so we need to clear them out of the way.

As we near the portage to Daniels Lake, Little Bear looks back at me, unsure of where to go.

"That's it Little Bear, gee!" I tell her.

She takes my command and veers onto the portage. As the sled slips across the portage behind my team, I grin. The dogs are running in silence, completely happy pulling me along. The cold air stings my cheeks, and my own breath makes my eyelashes freeze up. Occasionally a dog stops to leave its mark on a tree and the whole team bunches up. "On by, Beaver!" or "On by, Wallace!" I reprimand. But to myself I just laugh at how comical these dogs are. They are as giddy as I am to be racing through the winter woods.

At first, the dogs didn't take my commands as well as they do now. We trained ourselves using pure trial and error, and we are finally getting the hang of it after learning to obey two cardinal rules: never let go of the sled, and never *ever* put your hand in a dogfight. These seem like logical ideas, but they are easier in theory than in practice. On our first run of the year, Elissa and I became entangled in the woods because the lead dogs turned the wrong way. We didn't know how to turn them around, and a fight broke out among the dogs. We managed to break up the fight, but when I started to get back on the sled, the team lunged forward. I tumbled off and bashed my knee into a rock so hard I couldn't move, and the team took off without us. Elissa ran after them all the way back to camp, and I hobbled back, licking my wounds.

The next day we took a team of dogs out and kept them on the lake, but every time we tried to turn them back into the dog yard, they would run right on past. I would get out of the sled, while Elissa stayed on, and run in front of the dogs to show them where to go, and then I'd dive back into the sled. After several attempts, I realized I needed to run in front of them *all* the way back to the dog yard. Just when I was about to pass out from running through deep snow and trying to stay ahead of a whole dog team, we made it back in and parked the team.

The first few weeks were a series of such mishaps and calamities. There were broken sled brakes, runaway sleds, runaway dogs, and dragging bodies, but luckily there were no permanent injuries. Even now, I am always ready for them to go the wrong way, for a fight to break out, or for a massive tangle to occur—and there is still mass chaos whenever it comes to hitching up a team.

When we mushers arrive at the kennel to hitch up, we start pulling out sleds and harnesses, and the entire kennel erupts into a deafening noise of anxious barking and howling. As we start to harness, they really go wild. Each dog tries to tell us, "Pick me, pick me!" Buddy and Moe pose, front paws together, sitting on their back haunches, while Whitey and Beaver roll onto their backs in an effort to get our attention. Dylan and Deevers even stand on top of their houses to make sure we can see them. We take each dog off their chain, grab them by the collar, and run them over to the sled with their front legs in the air so that they can't pull us to the ground. Dogs like Whitey and Stymie are huge and strong, and if I let their front legs touch down, I will soon be dragging behind them. Whitey is so wild it usually takes two of us to harness him. Then there is Ram, who will actually walk beside me on all four legs and sit by the sled as I put his harness on. He even lifts each leg for me to put it through the correct loops.

We harness lead dogs first and command them to "hold 'em out!" They are supposed to hold the gangline between the team and the sled taut in order to keep things untangled while we hitch the rest of the team. But lead dogs like Little Bear don't seem to understand. She jumps up and over her partner William and sometimes turns around to socialize with the dog behind her.

Once they are all hitched up, the dogs begin leaping forward, barking incessantly, and pulling at the sled. I order my passengers to get in, make sure the teams behind me are ready, and then I pull the rope to release us. Immediately, there is silence as the team bursts forward. They are completely focused on running. But the dogs left behind in the kennel are not silent, and I can hear them barking until we leave Bearskin Lake.

Nearing the end of the Daniels portage, I prepare to go downhill, calling, "Whoa, easy now, easy!"

I put both feet on the brake and lean into the right side of the sled to keep it from tipping as we make a left turn. Then with a *whoosh*, we zoom down the hill and turn right, flying out onto Daniels Lake. Now that I understand how to steer the sled and brake adequately hills like this are a thrill.

Out on the wide-open surface of Daniels, the dogs have no trail to follow, so they prefer to stay next to shore. But this means weaving in and out of every bay instead of making a straight shot from one end of the lake to the other, so my passengers Gus and Jake take turns running in front of the team to show them where to go.

At the end of Daniels is the portage to Rose Lake that we call the Baby Grand. It is the longest portage in the Boundary Waters besides the nine-mile Grand Portage. The trail is mostly flat because it once was part of the railroad along the U.S.-Canadian border that allowed trains to haul out logs in the winter. It now makes a great dogsled trail. Partway across the portage we come to a waist-high downed tree barring the path—one of the obstacles we need to remove. I decide to let Elissa's group take care of this one and move on to the next tree, but this means I will have to jump it.

I stop my team, and they tug at the gangline, impatient to go again. I ask Gus and Jake to get out, and then I guide the dogs toward the tree. They jump right over without hesitation and keep going until the sled lurches up and over too, and I am airborne for a moment, hanging on for dear life. But I land the sled upright, stop long enough for Jake and Gus to climb back in, and then we resume our course.

At the next downed tree, I put in the sled's snowhook and tie the sled to a tree. The dogs can pull the snowhook if they really want to, so it's always best to tie off to a sturdy object. (This was also learned by trial and error.) In the half an hour it takes us to saw the log out of the way, the dogs bark and tug at the gangline, desperate to go, until finally most of them give up and fall asleep.

I brought a thermos full of hot chocolate laced with butter. Spending the majority of every day outside in the winter has increased my metabolism astronomically, and I eat huge amounts just to maintain my body heat. Drinking butter in hot chocolate is a great way to warm up, I have found, so we share sips of the rich brew between sawing stints.

As we finish moving the tree, the next team pulls up behind us—a cue for my team that they should perk up and get ready to go. I hop on the back of my sled and give Elissa's lead dog Monkey some kisses, which she returns affectionately. I untie the rope from the tree while Jake and Gus climb in, pull the snowhook, and the dogs instantly start to pull.

When we begin turning back to the Baby Grand portage, a sudden snarl erupts from Stymie, and I see him turn to and attack Ram.

"Stymie, knock it off!" I scream, but it does no good. "Gus, please come back here and stand on the brake, and no matter what, don't let go of the sled."

I grab the "jingler," a rope with washers tied onto it that jingles when I shake it, and I run up to the team where I grab Stymie's harness from behind. Elissa runs up to help me, and she pulls on Ram. Yanking and jingling for all we're worth, we get them apart, and I scold Stymie. Stymie is a world-class bully, and I regret bringing him on this run today. Ram is the sweetest dog around and doesn't deserve this attack—nor do I deserve the hassle of breaking up fights. I switch some dogs around, putting Ram in the middle of the team and Whitey in back next to Stymie, and we get going again before another fight ensues.

The ride back to camp is much slower than the first half of the day, even though the dogs now have their own trail to follow back. They are tired and often stop to rest of their own accord. Three people in a sled is a lot for a team of six to pull, so I jump out once in a while to run behind the sled and even push it to help the dogs.

As we reach West Bearskin the dogs pick up a more heavily used, packed-down trail, and they gain speed.

"Good dogs! Good job, Little Bear! Good job, William!"

Soon we hear the dogs at the kennel welcoming us back with a chorus of howls and barks.

Friends ask me what I love about dog sledding the most, and I have to pause. Certainly it's not the times I fell off the sled, not the dogfights, and not the occasions when the dogs turned the wrong way or broke loose from the gangline and took off without the sled. Or is it?

Honestly, I love the unpredictability of the animals—each dog with its own personality bringing excitement and adventure to the day. And I love that these beautiful dogs want nothing more than to run with me across frozen lakes and snow-covered trails.

Come summertime, when it's too warm for the dogs to run, I will dream of winter, eagerly awaiting snowfall and the chance to run together again.

Erin C. Altemus, a farm girl from Wisconsin, now attends a graduate program in non-fiction creative writing at the University of Minnesota. Besides working as a dogmusher she has also worked as a wilderness canoe guide, carpenter, waitress, teaching assistant, musician, and caterer, and she enjoys writing about all of these things. Recently she spent three months canoeing in northern Ontario in order to write a guidebook and hopes to find herself behind a team of dogs sometime soon.

MARY STUEVER

She Ran Calling Godiłtła

WHEN SOME PEOPLE HAVE A MIDLIFE CRISIS, THEY dream of owning fancy sports cars. My midlife daydream is a horse. Not just any horse, and certainly, similar to the fantasy sports cars of my peers, not a practical horse. No, I fantasize about owning a wild horse captured on the White Mountain Apache tribal lands where I work in east-central Arizona. It's something of an office joke that I am afraid has the potential to go a bit too far.

My job is to coordinate projects that address stabilization and rehabilitation on recently burned tribal lands. I work in ecosystems that seem devastated, but I am continually surprised and awed by their resiliency. In 2002, the Rodeo and Chediski fires burned just less than 280,000 acres on the Fort Apache Reservation, and in the aftermath of these fires, we planted trees, monitored vegetation recovery, stabilized eroding banks, cleaned culverts, built fences, and caught wild horses.

In order to allow the vegetation in the burned areas to re-cover, we try to keep browsing and grazing to a minimum. The area is excluded from livestock grazing for at least two years—longer if our plant surveys show we need to extend the furlough—and we try to keep the feral horse and maverick cattle populations in check.

Feral horses have a long history of running wild in these woods. Horses were often released by early settlers and historic road construction operations, and occasionally horses were lost and never recovered. Over the last century a wild population of horses has expanded on the reservation. Apaches hold high regard for horses, and they have historically tolerated large herds. In fact, the feral horse population had grown so large it was affecting vegetation years before the burns occurred.

Vegetation is the key to holding an ecosystem together. If too much plant tissue is removed too often, plants are no longer able to bind soil, protect hillsides, and assist water in soaking into the ground. Fortunately, the tribal range program had taken action before the burns to reduce feral horse and maverick cattle populations. In 1998 they trapped 700 horses and 130 cattle from the same area that would burn four years later.

Although there was some mortality in the feral horse population during the 2002 fires, the majority of the remnant herd survived the flames and was poised to threaten vegetation recovery if left unchecked. Once again, the range program stepped up and captured an additional sixty-one horses and thirty cattle.

Captured horses with brands are turned over to the appropriate livestock association responsible for managing the land. The feral horses must be sold off-reservation to ensure that they do not escape and find their way back into the burn. As the coordinator of the Burn Area Rehabilitation Program, I make sure the cowboys get paid for the horses that are removed. Here's where I got into trouble.

One day I just happened to mention that I would love to

own a black and white paint I saw months ago…and now the cowboys are chasing it down, aiming to please. I've tried to explain this possibility of me bringing home a wild horse to my friends and family as a simple mid-life crisis. My kids are horrified. My friends laugh. "Will you call him 'Wildfire'?" one friend asked, referring to a Michael Murphy song popular in our youth. I ponder. "Well, since the horse is clearly Apache," I muse, "I guess I'll call him Godiłtła, an Apache word that loosely translates to 'forest fire.'"

Like most mid-lifers, my daydream is totally impractical. I currently live on the reservation involved in a job that consumes all the hours a day has to offer—I have no conceivable time for a horse that would not be allowed to return to this land. However, when I consider the uncertain futures of most of these wild ponies bound for livestock auctions, I hope I can pull it off and somehow offer Godiłtła a home that honors his wildfire heritage.

Mary Stuever and her horse Godiłtła split their time between Arizona and New Mexico. Mary coordinates the Rodeo-Chediski Burn Area Rehabilitation Program for the White Mountain Apache Tribe. A forester, ecologist, writer, teacher, and wilderness enthusiast, Mary writes a monthly column, "The Forester's Log," which appears in various publications primarily in the Southwest.

* * *

The Adventure Family

MY AXE IS SHARP, SHARP ENOUGH THAT IF I MISS A stroke, if the blade glances off the log and continues toward my leg, it will slice through my heavy canvas pants and bite deep into my flesh. Forehand, backhand, forehand, backhand, each swing breaks through the strong fibers of wood, lifting out thick wedges of freshly exposed spruce. As the notch grows deeper, narrows to the bottom of the cut, I slow my pace and on the last stroke, I turn my double-bit axe so the less-sharp, beveled root blade makes the final cut, a cut that ends in the dirt.

"Hey Mom!" It's Jay, my eight-year-old. He's sitting on the side of the trail, leaning against his backpack and reading a thick paperback book. "Are ferrets the same as weasels?"

This is an important question for Jay but I have other things on my mind. It's late afternoon. We're working a trail we've never been on before and we need to find water before we stop for the night. My body is heavy with the deep physical fatigue that follows a day of non-stop hiking, chopping, and sawing.

"No, I don't think they are." I answer Jay's question as I sit down on the trail and push the freshly cut log with my legs, rolling it down below the trail. "I think ferrets are bigger."

"Oh." That's all Jay needs to know. He is gone again, back into his world of brave armies of mice battling evil legions of rats and ferrets. For my dreamy younger son, the summer trail-clearing job his father and I share is a succession of miles walked and minutes waited. He walks as we follow each trail, and he is a strong and willing hiker. And he waits, a few minutes or a few hours, while we chop or saw each tree out of the way.

Standing, I brush the dirt off my workpants, pants that are stiff with pine pitch and a month of hard work. While I'm putting my axe back in its leather sheath I glance over at Jay. He is relaxed and content, his ragged brown hair sticking out from under a dirty baseball cap, his water bottle dangling from his hand. He has no worries, except the fear that he'll get to the end of his book before we finish our week of trail work. He isn't carrying a spare.

I allow myself a sip of water and do a quick inventory of my water supply. Four plastic bottles poke out of the side pockets of my faded Kelty pack. I've less than a quart of water left, not enough to cook noodles but enough to get us through the night if we have a dry camp, a last resort option. It's time to consult the map again, something I do several times a day, like a fortune-teller gazing into her crystal ball.

We've contracted to clear over one hundred miles of trail and although we've worked in the Selway-Bitterroot Wilderness of central Idaho for years, this is our first journey on this trail. On the map a narrow red line shows our route, up from Warm Springs Creek and along the ridge all the way to McConnell Mountain. Blue-inked rivers and creeks wiggle across the map, but the smallest sources of water, the miraculous springs that bubble up high on dry slopes, are not printed on the paper. We have to search for those secret springs, lively trickles that spill out onto dark rocks made cool and slippery by the icy water.

"Jay, are you coming with me or are you waiting for Tom and Lee?" I have to say it twice as Jay is deep into his book, reading of the preparations for an animal battle. Tom, my husband, and Lee, our fifteen-year-old, are working on the trail behind us, sawing out a large dead White Bark Pine. Lee would be happy to be here, resting and reading with his brother, but he's our employee for the summer. We need his help and he enjoys the money.

"I'll wait." Jay doesn't even lift his head from the book. He loves the days when we have lots of trees to clear as it means he gets more reading breaks and does less hiking. I, on the other hand, know that our trail contract pays by the mile so I prefer days with miles and miles of hiking interrupted by the very occasional fallen tree.

I've got my pack on and my shovel in my hand when Lee arrives. He's a big kid: his belly rising above his hip belt, his massive head looking even bigger now with his bushy head of curly hair bleached a bright yellow. Lee is walking fast, his heavy pack tilting his body forward, and he stops abruptly when he sees the pile of fresh wood chips in the trail.

"Nice green chopper," he says, admiring the spruce I cut, his voice a trifle envious. For Lee and Tom and me, chopping a green tree is the ultimate trail work pleasure, as the soft fresh wood yields easily to an axe.

Tom is behind Lee, our crosscut saw bent over the top of his pack, the sharp metal teeth covered with a sheath made of thick fireman's hose and Velcro. The crosscut saw is fussier than an axe. Before using it we untie it from the pack, put on leather work gloves, carefully take off the long sheath, remove all vegetation from the sawing site, safely position both sawyers and finally, hope that both workers are ready to give and take on the saw, ready to pull straight and evenly. Tom and I work well together and the sawing goes quickly, almost like a dance. When I work with Lee we aren't always as fluid—the saw may catch in the wood and jerk our hands—and if we're tired we each blame the other for the roughness.

But even on grumpy days our razor-sharp, five-foot-long piece of metal is worth its weight in gold when we come across large dead trees. Two people using the crosscut can saw through the tough wood of a three-foot diameter dead tree without even breathing hard. Chopping through the same tree with an axe would produce gallons of sweat and long minutes of intense physical labor, with each stroke of the axe pounding into the dense wood.

Tom looks tired, his bearded face dirty and his eyes red. "Do you have any water left?" he asks.

I feel a moment of irritation. Let him drink his own water! It's been a long, hot day and the last water was at our lunch spot, hours ago. We sat on the edge of the trail by a shady stream and drank deeply of the icy water. After we ate our crackers and cheese we filled all our water bottles, but water is heavy and with our weighty packs we can only carry a few quarts. Tom is muscled and lean and sweats more that I do. He also needs more water.

"I only have a quart," I say and look at Tom. He must be very thirsty to ask for a drink. We are both fiercely independent and running out of water isn't something we would want the other to know. Asking for a drink is admitting a failure, a failure to be prepared for on the trail.

"I'm fine then." Tom says this lightly but I know he is craving water, his thirst even greater now that he knows we have so little.

Each year, as Tom and I and the boys return to Idaho for our summer jobs, some of our Forest Service friends are gone, lured to desk jobs where the work is steady and year-round, not just the three summer months. Many of the new employees we meet are kids still in their teens. What do they think of us, this nomadic family from New York State? Tom and I, our faces now creased with lines and hair going gray, worked here as seasonal employees before they were even born.

In the 1980s Tom and I worked together as a two-person wilderness trail crew for the Moose Creek Ranger District in the Nez Perce National Forest in central Idaho. At the time this was the only all-wilderness ranger district in the Forest Service. Since our district didn't have to worry about "getting out the cut," summer employees learned wilderness skills—low impact camping, hand tool use, and horse packing. Our summer season began with a two-day training hike up the Selway River Trail, a spectacular twenty-six mile path to the Moose Creek Ranger Station. Along the way we watched osprey dive for trout and found white sand beaches leading into the clear, icy water. At night, sitting around the campfire, we began intense friendships that lasted long beyond the summer season.

Our "Guard School" ended after ten days and the Moose Creek workers scattered, heading out to even more remote sites in the district—lookout towers, Forest Service cabins, and trails that hadn't seen a human footprint in six months or more.

We carried enormous packs filled with food, gear, and tools. These "mule packs" were so heavy that on the first day of each ten day "hitch" I couldn't lift my pack off the ground onto my back. I was lean and strong, but not strong enough to heft half my body weight. I had to drag the pack over to a tree and lean it against the bark with the strap side facing out. Then, sitting in front of the pack, I'd slide both arms through

the straps and lean forward onto my knees. After an intense
struggle for balance I would rise slowly to my feet, staggering
under the weight of a sixty- or seventy-pound pack.

At lunch on our first day we sorted through our food,
choosing the heaviest edibles—a fresh loaf of bread, an apple,
a bag of fresh-baked cookies—for a first-day feast. We joked
about drilling holes in our toothbrushes to save weight, but
we didn't really mind carrying the heavy loads. Those bulky
packs, bursting with jars of peanut butter and bags of granola,
represented our freedom, freedom to range far away on
wilderness trails where the most frequent users were moose
and elk. Every day we would walk and clear trees, stopping before dark at a flat streamside campsite, or if need be camping
alongside the trail on a rough patch of ground. We felt as light
as leaves in the wind, ready to dance into new adventures.
Where would we land, the two of us? Our freedom lightened
the load, made us ignore the chafing of a shoulder strap or
hip belt.

Our work was simple, and very complicated. We were to
open up the trails and make them passable and safe for pack
strings—heavily loaded horses and mules. In federal wilderness areas motorized tools are prohibited so instead of a chainsaw we carried a crosscut saw and we each had an axe. Trees
that could be quickly buzzed through with a chainsaw might
take hours with our tools. The fallen trees hung across the
trails, taut with hidden stresses and pressures. If we misjudged
a cut, the tree might twist or pinch our saw blade into the
wood, trapping it in the interior of the tree. And after we cut
a piece out of the tree, we had to move it out of the trail. A
ten-foot long log from a huge green spruce weighs hundreds
of pounds.

Over the years we gained more skill, learning at what
angle to cut a tree so the log would roll free and not get stuck,

learning how to use a stout branch as a pry bar when a tree or rock was too big to move without mechanical assistance. And we learned how to go light, leaving behind everything but the barest of essentials. Often we didn't bring a tent, counting on the dry, bug-free weather of an Idaho summer. On the tenth and last day of our work "hitch," we raced back to the ranger station, our empty packs banging against our backs, our empty stomachs aching for food.

For three months we stayed in the woods with our Forest Service friends, refueling with marathon potlucks on our days off, washing our filthy trail clothes in the wood-heated water at the bathhouse. Then almost as soon as the clothes were dry, putting them on again to start the next hitch. Every day we walked. Every day we explored the vast woods of the wilderness, from the dark silence of an ancient cedar grove to an open ridge dotted with the silver snags of burned trees.

After graduating from college, Tom won a travel scholarship and we lived in northern Japan for most of a year. In our primitive Japanese we tried to explain our summer work in the Rocky Mountains—trails, trees, rivers, mountains, axes.

"Ah so!" Our new Japanese friends nodded in understanding. "Like *Adventure Family!*"

It was our turn to look puzzled. We learned that *Adventure Family* was a TV show featuring an intrepid family who week after week took on a wilderness challenge—whitewater rafting, hiking, rock climbing. Now we had a new shorthand way to explain our livelihood to our Japanese friends. Yes, we were like the Adventure Family, only we didn't have as many disasters as they did. And we didn't have any children.

"Mom? Can you tell a Little Boy and Big Dog story?" Jay is ahead of me on the trail, his strong legs walking almost faster than I want to go. We are still climbing up to the ridge and still looking for water. In this thickly-wooded area, golden shafts of light alternate with deep shadow; it is time we stopped for the night.

"Sure." I make my voice sound enthusiastic, though I am tired of telling endless improvised tales as we hike along. Jay's legs, underneath his blue REI kid-sized pack, give a little skip of anticipation. "Once upon a time there were two friends…" The stories always begin this way and Jay and I have created a detailed cast of characters to populate The Big Woods, our story world. My favorite is Millie Yana, an adventurous girl beaver who heats the water of her beaver pond for year-round swimming comfort and keeps her refrigerator stocked with cases of root beer.

Tom is behind us. He interrupts our story, "Any more trees, we save them for the morning. We need to find a flat place to camp." His voice is strained.

Lee's voice asks, "What about water?"

Tom sounds grim, "We'll find it in the morning."

A silence from Lee. This is rare, as Lee is always arguing or discussing something with us. He must be tired, too.

Water defines this country. To the east and west of these mountains are dry plains, exposed landscapes of cacti and sagebrush that rarely get more that a few inches of rain a year. Here in the Selway country, south slopes are dry and vegetation is sparse. Towering Ponderosa Pine, with flaky reddish-tan bark, watch over open slopes lightly seeded with grasses and shrubs.

Yet trees crowd the northern exposures and river bottoms, thick stands of Grand Fir, Douglas Fir, Engelmann Spruce, and Western Cedar. The soil is dark and rich and the shiny heart-shaped leaves of wild ginger crush underfoot leaving a thick scent of spice. The rivers and creeks that bisect the mountains roar during spring melt then grow calm, their water clear and cold. By midsummer many small rivulets are dry, their narrow streambeds empty until the cold rains of autumn.

As travelers in this wilderness we must remember the unequal distribution of water. Once, in early June, Tom and I had instructions to clear the trail up North Moose Creek. When we reached the crossing we found a raging torrent, with dangerous icy water surging past our waists before we were even halfway across. We turned back and decided to fell a tree to create a temporary bridge. After an hour of sawing, our tree dropped perfectly perpendicular to the water but the swift current took the long tree and pulled the tip downstream, drawing the whole tree into the current and sailing it out of our sight. We gave up and walked, in the dark, the ten miles back to the ranger station to receive a new trail assignment.

Most stream crossings aren't as desperate, but even a narrow crossing can be dangerous when traveling with an eight-year-old. Fast water that rises to the level of an adult's thigh can easily tear a child off his feet.

The four of us have developed a strategy for times when our dry land trail dips across a creek. First we remove boots and workpants and stuff them into the tops of our backpacks. Lee is always eager to go across first and I'm happy to let him. He is a good swimmer and with his smoothly padded body he stays warm longer in the cold water than the rest of us. Using his shovel as a walking stick Lee finds a path across, drops his pack on the other side and returns to help me with Jay. To save weight we don't carry sandals but to save our tender feet from the sharp rocks we wear our wool socks. We look like storks, our bare white legs topped by giant backpacks. Lee carries Jay's pack and Jay walks between the two of us, gripping our hands for support. If the strong current knocks Jay off his feet we are there to keep him from going under.

Meanwhile, Tom carries his pack over then returns to "rock the ford," pulling any rocks he can out of the path the horses will take when they come across. On days when the strong summer sun blazes into the river canyons these water crossings are welcome, but on cooler days we shiver as we put our boots back on and hurry to walk again, grateful for the warm weight of our heavy packs.

Today we have not crossed any sizable streams. We're in the "high country," walking on ridges where water and vegetation are sparse. Now the trail angles up through a stand of lodge pole pine. The even-aged trees with tidy undergrowth sprinkled beneath them seem to belong in a city park, not this remote ridge in Idaho. How fine it would be to find a public water fountain here, perhaps one made of white marble, spraying out cold clear water. Nothing in sight though, not even any of the broad-leafed plants that can indicate damp soil. Now my mouth is dry also.

Jay chatters away. "Then Millie Yana, Little Boy, Big Dog, and Skeleton Boy swam across the pond to Millie Yana's house and climbed up the ladder to her deck." Jay is in full stride now. "Then they ate cinnamon buns and scrambled eggs for breakfast."

"I wouldn't mind a cinnamon bun," says Lee, interrupting the story. "What's for dinner?" Lee is very interested in food. For his birthday he asked for a subscription to a cooking magazine and at home he often prepares elaborate feasts. The dry noodles and soup powder we carry doesn't offer him much opportunity but he's perfected a superb trail meal of pesto pasta.

"Hey! Lee, be quiet." Jay resents conversation when he is telling a story. "Then Millie Yana showed them photos of

Underwater City and Big Dog noticed there were mermaids swimming around."

I'm not really listening, though I do hear just enough to be able to take over the plot when it is my turn. This slope is beginning to feel endless. We've been climbing for hours and hours, with stops to clear out trees. I shift my pack, and shrug my shoulders to loosen the ache. At least our packs aren't heavy—no extra water and very little food left by our fifth day on the trail. We've made good progress and tomorrow we hope to clear to the end of this trail, stopping at a trail junction near Lost Knife Meadows. That will put us at our farthest point from a road, a long two-day walk in either direction. From there we'll turn around and re-trace our route.

With our work done, we can relax and become backpackers, though we always find a few limbs to cut that we missed on the first time through. And most backpackers don't carry such an arsenal of tools—a crosscut saw, two axes, a Pulaski (a fire tool with an axe blade on one end and a digging tool on the other), a shovel, a hoe, a file, and a sharpening stone.

Jay carries a trowel. We bought it so he could help dig out water bars, diagonal barriers of wood or rock that divert water off the trail. Digging out water bars is not our favorite trail work task, especially when we encounter sections of the trail where zealous trail builders set in hundreds of these water diverters. To do a good job we must take off our packs at each water bar and the continuous twisting and heaving leaves us more tired than the actual digging out of the trench, the scraping out of debris that makes the trail into a wide-open angled gutter. Jay, though, has found his trowel to be most useful in creating barricades and trenches for his plastic army of cowboys and Indians.

"Yahoo!" It's Lee, on top of the ridge. He barreled by the rest of us after Jay reprimanded him and kept up his momentum, heading for the top. When Jay hears the celebratory whoop he picks up his speed and in a few minutes we're all out in the last of the sun, looking out at a long expanse of ridges and summits. The view makes me giddy, so much distance and space.

Lee has his pack off and is scouting for a campsite. He returns with news of a flat spot, not huge but big enough for our two small tents. He's also found an adjacent site with a flat rock where we can cook dinner.

Dinner? Tom and I exchange looks again. I think we have enough extra crackers and peanut butter to make a small meal, though we don't want to eat anything too salty; it will only make us thirstier.

It doesn't take long to set up camp; we've done it so often we could (and have) put up our tents in the dark. Lee shows me the cooking spot he's chosen and it is perfect, a flat bedrock outcrop where we can easily make a small campfire without disturbing the fragile topsoil nearby. "Perfect," I tell Lee, "the only problem is we don't have enough water to cook anything. We'll eat a bit of lunch food and save the water for drinking."

Lee looks at me, puzzled. "What? I've got plenty of water." He rushes off and returns with his half-gallon water bladder, almost full. I give him a hug, but then scold him for not drinking enough during the day. Lee gives me a what-are-you-talking-about look and goes back to his pack to retrieve two empty quart bottles. "I've been swigging down water all afternoon. It's just that I am *prepared*, unlike you and Dad, obviously."

I decide not to answer. His teenage ego is strong and, this time, he is right. Tom and I usually carry two quarts, or four pounds, of water, and expect to find another water source within a couple of hours. We should have been more cautious on this new trail.

Jay comes bounding over. With his pack off he is lighter than air and full of energy. "I found a cool place to set up my armies!" Lee drops his water bottles and gallops after Jay, ready for a break from adult preoccupations.

I sit on a silvery log, smooth from years of wind and rain. The boys may not be tired but I am. Tom is off scouting ahead, looking for water. Now it doesn't matter if he returns defeated. We have plenty of water for tonight and we'll get an early start in the morning, walking before breakfast. The map shows this ridge continuing for a couple of miles then gradually descending to a low spot where a stream crosses the trail.

I can hear Jay explaining the new rules to his game, his voice high and excited. Occasionally Lee's new bass voice interrupts. The two-dollar bag of lightweight plastic figures Jay begged me to buy in Missoula was the best investment of the summer.

In a moment I'll look for firewood, but for now I throw back my head to take in the wide sky growing dark, to breathe in the deep silence of the sturdy outlines of spruce and fir trees. I'm suddenly filled with joy, that uprising of happiness that comes like a gift. Here we are, together, on a remote mountain ridge in Idaho. Here we are, the Adventure Family, at home in the wilderness.

Betsy Kepes lives in the northern Adirondack Mountains of New York state during the school year and works as a piano teacher and freelance writer. In the summer she and her family migrate to Idaho where they become a wilderness trail crew and forest fire lookouts. In her spare moments she runs marathons, writes children's books, and does historical research and reenactments.

ELIZABETH DAYTON

✶ ✶ ✶

Hours Till Dawn

JUST AS I PULLED INTO THE CAMPSITE, I SAW IT: A BIG, bumbling, furry creature, scrambling up the slope to get away. Every time I'd seen a bear it had been just like that; I'd only catch a glimpse of the animal's furry behind as it escaped my human presence. It was obvious the bear was scared of me, terrified in fact. But still, I had studied that carnivore's jaws in mammalogy lab until I memorized the tooth formula and the shape of the bones in the palate. I had stroked the razor-sharp canines with my fingers, pressing one of the huge pointed teeth into my thumb pad and then pulling it away to watch the whitened area of my flesh slowly give way to crimson as the indentation filled with a tiny pool of blood. I'd held a bear's claws in my hand—five blades the animal could use to rip my flesh with one brusque swipe of its heavy paw. I knew that a black bear would rarely attack a person, unless it was sick, starving, or thought that its young were threatened. Still, the vision of a creature that was so close to the top of the food chain poking around so close to my tent made every hair on the back of my neck stand up.

I swung the truck door open and stepped out onto damp earth. The bear's tracks were all around my campsite, circling the one-man tent. For the first time I noticed scratch marks deep into the heartwood of some of the trees that surrounded me. Strips of bark lay in shreds at the base of a large redwood, the trunk left naked and lined with deep tooth marks where the bear had eaten away the sugary sapwood. It seems I'd unknowingly set up a bivouac in the bear's territory. Perhaps I should have unhitched my tent, packed my sleeping bag back into its stuff sack, and moved my camp to a new resting place for the night. But after a long day of sampling the creek for amphibians, I was wet, weary, and hungry. The sheer physicality of working in the headwater streams of Northern California always made me feel this way. My calves were tight from the long hike to and from the creek, my arm muscles were sore from climbing up boulder-strewn waterfalls, and my back ached from hunching down beneath overgrown vegetation. This is why I had set up camp earlier that morning, when my energy level was high; I knew by day's end the last thing I'd want to do was pitch my tent. The thought of moving my camp now, when the sun was just starting to creep behind the hills, made every cell in my body scream in protest. Besides, it was just a bear, like so many I'd seen before. A bear scrambling to get away from me, more scared of me than I was of it. I decided to stay.

I whistled a high-pitched trill and Dezzie, my yellow lab, came bounding from the bed of the pickup. Long hours in the creek could get lonesome, so I often took her along for companionship. It felt better just knowing someone was there. Plus, it was widely known that bears disliked and tended to avoid dogs. She immediately made a funny noise in her throat, almost a growl, and I could hear the heavy thump-thump of air going into her nostrils as she sampled the scent particles all around the bear's tracks. As I unpacked chicken and tortillas from the cooler she quickly lost interest, sitting in a diligent begging position at my feet.

This was the first time I'd camped out while I was on the job. Most of my sites were closer to home, but these creeks were up in the Klamath River drainage near Oregon and it just didn't make sense to drive back and forth. My boss agreed that I might as well camp out, even though I could tell it made him nervous. He didn't usually worry when guys on the fish crew had to camp overnight or when the owl crew was out into the wee hours of the morning. But I was a woman, and I was alone. The fact that he was worried made me even more determined to prove that I could do it. Being the only woman on the macho wildlife crew of a timber company often made me feel as though I had to prove something of my 110-pound self. Plus, it sounded fun: an adventurous night in the woods, just me and my dog beneath the stars. I decided to build a fire.

As I stirred a pot full of beans over the flames, Dezzie drooled all over her paws. The sunset made a dramatic backdrop, flushing red like grenadine across the deep orange sky, giving the effect of a cheerful mixed drink. I held up a scratched old Nalgene bottle, half-full of lukewarm water, and made a toast to my first night alone in the wild. I took a swig and nearly choked on a waterlogged moth. I spat the dead, wet insect into my palm, wondering how it had gotten into my water bottle.

After wrapping the beans and some chicken in a tortilla, I sat down to eat my dinner in the waning light, tossing some meat to my dog, too, which she eagerly devoured. My body was tired, my muscles sore, but it was the good soreness that comes from hard work and sets in only after you're done for the day, the type of soreness that comes with a sense of accomplishment. I exhaled, stretching my legs out in front of the camp chair that held my body like a sling. The food tasted warm and good. In the distance I could hear the sounds of night beginning to unfold: the chorus of Pacific Treefrogs serenading females in the dusky stillness, the chirping of crickets, stroking their back legs together like bows across violins. Even in the Pacific Northwest, where the summer nights are cool and damp, the dance of life thrums on as lonely voices cry out for potential mates. Still, I felt good in my solitude. I felt whole and strong and totally at peace. Visions of the bear far from my mind, this was just how I'd pictured it—me and my dog, sitting beside the campfire. As curtains of night began to draw on the sky above, I saw a star sparkle in the twilight.

I heard the first sound as I was cleaning up my dishes. It was a rustling in the brush. Darkness had encircled me and I couldn't see anything beyond the glow from the fire. I heard it again, and this time Dez perked up, her ears pointed forward, head cocked to one side. A low growl emanated from her throat. She barked and the sound pierced the night like a dagger, making my skin bump into gooseflesh.

"Ssssshhhhh!" I hissed at her, giving her my most evil of looks. I felt like whatever it was might continue on its merry way if we didn't antagonize it.

Something went crashing through the brush, and whatever it was, it sounded big. I knew of course that what sounded like a crash was more likely a scampering and that little creatures can sound very big when they are moving over dry leaves. Still, what the head knows the heart often can't comprehend, and mine was pounding with fear as a shot of adrenaline rushed through my veins.

My breathing felt heavy as I moved quickly, silently, getting the dishes back into my little camp kitchen box. The wind began to stir. I secured the food in the cooler and placed it inside the truck cab, out of reach of the bear, which loomed in my mind now, dark and shaggy. Though I had only seen the hindquarters, I pictured the teeth and the claws, red and bloody. Ridiculous, I know, but the mind does strange things when left alone in the dark.

How quickly a scene can change when your thoughts get reeling. I perched in front of the fire with Dez at my side, and the warm relaxation I'd felt earlier was replaced with clammy tension. I tried not to stare into bleak shadows, ears homed in to each crackle of twig or rattle of wind. The trees that had previously appeared low-limbed and friendly now looked forked and twisted in the flicker of campfire, making me feel claustrophobic yet at the same time very, very exposed. I heard the call of a Western Screech Owl, and I jumped. Funny, I'd helped out on the owl crew dozens of times, hooting for owls, catching them, banding them—it was always with a sense of wonder that I heard their calls during those times. But now, alone in the woods, they sounded spooky, sinister. I hugged my legs to my chest, feeling cold despite the fire.

Pathetic, I thought. Here I was on a camping trip in the forest where I comfortably spent most every day, and I was jumping and twittering at each little noise. Dez had fallen asleep by the fire, but I was awake, biding my time until I could go to bed with some semblance of self-respect. I had envisioned myself gazing at the stars, sipping a cup of hot cocoa, writing in my journal. But the truth was I couldn't leisurely gaze, sip, or write because I was scared. I was scared, and I hated it. I wanted to be a strong woman, braving the wild without fear, but I felt like curling up deep in my sleeping bag until dawn. The fire had consumed the wood to mere embers that appeared to writhe and hiss like a living creature. All around me the forest was in shadowy motion; gusts of wind turned tree branches into gnarled arms and fingers, reaching toward me.

That first night alone in the woods was one of the longest of my life. I lay awake in my tent, listening to Dezzie's snoring and trying to ignore the scrapes and creaks and weird animal sounds that seemed to surround us. I would just drift off to sleep, my sweet refuge, when a loud crackle of brush would pull me back to wakefulness. I would push the button on my watch to illuminate the display and count down the hours till dawn. Once I woke up with an intense urge to pee, but I held it because I heard something, some creature, shuffling and snorting around the tent. I thought to myself that the bear must be back. I knew if I heard a loud noise it would not be a Mountain Lion. No, those cats are sleek and silent, ambush predators who hide and wait for unsuspecting prey to come along before they pounce and make their kill. But I did hear once of a woman who got attacked by a lion while in her sleeping bag. The cat must have been sick, or perhaps very old, because such behavior was uncharacteristic. There were a lot of lions out here, though; I often saw them while driving the logging roads. What if one of those anomalous individuals had sniffed me out for an easy meal?

Just then, I heard another noise. A scratching. Dez lifted her head and growled. I reached for my headlamp, strapped it on my head, and peered outside through a small opening in the tent zipper. I turned the toggle switch on. There, in the shine of my headlamp, was a pair of ghoulish green eyes staring right at me. I pulled back into my sleeping bag like a turtle retracting its head into its shell, willing my body not to move, barely able to breathe, just hoping and praying that the creature— whatever it was—would leave. Dez was whimpering beside me, perhaps sensing my tangible fear. She growled again and I wished she would stop. What was out there? A lion? A bear? The only thing I knew it *wasn't* was a man because the gleam of my light reflecting in those eyes indicated the presence of tapeta lucida, the mirror-like layers of light-enhancing cells found only in the eyes of nocturnal mammals.

I lay there for a long time, trying to calm myself. *This is ludicrous*, I thought. *I am a biologist.* Rationally, I knew that the animal was most likely a harmless, hungry critter who smelled the scents that were left around my campsite after dinner. It was probably a deer or a raccoon. Maybe a coyote or fox. It could be any number of animals that presented absolutely no threat to me. My breathing began to slow as my mind calmed. I knew I would look back on this night with humor—my first night alone in the wild.

I didn't grow up surrounded by wilderness, or even in the countryside. I grew up in the city, the suburban jungle of southern California, where a scant bit of remaining coastal sage scrub habitat offered only an occasional lizard to catch in my backyard. That was it for wildlife, and I watched the last of the habitat and its creatures disappear as the years passed. Growing up in suburbia, it's easy to feel as though you are separate from nature. But, as an adult who chose to become a biologist and spend so much of my time in the forest, I now felt very much a part of nature. I had come to depend on its existence for my work, my life, my sanity. The wilderness was now the place I felt most at home, and I reminded myself of this as I huddled in my dark tent.

I couldn't hold my bladder any longer so I unzipped the tent and stopped to listen for a moment. Nothing but the wind hushing the trees. I crawled out into the soft dirt and ambled toward a Douglas fir tree. I squatted, pants bunched around my ankles. It really was beautiful here, the sky filled with millions of stars that blinked through the space between tree branches. The air was heavy with the pungent scent of spruce and fir. I breathed deeply, relaxing. Then I heard a sound that caught my breath in my throat again, made my leg muscles quiver. It was a shrieking of sorts, a wild lunatic sound like a howling, cackling scream. It was part coyote, part loon, part rabid madman. Dez began to bark, fierce and guttural, and the sound echoed throughout the woods. I was left naked and terrified, feeling exposed as though whatever it was could see me and was watching me right that very instant. My pants weren't all the way up before I bolted upright and dove into the tent. I wildly zipped up the tent flap and curled into my sleeping bag.

I could feel my heart throb, my breath coming in shallow gasps. Each moment slithered by like a weary serpent as I waited for dawn. My dreams for the remainder of the night were tormented and fearful. I'd awaken in a cold sweat and then gaze out at blackness that seemed never-ending. The woods were alive with crackling, popping, shuffling noises that made me stiffen and sweat in my sleeping bag, praying for morning. Then at some point, as I slipped from a dream state to wakefulness, the sky turned a soft mauve as dawn raised the curtains of night, and the tent filled with a rosy, welcome light. It was glorious. I felt as though the light was streaming into my pores, bathing my body in its splendor, filling my lungs with energy. The scratching and creaking from the night before were replaced with birdsong: the long, low steam whistle of a Varied Thrush, the playful call of chickadees, the bouncing notes of a Winter Wren. Dezzie was snoring heavily beside me. I stretched lazily and reached over to give her a scratch.

Unzipping the tent, I stepped into gilded morning light. Sunshine was pouring from behind trees that appeared friendly once again. My eyes followed a trail of tracks running in a straight line, one foot in front of the other, to a stump that stuck out of the ground where I'd seen the eyes shine. I walked over to the stump and saw paw prints, each about two inches long and tipped with little claw marks. They were from a fox. At that moment I recalled hearing that foxes make strange, eerie vocalizations in the night. It dawned on me that a fox must have been what I heard. I had to laugh at the mental picture of myself horrified, half-naked, and jumping into the tent over nothing but a fox.

I started up my gas stove and made a cup of strong, black coffee. The fear from the night before seemed far away as the sun rose higher in the sky and I could feel its warmth through the flannel shirt on my skin. The night had been difficult, like any new thing was difficult. I remembered my first week on this job, my first job as a wildlife biologist. I had been intimidated to be the only woman on a crew of men, fearful of getting lost on the winding logging roads, nervous to work all day in the field by myself. But I found strength as I grew out of my fears and eventually grew to love my hours of solitude. My time alone on the creek was reflective, empowering. I looked forward to my long, peaceful drives, and even when I got lost I discovered someplace interesting—and I always found my way back home.

After breakfast, I packed up camp and made my way to the truck. Just as I started it up, my boss came on the radio.

"How's it going?" he asked, checking up on me.

"Great," I said. "Couldn't be better."

And I meant it.

Elizabeth Dayton is a writer and educator who has worked as a field biologist in the Pacific Northwest, Southern California, North

Carolina, West Texas, and México. She received her bachelor's degree in zoology from Humboldt State University and her master's degree in Education from Texas A&M University. She currently lives in California with her husband, Gage, and their two daughters, Savanna and Camille.

Big Lesson, Little Island

THE HUMAN CAPACITY TO HABITUATE NEVER CEASES TO amaze me. We can take even the most spectacular circumstance for granted in record time and render the magnificent mundane. I speak in generalities but with the certainty of one who has had to knock herself upside the head, as they say, more than once to remain humble and appreciative of the life she leads. There is, after all, a lucrative industry devoted to allowing the average person to experience a scaled-down version of my job for an afternoon. I study whales, and not just any whales, but humpback whales, which are in my opinion the sexiest, most exciting whales around. And I don't study them just any old place, but it in a remote cluster of islands that lies hundreds of miles off Mexico's Pacific coast.

I realize that sleeping in a sandy tent for several months, sometimes passing night after sleepless night as the screaming wind collapses your shelter on your face, or bathing in cold saltwater, or dining in a kitchen where you check your rice for roaches before each bite, is not the universally accepted idea of an island paradise. But despite its inconveniences, Isla Clarión is very much my little corner of heaven on Earth. Or so I was busy reminding myself one late February a few years ago, in the middle of what was proving to be my crew's most ill-fated field season to date.

Things had not begun well for us that year. Our research usually commences in the middle of January when we catch the bimonthly supply ship from the Mexican naval base in Manzanillo, which leaves on the 1st and 16th of each month. A day or three later (depending on the number of functional engines and man-overboard drills performed en route), the ship stops at Isla Socorro, the largest of the four islands, to leave food, personnel, and supplies, then continues another day west to tiny Clarión. That year we were behind schedule from the outset. We lost the first fifteen days, or *quincena*, of our field season (and a significant amount of money) while wading through the sea of red tape that lay between us and the research permits necessary to work in Mexico, at a biosphere reserve, on an island and a military base, and with an endangered species. After two bureaucracy-ridden weeks in Mexico City, our crew of eight had reconvened aboard a gracefully aging World War II-era gunboat, chugging blessedly westward, reveling in the familiar salty stickiness that is being at sea in the tropics.

Our original intention was for the entire crew to spend the first *quincena* at Socorro, setting up the more technologically involved project there. Then four of us would catch the subsequent transport to Clarión and spend the next couple of months working with the whales around that island. Having been robbed of that crucial set-up period, we finally opted to send three of us directly to Clarión to get started, and Jeff (our fearless leader, capable of building or fixing absolutely anything) would remain at Socorro to assist until the February 16th transport.

When our ship stopped at Socorro, we had one frantic evening to relocate all our stored equipment from the previous season, inflate our noble research vessels, fire up the outboard engines for a quick test drive, divide up food and cameras and film and chemistry and recording gear and biopsy equipment, and get our half aboard for the continuing journey to Clarión. It was controlled chaos, but the following morning when the dust settled and I watched Socorro slip away behind us, a steamy silhouette in the warm dawn, I sighed and smiled back at the bottlenose dolphins surging along at our bow. It felt like going home at last after a long year's absence.

The passage was tranquil, and I spent it watching aerial acrobatics of masked boobies as they assaulted flying fish that were scared skyward by the passing of the ship. I ran mental checklists of what would need to be done to get our project up and running as quickly as possible, and let my brain sink back into Spanish, as I was the only native English-speaker for a long way in any direction. We arrived early the next day to find Isla Clarión resplendent in the morning sun, her slopes still donning the last green vestiges of the previous rainy season, which would soon fade to golden.

Getting people and goods ashore at Clarión involves navigating a rocky beach break and is an experience that can range from mildly amusing to life threatening depending on the conditions and aptitude of the personnel undertaking the task. That day the surf was manageable, so we and our things made it ashore without incident, as did a new team of ten *marineros*, and all the food and drinking water to sustain the thirteen of us for the next fifteen or so days. The Mexican navy outpost on Clarión consists of one rectangular cement building, which is divided into a large sleeping area with bunks and lockers for the *marineros,* a kitchen, a bathroom, a small medical room with a meager complement of aging supplies, and a separate bedroom with its own bathroom that is usually reserved for the commanding officer on the island. By virtue of me and one of my co-workers being female, the biologists earned the honor of using that room for the duration of our stay. Our sharing a bathroom with the boys was clearly not an option anyone wanted to entertain. So that became our center of operations, a place to plug in computers (a diesel generator provides electricity during the day) and develop film and store supplies. But the beach was my bedroom.

That afternoon I took my little tent down the familiar trail to the beach and set about finding large enough chunks of coral to which I could tie the corners of my tent and then bury them in the sand as an anchor against the occasionally intense winds. I carefully affixed my A.B.C.D. (Anti-*Buo-Cuervo*-Device), a square patch of canvas salvaged from an old boat cover which served to protect the delicate material of my rain fly from the talons of the *buos* (burrowing owls) and *cuervos* (ravens) who so loved to perch atop my home. I positioned my tent with the mesh door facing east to the gap in the hills where the sun would rise each morning. That done, I trekked up to the *faro,* or beacon, atop the highest hill on the south side of the island to look for whales. I saw only two small groups: a pair of whales a kilometer or so directly offshore and a solo doing long, sleepy dives off a point to the east—perhaps a male singer or a lone, pregnant female getting ready to give birth. It was still early in the season, so the scarcity of animals was not alarming. I looked forward to an early start on the water the next day.

I dined in the mess hall that evening with the contingent of *marineros* with whom we would live like family for the next month until they were replaced by a new group (and who thought us insane for volunteering ourselves to the exile of the islands), and retired early to my tent. But as I lay in the darkness, the north wind sighed down off the plateau like an omen. Its presence steadily increased throughout the night, scouring the surface of the tent with fistfuls of sand, until I found myself scrunching farther into my sheets with my roof plastered down on me. Resigned to wakefulness, I put my mental energy into fervently believing that this wind would die down mid-morning, as it often had before, allowing us good working conditions throughout the afternoon and a productive first day of work.

But die it did not, and after a leisurely breakfast and nearly an hour of staring at the backs of whitecaps racing out to sea, scanning for whales in the chop, I decided, "Screw it, we're going out anyway." I rallied my companions and down we went to our waiting boat. I had seen the same solo whale to the east that morning, and from what I could make out through the binoculars of its mostly white fluke, which it lifted clear of the water when it dove, I suspected he might be an old friend of ours, and the curiosity was killing me. We loaded cameras, recording gear, and crossbow—basic tools of the trade—into our ancient Zodiac and orchestrated our launch through the surf: hold the boat steady, jump in and start the engine, push off, and gun it out through a break in the waves. Once beyond the breakers we would unscrew the transom-mounted wheels used to pull the boat ashore, reposition them out of the water, and be off.

Wind is the arch-nemesis of those who study anything at the air-sea interface. Aside from making navigation slow, clumsy, and wet, it makes it very difficult to spot whales at all. In calm conditions, the visible cloud of a blow, which a whale produces with each warm, moist breath, collides with the cooler air outside and lingers like a fuzzy flag on the horizon for a few seconds, but it is virtually invisible in a strong wind. The telltale glisten of a shiny black back can be nearly indistinguishable from the glare off the lumpy seas around it. So you have to be somewhat lucky and blunder quite close to even locate your study subjects on a windy day. Once you have locked on to a target group, the goal is to position the boat behind each whale and capture a photo of the underside of its tail flukes as it lifts them in the terminal dive of a surfacing. We use these photos to keep sighting histories of individuals, as no two whales have the same unique pattern of coloration, scarring, and shape (although some can be frustratingly close). If a whale surfaces at a good distance upwind, it can mean a rough dash, water flying everywhere, trying to keep the camera dry, barely getting into position, only to have a wave jar the whale right out of the view finder at the critical moment. So you get to wait for him to come up once more and give it another go.

That was more or less the theme of our first day out that year, and our perseverance was repaid by a successful identification of whale #155, just whom I was expecting, singing in the waters off Punta Cola. Had it been calm enough to not rapidly blow sound out of earshot, we would have dropped a hydrophone and recorded his season-opening songs. Instead, we patrolled the more protected waters of the south side for about five hours that day. We encountered a mother with her brand new calf and an amorous male escort in attendance, a trio from which we obtained just one useful photo, and we saw another lone whale that we were never able to approach successfully. Not a wholly unproductive day, but far from a stellar start to our field season. We returned to shore to find that three of my four sand anchors had failed and my tent was upside down, having very nearly followed me out to sea that day.

I dug my tent in deeper and endured another sleepless night like the previous. In an unrivaled stretch of foul weather, the wind did not subside for a week, and after about the fifth night I even abandoned my tent for the outpost, preferring the echoes of snores in cement hallways to the relentless crush and howl of the wind. We launched the boat each morning for the first couple of days and withstood a few demoralizing hours at sea, then decided our time was better devoted to maintenance than the futile pursuit of whales, and we granted ourselves a couple of shore days.

Which brings me to the subject of our boat, little old *Tsitika*. Fourteen feet of fading gray Hypalon, which allowed air to quietly escape and water to consistently intrude, *Tsitika* was probably eligible for retirement ten years earlier. Yet, through persistent stitching and patching, she had been returned faithfully to service season after season. I believe that year was her twenty-third. We knew her days were numbered, but as long as we had patches and Hypalon glue, and as long as our research subsisted on the proverbial shoestring, we just couldn't bring ourselves to lay her to rest. She did, however, require a sometimes undue amount of maintenance. That year the precocious ravens had discovered a new pastime. Having been thwarted in their attempts to shred the top of my tent, it had become all the rage to spend their afternoons systematically picking patches off our research vessel. This was an insult above and beyond that of the wrens that nightly built nests in our gas tank box and the Clarión doves that dauntlessly attempted to nest under the floorboard in the bow. So we spent a couple of windy days cleaning her up, replacing her patches, adding a few new ones to the collection, and creating a raven-proof boat cover. And we were feeling quite good about the prospects of the season when the wind finally abated, on the 13th.

We rushed down to the boat, loaded up, and then stared out with trepidation at the rowdy surf for several minutes. The wind was down, but the swells, spawned by winter storms far to the north, were definitely up. And the tide was out, which meant carrying the boat a fair distance over the rocky exposed reef to reach deep enough water to start the engine and climb aboard. Certainly not the most trying conditions we had faced, but not a day to miscalculate. If our boat were to over-turn, the damage and the potential loss of gear would be cat-astrophic to our study. Getting injured while separated from the nearest hospital by over six hundred miles of ocean was ill-advised as well.

After a few minutes we had the sets timed and had confi-dently lugged the equipment-laden boat into the surf. Since I was the tallest, I generally had to stabilize the boat until the last possible second and then haul myself up over the side, and I had just done so when we passed through the trough of a wave and felt a sharp thud of something catching on the un-even bottom. I glanced back at my companion at the tiller, and he looked quizzically at me for a moment before we redi-rected our attention to the immediate task of clearing the out-side break. But not a moment later, the boat drifted sideways into the coming waves, and I whipped around to see what was wrong. We were flooding, and the engine was caught in some-thing—the wheel, it seemed.

"Shit!" I elegantly proclaimed as a wave nearly high-sided us. "Turn us around and get us out of the surf!"

I leapt to the stern and did my best to pull the errant wheel clear of the leg of the outboard so we could get outside the break and assess the situation. Once clear of imminent danger, and ankle deep in water inside the boat, I found myself hang-ing over the stern staring through a silver dollar sized hole in the lower port side corner of the transom where a mounting bracket of the launch wheel had once been attached. "Shit," I said again, for good measure.

Frustration tumbled from my brain in a cascade of ques-tions. How would we get back through the surf? How would we carry the boat, heavy with water and minus the support of a wheel, ashore? What possible solution was there to repairing the gaping hole in our boat with our pitiful assortment of supplies here at the outpost on Isla Clarión? I directed that last, and by far most troubling, question into an eddy in the backwater of my mind, and worried about just getting in. Too wet for duct tape, we resorted to cable ties as a means of attaching the wheel to the side of the boat so we could at least steer. The best solution I could come up with was to chain together several long ties and then use them to bind the wheel strut to the pontoon. That arrangement didn't inspire much confidence so I tied the whole affair up with the stern line as well.

We limped in and heaved and cursed the boat ashore. I grumbled as I sat cross-legged in the sun with a screwdriver and wood file excavating the soggy, rotten wood that had finally given up holding the wheel on. Had I known how much more involved the whole fiasco would soon become, I might not have indulged as much of my foul humor as I did that day. At that point I was forced to concede that the timing had not actually been so bad. It was the 14th, and we still had time to contact the mainland for supplies by calling the base at Socorro on the single side-band radio, which in turn contacted the base in Manzanillo by satellite phone. We requested that a sheet of marine grade plywood, some hardware, insoluble wood glue, and marine varnish be sent on the next supply ship, which was scheduled to depart Manzanillo on the 16th. That meant that after the trip to Socorro to collect Jeff (actual proprietor of *Tsitika*), and then to Clarión, plus a day or two to fix the boat we could conceivably be back in business in five or six days. Meanwhile the *marineros* had offered to drive us around in their *panga*, a massive, leaky fiberglass affair that was moored in the bay, poorly suited to chasing whales but preferable to staying ashore. It also gave the guys, bored out of their minds, something more interesting to do than cutting grass with *machetes*.

We worked a couple of exceedingly ineffective days that way, until the 19th, which we spent eagerly preparing for the much-anticipated arrival of the supply ship. We knew the boat had left Socorro the previous day, and we were quite puzzled when its E.T.A. came and went and the boat never materialized. Finally, a call came over the radio explaining everything: the Mexican navy, or *Armada*, had received notification from the U.S. Coast Guard that there was a vessel somewhere in the vicinity of the islands that was suspected of transporting drugs. The supply ship (the *Ortega*, which incidentally took great pride in the distinction of having made more drug busts than any other ship in the *Armada*) was ordered to change its route and pursue the suspect boat, which it eventually caught up to four or five hours east of Socorro. They boarded the boat, found traces of cocaine, arrested the crew, commandeered the vessel and headed back to the mainland with Jeff, the materials to repair our boat, and all our food and water for the next two weeks aboard.

The stated plan was for the *Ortega* to escort the vessel back to Manzanillo, stay a "little while," then turn around and come back out to the islands, arriving at Clarión sometime on Thursday the 24th.

We bitched, moaned, whined, and then finally resigned ourselves to keeping busy working in the navy skiff. But then the command came from on high for the guys to get busy cleaning up the base (which generally deteriorates from a boy scout camp kind of feel to something out of *Lord of the Flies* by week two) because we might be having "important guests." In other words, the president of Mexico was probably thinking about coming out to Clarión to go diving—

stunning timing for us. So I didn't have huge hopes of going out on the 21st, but was thinking just maybe I could beg for a few hours of boat time. That was until I got up to the base that morning and looked out to see only the very tip of the bow of their skiff visible at the moorage. Overnight, a strong north wind had combined with an unusually low tide, an unusually large swell, and a too-short mooring line to sink the boat, motor and all. It took a monumental Mexican navy drill: ten *marineros*, one decrepit six-wheel-drive vehicle, three hours, and countless futile acts of mindless machismo to eventually drag it ashore. It would be awhile before their skiff was in any sort of working condition: the engine was flooded, and there were holes in the hull where it had been banging against the bottom overnight. We were completely boatless and utterly deflated. Our only consolation was the thought of poor Jeff, unwittingly trapped aboard the *Ortega* until further notice, who had it undeniably worse than did we.

We took stock of our situation. We had enough drinking water, provided we were mindful of our usage, to last us at least another week, maybe even two. We had enough rice, beans, and feral animals on the island to last a hell of a lot longer than that if it came down to it. When word came that they had decided not to send the *Ortega* and its prisoners to Manzanillo but to the port of Lazaro Cardenas, another twelve to fifteen hours south, we just shook our heads. They said we could expect the ship Monday or Tuesday. Our last day of work had been the 18th, which meant a loss of at least ten days, a significant chunk of our two months to work at Clarión, and during the peak of the humpback breeding season.

And so I found myself in the deepest of funks on Isla Clarión. All was wrong in my little world. I had developed, reviewed, scanned, and entered the data from the whopping six rolls of film we had shot so far that season. There wasn't much else work I could do, so each day, after breakfast, I loaded my backpack with water, an energy bar, a journal, and binoculars and set to wandering about the island. I usually wound up back at the more remote beach to the east of the base in the early afternoon. The day of February 24, I had picked my way through the tide pools to the end of a rocky outcropping that was the eastern boundary of the beach. There I sat with my boots at my side, my feet dangling over the edge catching the occasional wash of the surf, and watched a mother whale, her young calf breaching exuberantly alongside, swimming lazy circles just a couple hundred meters away from me. So close, yet so far, as they say. I saw another group of adults, probably three or four, steaming their way east farther offshore.

Watching my work parade by while I sat landlocked only worsened my mood, so I climbed down and kicked my way along the beach of chunky white coral. It was hot and I was dirty from hiking dusty trails, not to mention sticky with a toxic sap that I knew from experience would blister my skin if I let it sit too long, so I ditched my clothes and waded into the ocean. It was lunchtime, so I figured the chances of any-one from the base stumbling across my path were pretty re-mote. I thought wistfully of my home far to the north, where the ocean was dark and cold and storm-tossed, as I watched bits of purple shell swirl around my feet through the brilliant lens of clear water. Feeling clean and deeply refreshed, I lay in the sun for a while and allowed myself to melt.

I let go of my expectations and accepted that I was exactly where I was meant to be in the universe at that moment: on a gem of an island that an infinitesimally small percentage of the human population even knew existed. I was on vacation! No work to distract me from knowing Isla Clarión as an un-encumbered soul on her softening volcanic soil. And the whales were on vacation, too, from the presence of our noisy little boat, an aspect of our work I have always regretted. I chided myself for the shamefully jaded state I had allowed myself to slide into, for complaining when I stared down at the hulking shadow of a resting whale, suspended sixty feet below me in the bottomless expanse of turquoise for twenty minutes, when all I wanted was for it to surface so I could get its picture and get on with my day, as if it were another tiresome piece of paper on my desk. I renewed my vow to cherish my life like the gift it is, to remain conscious and never take a moment for granted, no matter how magnificent or insignificant.

The *Ortega* finally arrived Monday, February 28th and deposited an exhausted but elated Jeff into our midst (along with a two-week supply of drinking water that was tainted with gasoline). We went straight to work on the boat and were able to put that extra day in February to good use, even managing a few hours on the water that afternoon. I can't say *Tsitika* was as good as new, but she was fully functional again.

Calm weather and plentiful whales prevailed throughout the month of March and we did our best to make up for the lost days earlier in the season. By the time we departed the island at the end of the first week in April, the tribulations of February were little more than a series of amusing stories for the crew awaiting our reunion at Socorro.

Erin Falcone is a currently working as a biologist for Cascadia Research Collective, a small non-profit organization in Olympia, Washington that specializes in the study and conservation of marine mammals. Humpback whales are the species with which she most often works, and she has studied them from Central America to Alaska, and most points in between.

KATHLEEN YALE

Bone Boiling

OVER THE LAST FEW YEARS I HAVE SPENT SEVERAL
seasons working on wildlife field projects. A lot of people au-
tomatically think *ranger* when I say this—pickle-green suit,
funny hat, shiny badge-wearing ranger. The general consensus
seems to be one of respect, and at the very least there is a level
of esteem associated with the title. But I have never been a
ranger, have no desire to be one, and don't mean to lead people on.

When I describe my work of the moment, polls reveal that
the most common responses I usually receive are either the
envious "I wish I got paid to do *that*," or the bewildered "Oh,
well, that must be nice for *you*." As in, "You spent the fall collecting bear scat? Well, that sounds perfect for you." Never
mind the fact that someone might actually think my ideal purpose in life is to retrieve animal excrement. You see, while
some imagine the world of biological field work as one full of
petting baby animals, making daisy chains, and working on
your tan in a sort of *the-hills-are-alive-with-the-sound-of-music*
state of ecstasy, let it be known that there is a far more seedy
underbelly to it all. Grunt work, clean up, whatever you want

237

to call it, there are a great many cogs that need to be kept greased in order to run a successful project. And the greasing gets you dirty. Sometimes disgustingly so.

When trying to one-up a task that involves "homogenizing" a scat sample (read: squishing it in your hand for two or three minutes, eyeing it for bugs, bark, and berries until your gloves are stained a number of colors), there are only a few pegs on the ladder of revulsion to ascend. My family thought the process of bottling fermented cattle blood and fish guts as liquid bear lure—*you have to scrub the maggots off before you fill the bottle*—took it up a notch, if not several widely spaced notches. That was for a project in Glacier that tried to entice grizzly bears into certain marked areas where they might rub on trees and roll around in said concoction, leaving bits of DNA in strands of hair and piles of scat for our collection purposes. Obviously in the game of gross-out, two-month-old fish guts and greedy, writhing maggots were hard to top.

Until Yellowstone.

A couple of years ago I began working on the Gray Wolf Restoration Project in Yellowstone National Park. The job entailed many different responsibilities—observing and documenting wolf behavior, radio-tracking and mapping individuals' locations. One of the project's focal points is documenting wolf kill rates, so we spent a lot of time looking for prey carcasses and doing necropsies on disarticulated bison, deer, and most of all, elk. It is possible that you really haven't lived until you've gotten your hands dirty in a gooey, gangrenous elk carcass.

At every kill site we recorded the sex, age, and condition of the animal, examining bone marrow and looking for any abnormalities before taking a souvenir back to the office in the form of an elk leg. Eventually the metatarsus bones (the elk equivalent of the human bone that connects the base of the toes to the ankle) are measured for general record keeping and as an index of vulnerability in regards to elk population and health within the park. These bones are supposedly some of the last long bones to finish developing in a fetus, and by comparing bone lengths from different individuals we can get an indication of the overall health of these animals and the health of their mothers during pregnancy. But between collection and measurement lies a crucial step in the process: bone boiling.

In truth, a more accurate description of the task would probably be along the lines of "putrid flesh boiling" or "experimenting with malodorous scent tolerance," but that's just the bleating of a finicky stomach.

Right. So the day begins with the unceremonious lighting of a propane fire and the filling of a large, much dented tin garbage can with many gallons of water. It usually takes an hour or two before the pot is finally boiling, and the real task begins.

Imagine a maintenance area—well, junkyard really—located down, down, down at the dead end of a winding road in the Mammoth Headquarters neighborhood of the park. There sits a large chrome freezer, the walk-in kind the size of (or sadly, perhaps larger than) my seasonal dorm room at the time. This particular freezer's favorite game is "let's break down again," which it is very good at, and has successfully completed multiple times in the past. The most lasting result of this game, beyond emotional scarring for the poor soul that must mop it out, is that often the contents within the freezer don't necessarily stay "frozen." The very location of this exiled freezer is a pretty good indicator of how the rest of the park feels about the matter. It is my personal belief that they are trying to forget it exists.

And what does said freezer contain? Hmmm. Well, there is usually a wide assortment of animal heads, bodies, and parts—

many waiting to be examined at a wildlife lab, or used as evidence in poaching cases. There are also many, many tissue and bone marrow samples and many, many, many elk legs. And that is what we were after—the elk legs and the metatarsus bones within them.

These legs (and I really don't mind calling them "legs," as unscientific as that may sound, because they still have flesh and blood, and hide and hoof attached) usually live in the aforementioned freezer for between three weeks and three years, depending on how long crews can procrastinate bone boiling. Wisely, the park policy gods and biologists have deemed that boiling can only take place in the winter months when the resident grizzly bear population is denned up and asleep. Otherwise things might really get interesting.

Anyway, when the water is boiling we bring the elk legs out. In truth, entering the cooler is a job that I try to avoid at all costs, as just opening the door releases a powerful stench—cool, stale, vivacious. So when I say *we* bring the legs out, what I usually mean is: *I hope someone else* brings the legs out. Upon disentangling each leg from its respective garbage-bag wrapping, we check to make sure the metal-tag labels are secure before tying a thin wire around each leg. Dangling from these spindly hooks, the legs are lowered into the pot, where they will remain, submerged, boiling like a witchy stew for about an hour.

Now picture four spry wolf project volunteers. Think of the prestige associated with that affiliation, the glamour. Visualize us all wearing matching canvas Park Service coveralls. Yes, they are of the classic pickle-green variety. I'm the one in the middle, my jumpsuit borrowed from our project leader who happens to be about 6' 2". I am about seven inches too short. I look ridiculous. Picture us all lined up in front of a makeshift table—a long, wooden plank resting on top of upturned garbage cans, lined with old outhouse toilets for optional seating. Here we are sharpening our dented, rusty knives, wincing at the screechy sound. Now we are slipping rubber gloves on over wool ones. Imagine that three out of four of us are vegetarians.

Time is up. We lift the lid, releasing a rank, billowing steam directly into our faces, and begin pulling out legs.

First you have to cut off all of the hair and all of the flesh. If the leg has boiled long enough, that isn't hard—the flesh just sort of falls off. Then you have to cut the veins and yellowy ligaments, which recoil like rubber bands released, and slide up the bone, eerily moving on their own. This is the time when you are most likely to get squirted in the face by your elk leg or the one next to you. And you won't really be able to adequately wipe yourself clean, because your hands and sleeves are soaked in juices, and you are standing in a puddle of cooked-leg water. This might even lead to a nasty eye infection, as my co-worker Janice learned the hard way.

Some of the legs are still bloody, possessing a reddish hue that contrasts with the grayish flesh, some smell musty and freezer-burned—and some really aren't so bad. Nevertheless, this is also the time when you might need to take a break for a minute or two, sit down and re-evaluate your career choices.

Occasionally you recognize the number on one of the tags and catch yourself remembering the place where this animal took its last breath. You try to avoid thinking about it too much, respecting the individual and realizing the importance of the connection, but needing some distance just to get through the process. I've been told it's kind of like eating a hamburger at McDonalds. You just don't want to think about it too much while you're doing it.

Once the skin is off, you work the joints. In the most barbaric moment you must whack the leg against a rock or cement wall to loosen the joint and pop off the hoof. Still, there is something primal about this whacking that ignites a small, smoldering spark in your gentle, herbivore heart—and it all starts to feel pretty good.

The hoof is then tossed, with the other hooves, into a gruesome pile of feet and loose hide. At this point the magpies are already flying closer, leap-frogging in from behind wintering sagebrush, occasionally nabbing a morsel with a bold beak. From here on it is just a matter of scraping the fine connective tissue off and properly cleaning the bone up. The entire processing of one bone takes between fifteen and thirty minutes, depending on how long it boiled and how sharp your knife was. And at the end of the day, you can step out of your little puddle, and look at your small pile of shelf-worthy bones with the kind of satisfaction that comes from contributing something to this world.

Eventually the bones will be measured and categorized, and the data added to our working knowledge of how the Greater Yellowstone ecosystem functions, and hopefully, it will ultimately help to preserve the species within it. Because metatarsus bones reflect physical and environmental health and growing constraints, they can in effect act, as tree rings do, like clues to the conditions under which an animal lived.

One of the most wonderful aspects of the Wolf Project is the time you spend watching individual animals interact with each other. Through the use of radio-collars and with the aid of spotting scopes, if you sit still long enough, shivering and cold to the bone, over many days, you can recognize individual personalities and behavior. And you *will* feel affection for these animals as you rub your scabby wind-burned face, applying more Vaseline. You will come to love the wolves, and also the coyotes and cougars, the elk and bison.

Ecology shows us that while there are individuals, there is also the whole. Each species is unique, but also part of a larger system, and they are all dependent on one another for survival. And this is the greater meaning. This is why I am willing to boil bones, squish poop, and brush phantom maggots off my skin for hours after the fact. Like planets in the solar system, they are all the necessary components of a bigger picture. I still don't have a funny hat, don't even want one, but my dog loves that lively *eau de bone* fragrance I wear home.

Kathleen Yale holds a Bachelor's degree from the University of Wisconsin in Conservation Biology, and a Master's degree in Environmental Studies from the University of Montana. Her essays and poetry have appeared in Camas: Nature of the West, Moon City Review, *and* High Desert Journal. *She is currently living in western Montana, where she has spent the last several years following around wild animals under the guise of a wildlife biologist, swimming in cold water and poking around in the woods.*

* * *

A Hawk Is My Weapon

As I sit on a rock beside a frozen pond, the trained red-tailed hawk is somewhere in a tree across the snow-covered meadow—far enough that I cannot see him at the moment, but close enough that if he moves anywhere, I will hear his bells. The snow begins falling as the wind rises, swaying and creaking the leafless black hardwood trees in the forest behind me.

It's been below freezing for over a week this January in southwestern Virginia. The fresh snow skitters across the icy surface of the pond; it catches in the depressions left by animal tracks in the old snow. I've been outside participating in this art or sport called falconry for over an hour, tromping through the woods and field edges followed by the hawk aloft, looking for prey. Steely clouds gather in the west, increasing their mass as I watch, creeping across the sky to close out the listless blue, now in retreat. Anticipating the wavering weather, the woodland critters seem to have holed up for the day: we haven't jumped anything. Nevertheless, the hawk and I are enjoying blending into the rural landscape, now cast in the faltering light of a dimming afternoon.

For his part, the hawk is probably savoring his high vantage point, standing with a leg tucked into his feathers, swaying with the wind on a tree limb. On the ground, I'm wondering if I should continue to roust rabbits or just pack it in, as the sky grows more ashen and the pond ice *thunks*, making mystery movements to my left.

I've seen lots of rabbit and squirrel sign in the territory I've so far covered. State regulations confine my hunting season to the cold-weather months. But I don't object. I love hunting in the snow because it's so easy to see the recent history of activity in the area. Not only were rabbits and squirrels moving about on their daily rounds earlier: tracks of deer, dogs, mice, even a raccoon were in evidence.

Often by this time, if we haven't found anything for the bird to chase, he gets somewhat antsy. He has limited tolerance for my pedestrian efforts toward flushing prey. On those no-flush days, he'll spot a likely patch of brush or a nice stand of nut trees, and suddenly I'm following him, rather than the reverse. I've grown to trust his eye for likely habitat, as he seems to (mostly) trust mine. Of course, he can see a squirrel in a distant tree much better than I can, not only because of his superior eyesight, but also because of his lofty vantage point.

He used to buzz me when we were unlucky—he would fly close to my head, hoping to flush a tasty tidbit from my pocket. Snacks never appeared in those circumstances, of course, as that would have reinforced unwanted behavior. In a few respects, training raptors for the sport of falconry is like training a dog: when a young dog barks to get your attention and you go outside (even to scold him) the barking behavior is reinforced.

On the other hand, training wild raptors is very different from training a dog; the raptor never becomes domesticated or emotionally dependent on its trainer. Saying "good boy," to a

raptor and petting it, as one might to praise a dog, gets the falconer exactly nowhere along the training curve. We sometimes do it anyway (if the bird will stand for such treatment)
because it makes us feel better.

I'm not a professional trainer, but I imagine training birds
of prey might more easily be compared to training other wild
creatures: whales, tigers, bears, dolphins. A relationship of sorts
develops (especially with pack- or flock-oriented animals), but
it is not like relating to a domestic animal. With wild animals,
the relationship is lopsided: the human grows attached to an
animal that can do without the fumbling biped.

With birds of prey, the training is based on quick and easy
meals—the hawk learns that I am a sure source for dinner,
whether we're out hunting or at home. In falconry, training is
all about building this food relationship and getting a raptor
accustomed to your presence.

That bird in the tree across the meadow from me is
"trained" in that he has grown to tolerate having me around.
Sometimes I prove useful while we're out on our romps: a rabbit or squirrel will jump from its feeding grounds because I'm
crashing around its habitat like the clumsy humanoid I am.
During that mad rush when the prey streaks for cover, the
hawk gives chase. Sometimes the rabbit wins, sometimes the
hawk wins, just as if I wasn't present. If the hawk wins, he allows me to approach—something no untrained raptor would
permit. If he loses (and if he's sure the prey has really escaped
and is not simply hiding), he'll return to my glove. On occasion, he'll find a tidbit of meat there as a reward for his efforts.

Every bird I've worked with (so far, I've trained five redtails and two captive-bred hybrid falcons in my tenure as a
falconer) behaves somewhat differently in similar situations.
For example, one redtail of my acquaintance loved to bathe
in our stream—splashing water like a finch in a birdbath—

while another wouldn't bathe, but would drink and play with bits of flotsam he'd find. Another bird would react as though he had never seen me before if I wore a billed hat, while several others couldn't have cared less about my headgear.

Without anthropomorphizing too much, I now see these as differences in each bird's temperament and personality. Some of it, admittedly, is training. When I was serving my federal- and state-required two-year apprenticeship for falconry, I must confess that the birds trained me more than I trained them.

One of the first red-tailed hawks I worked refused to hunt for more than one hour. Raptors are very routine-oriented— after one hour of unsuccessful hunting, this bird would also buzz my head, anticipating a snack. When that produced no results, he would fly to the ground around my feet and start jumping up and clinging (with his talons) to my jacket, where he knew I kept the tidbits. Yes, he trained me very well. In my innocence as an apprentice, I would become flustered and give in, wondering what on earth was going wrong with this falconry business. Before I learned better, I would quit the hunting session, take him home, and feed him: exactly what he wanted me to do. He'd already discovered that being fed on my glove was easier than having to catch his own dinner. A raptor, like all wild animals, is opportunistic.

Five years later—years of daily hunting expeditions during the falconry season, of reading everything I can get my hands on, of handling and feeding various raptors, of educational programs and demonstrations—I'm more confident of my falconry skills. But I know that I still have much to learn.

I was jolted into an awareness of my limited falconry knowledge when I spent a summer abroad as a working pupil at a falcon breeding and training facility. There, I learned bits and pieces of falconry methods practiced in Spain, Afghanistan, the United Arab Emirates, Mexico, and the U.K., as well as in Maine and America's West. I trained a gyrfalcon hybrid and a peregrine/saker hybrid—a gyrfalcon is a large arctic falcon, historically viewed as the King's falcon due to its size and "nobility;" a saker falcon is a dry-climate species found in the Middle East. Two other birds, also captive-bred at the facility, I "manned." Manning is the initial stage of training in which the raptor gets used to being around humans.

My internship under Dr. Nick Fox, one of the foremost raptor biologists in the world, exposed me to the captive breeding and re-introduction of raptors to the wild. Along with many others, Dr. Fox is responsible for newly growing wild populations of the native (and nearly exterminated) red kite in southwestern England and Wales. At his facility, raptors are bred for conservation purposes and also as a business, in which selective breeding is undertaken to produce quality falconry birds for sale to falconers around the world.

One of the primary things I learned from my experience abroad was that it is dangerous (in emotional terms) to become too attached to a wild thing. "Never release a falcon you're not prepared to lose," Dr. Fox says—and I became sadly aware of how many ways a handler can lose a bird. Fatal heat exhaustion, electrocution, cow-stomping, genetic disorders, fox-mauling, and one never-explained disappearance all played a downside role in his large-scale raptor breeding and training program.

Back here in Virginia, falconry seems much more humble, at least the way I practice it. Here, it's just the bird and me, outside, alone. While sitting on this rock in the snow, I contemplate this sport, a natural history training ground that opens my eyes to new lessons every day. I'm learning not only about raptors, but about prey species habitat, and how that can be disrupted by simple things we take for granted. The deer and cows compete with rabbits for food. Neighbors cut down trees to fuel their stoves or build their houses, thinning the squirrel habitat. Packs of loose dogs roam over the countryside disturbing the feeding patterns of rabbits and forcing them to become even more nocturnal. In some areas around my home, if I find the telltale signs of a rabbit that succumbed in that age-old battle for survival, I suspect that the predator was an owl, not a redtail.

I see evidence of a fawn's birth, a poached deer, a rabbit in heat, a lightning-struck tree split lengthwise and scorched, and a fox marking its territory. A scattering of songbird feathers hints at a recent Cooper's or sharp-shinned hawk's meal.

I'm learning to identify trees by their bark rather than their leaves; the preferred (or at least most plentiful) nuts for squirrels and where they like to eat them; that I'm unlikely to find anything other than raccoons, songbirds, and deer near a woodland winter stream. I've even seen a trained redtail steal a half-eaten crow from a wild Cooper's hawk, a plentiful but secretive raptor in this region. In addition to redtails and Cooper's, Virginia's west boasts native populations of red-shouldered hawks, sharp-shinned hawks, and kestrels; some re-introduced peregrine falcons; a wide variety of owls including great horned and screech; as well as migratory populations of many other raptor species such as osprey.

It is wonderful to live in a region so rich with raptors. I thrill to the high *keeee-eerrrr!* of a soaring redtail; count sightings of hawks in my region; and note the progress of raptor fledglings in the woods near my house. I take every opportunity to educate my neighbors, not only about the laws protecting raptors, but also about the dangers posed to raptors when they use poisons to control problem rodent and bird populations. Like most falconers, I have a deep, awestruck love for wild raptors, and do as much as possible to protect the local raptor populations.

A similar appreciation for raptors is what prompts many people to investigate the sport of falconry. But many don't realize how demanding falconry is. A falconer must pay attention to the details of weather patterns, facility and equipment upkeep, and the bird's needs every single day of the year. The demands increase during the long falconry season itself.

Every day during hunting season, I weigh the bird. This weight is calculated against the ambient temperature so I can judge his metabolic demands and the initial onset of hunger. If not hungry, a hawk will loaf around and be uninterested in hunting (like wild raptors, it conserves energy whenever possible); and if too hungry, the hawk focuses more closely on me, or on opportunities for an easy meal (a redtail is not averse to carrion-eating). Finally, I look at the sky and make more judgments: Too windy? Too foggy? Too bitter? How long until the sun sets?

These assessments compose an elaborate process leading to a very simple relationship: that between predator, prey, and observer. Any factor overlooked or misjudged, and I lose a hawk. At any moment, the bird could dispense with our "relationship" and wing off over the nearest hill, never to be seen by me again. If this happens, he will easily revert to his wild state, feed himself (as he mostly does even in my care), find a mate, soar the thermals, sit in the tops of trees, and do all those raptor-like things it is in his nature to do.

To me, this quality is actually a huge bonus to the sport of falconry. It is my practice, after a few years working with an indigenous bird, to release it back to the wild. I merely "borrow" the bird; I don't own it. I avoid referring to it as "my" bird, because I don't feel that it is.

My personal philosophy about falconry is this: I take a bird from the wild—law requires that the redtail I take be nothing other than a juvenile in its first year plumage—train it, exercise it, provide it with quality food, give veterinary care if needed, shelter it safely, and in general take a few years to build it up in health, fitness, and skills. Then I return it to the wild so it can breed as it would naturally, and it lives out its life as the wild creature it is. In this way, I've taken a young redtail (80 percent of which don't survive their first winters) and tipped the survival scales in its favor. In return, I get the thrill of a lifetime—I'm allowed to be present when one of nature's oldest battles takes place; when winged predator and prey engage in a fight for survival and the odds are fifty-fifty.

I get up from my rock as the wind sighs through the tops of the trees. It's snowing harder now, and I've decided that the rabbits and squirrels are much smarter than I am today. They have the sense to stay sheltered and warm instead of romping about in the chill landscape. I place a whistle in my mouth, transfer a tidbit from my pocket to my glove, and lift it high enough for the hawk to see. I blow one piercing note and hear the tinkle of the bells as he leaves his perch. It takes a moment until I can see his form sweeping toward me, even though I know (more or less) where to look. The wind puffs at the last moment, making his landing on my fist ungainly. But his talons catch hold and he bends to snatch up the tidbit.

"We're calling it a day, old son," I tell him, and we head home.

After feeding him an amount of meat I have learned is enough to keep his weight steady for twenty-four hours at this general temperature (in anticipation of tomorrow's hunt), I put him into his outdoor enclosure. This is a large cage that protects him from anything that might try to do him harm; redtails and great horned owls are deadly enemies—they compete for food and habitat, and will eliminate one another if their territories cross. This enclosure also lets him survey his environment if he chooses, or perch in a nice shelter if he doesn't.

He contentedly "feaks his beak," or rubs it on the rough perch as if polishing it. Then he "rouses," fluffing up all his feathers and giving himself a good shake. Both feaking and rousing are signs of contentment for raptors, so I leave him for the night. As usual, I walk away freshly amazed by his behavior, his coloring, his habits, his smell—but mostly by the fact that he allows me to be here, doing what we do together.

A. Lee Chichester has been a professional freelance writer for twenty-five years, working primarily in the construction trade magazine industry. She's been a licensed falconer since 1992 and is an outdoors education instructor certified by the Virginia Department of Game and Inland Fisheries. She has published a memoir of her falcon-handling adventures in the United Kingdom, Falcons and Foxes in the UK: The Making of a Hunter.

Beyond Thunder Mountain

A CLOAK OF MIST WRAPPED THE WILLOW FLAT AND DEW-beaded spider webs flickered with the first rays of sunlight. Two thousand feet above the valley floor, Hawk's Rest pointed cliffy fingers toward the sky. At my feet, fringed gentians strung a violet ribbon along the sweet, damp earth, where flowed the Yellowstone River.

The Yellowstone: haunt of wolves and grizzly bears, legendary trout water, carver of waterfall canyons in the world's first national park. From deep in Wyoming's Teton Wilderness sprang the headwaters of 700 miles of free-flowing river.

My task that week in the backcountry was to evaluate the headwaters of the Yellowstone for its potential as a National Wild and Scenic River. Though I'd been eager to conduct a river study, I did not anticipate my discomfort as I stood in the unfamiliar position of judge.

Hawk's Rest, an all-day ride from the trailhead at Turpin Meadow, was as far up the Yellowstone River as I had ever gone. On past trips I would slip away from the Forest Service patrol cabin and watch the glassy current slide beneath the pack bridge. From there the Yellowstone meandered in elaborate loops, dawdling over its shallow bed as if in no hurry to leave the remote backcountry. The river flowed from the mountains to the east, and far upstream at the end of a summer evening a ruddy alpenglow hovered on the west face of Thunder Mountain. How I had longed to follow the river around the mountain and beyond, to where it split into twin forks cascading from the crest of the Absarokas. The Yellowstone flowed from the most inaccessible wilderness in the Lower 48, as far as one could get from a road, but Thunder Mountain blocked my view of those mysterious headwaters. Today, at last, I would see what lay beyond it.

The river fog had dissipated by the time Ray and the mules filed onto the trail ahead of us. I rode between Jamie, an archaeologist with a knack for finding stone tools at every rest stop, and Rebecca, who oversaw field management of the Teton Wilderness. Ray, a veteran ranger, worked for Rebecca.

Dust boiled in a powdery storm behind the mules. Ray twisted in his saddle, watching for loose ropes and shifting loads. Jamie eyed the ground, watching for glints of obsidian. Rebecca and I alternated between conversation and reverie. As we followed the river upstream, I stood on one stirrup for photographs, vainly trying to keep my horse's ears out of the pictures. In a spiral notebook I recorded aspens sprouting from a forest fire's blackened snags and riverside willows flashing the signature forms and colors of their species. One spread upright branches, its thick and glossy leaves already flecked with yellow the third week in August. Another variety waved spearhead leaves from ten-foot wands. A compact, silvery species hugged a dry channel like a row of porcupines. Together they wove a tapestry, threading the meanders with a cloak of dense foliage. I jotted the names—Booth's, Geyer's, whiplash, coyote, Wolf's.

Hours passed as the horses carried us along a trail they knew by heart. Hawk's Rest receded into the distance, then disappeared behind enclosing curtains of cliff. Ahead lay a great wall of carved volcanic ash: Thunder Mountain. It unfolded across the sky like an accordion.

We stopped for lunch at Castle Creek. In the miles from Hawk's Rest, the river had dwindled from a maze of oxbows to a shallow, quick cascade. I wandered along an emergent bar where Castle Creek met the Yellowstone.

Deltoid imprints of Canada geese crisscrossed the shoal. A necklace of branched impressions like fossil dinosaur tracks marked the path of a sandhill crane. Knob-toed bear prints were inscribed by the tiny glyphs of water beetles. Cloven tracks dented the fresh mud—a pair of elk, a skittering of deer. Traces of a moose overlay them, the deep, wide saucers of its hoof prints filled with river water.

As I studied the archive of wildlife crossings, I thought about the stack of river inventory forms waiting in my saddlebag. *I should be writing this down.* But the August sun combed and teased the riffles and iridescent dragonflies darted at the river's edge. I closed my eyes to absorb the heat reflected from the face of Thunder Mountain. I was struck by an urge to undress and jump into the water.

I took a few photographs and scanned my notebook and wondered what equipped me to evaluate this river, to answer with certainty the questions on my inventory form. I was attempting to quantify the ineffable—beauty, wildness, the river's capacity to inspire. I was supposed to restrict my attention to the half-mile river corridor, a problem I had not resolved in two summers of Wild and Scenic River surveys. Taken out of context, each stream varied from all the others only in minor detail—the kind of rocks and mix of willow species, the shade of blue or green that settled into the deepest pools. But a river was more than flowing water. It included everything in sight: water, floodplain, cliff bands far above. Cranes and geese and moose and bears, the slice of sky visible between the canyon rims.

And, as surely as it carried water, the river carried human imaginings and dreams, history and legend. I could not enter the portal of Thunder Mountain without falling under the spell of the Yellowstone's particular beauty and the overlay of my own sensibility. The earliest trappers and mountain men passed this way, the famous and the notorious: Buffalo Bill and Beaver Tooth Neal and dozens of other men of the mountains for the past two hundred years. This river bore the name of the world's first national park. I could not separate this knowledge from the water that passed before me.

Pay attention, the river seemed to say. Pay attention in bear country, especially. I focused on a set of tracks at my feet and imagined the grizzly that had recently left them in the slick mud. It probably dozed in some cool retreat under the willows, not far from where I walked.

A sudden shriek spun me around. Had I flushed the bear off its day bed only to have it stumble onto my riding partner's lunch? Did Rebecca have the pepper spray handy or was it in a saddlebag? Another cry, wild and joyful, followed the first and I knew there was no bear. I shouldered downstream through the willows and found her shirt, shoes, and jeans in a pile beside the river as she bounced from the water and laughed with delight.

I slid my hands into the icy current with a pang of yearning. On backpacking trips in my twenties I was the first to shed my clothes and dive into a mountain lake and I didn't care how cold the water was. It was a measure of the wildness around me that I never worried that a stranger might happen along and see. It was a measure of the wildness in me. The alpine lakes of long ago gave me a form of baptism, a ritual of savage consummation. But I'd spent the bulk of my life since then cultivating the reserve that now seemed out of place beside the untamed Yellowstone. I watched Rebecca shaking out her damp hair. *That used to be me.*

Beyond Thunder Mountain we entered a narrow gorge. The enclosing forest brought welcome shade after the hot brilliance at Castle Creek and the scent of conifers followed as we rode beneath the brow of the Continental Divide. High above, platinum blonde grass rippled between dark volcanic cliffs on a breeze that did not reach the canyon floor.

The sun hung low over a basalt rim by the time we trotted across a meadow to make camp. Released from cinches and woolen saddle blankets, the horses rolled in the grass and shook like wet dogs. As I unfurled the tent beside the river, a sequence of chords floated on the warm late-summer air as Rebecca strummed the guitar she'd top-packed for three days across two panniers full of grain.

Our campsite was splendid but the trail continued upstream. Tired as I was, the Yellowstone still beckoned. I started up the trail.

A half-hour from camp, I broke out of the forest into a meadow with a view straight up the river. A strong wind ripped with a sound like falcon's wings among the spires of overhanging rims. Strands of cirrus streamed across the spires, making them appear to sway, making me dizzy to watch. A wedge of mountain cleaved the valley and split the current in two. North Fork, South Fork—here lay the birthplace of the Yellowstone. Like eager twins, the branches of the Yellowstone tumbled from the arms of the Absarokas. Between them Younts Peak shone like brass in the evening sun. I imagined sitting up there in the wind at nearly thirteen thousand feet to watch the sunset. No matter how far I traveled up the Yellowstone, it would always call me farther.

I stepped onto a slab of polished stone, then another, until I stood in the middle of the river, where the waters of its forks had not completely mixed. Shadows climbed Younts Peak as blue dusk filled the canyon. I bent toward the river and dipped my fingers. On its way to North Dakota, the young river rippled down the mountainside with purpose, rushing toward important errands: to wash spawning gravel for cutthroat trout, to float rafts and dories, to water corn and sugar beets. I cupped my hands and drank.

Back in camp, I pulled out an inventory form and laid it on my clipboard. The first question droned like a jaded postal clerk: "Scenic quality outstanding for most of the river segment?" I paused at boxes labeled *Yes* and *No*.

Scenery: the word seemed out of place, a mere backdrop to observe from the window of a speeding automobile, a distraction for bored tourists, a postcard of false-front mountains and a faded sky. There was nothing like that here. The river I had followed from the gentian-splashed flats at Hawk's Rest had enveloped me with wind and sounds and smells. It absorbed our little survey party into its timeless flow. Here I stepped into the sublime and drank from the cup of history.

There wasn't room to put that on the form; instead I checked the box, *Yes.*

Next question. "Evidence of human influence on natural processes minimal?" *Yes, yes.* Of course—the hoof prints we left in the trail were already covered by bear tracks.

I would answer *Emphatically, yes* to all nine questions on the form. I imagined calling Rebecca over to announce, "Hey look here. I just filled out this form, and guess what—the river is a Nine." She would nod, gaze past me with a vague smile, and go back to playing her guitar.

I put the clipboard away and unfolded a topographic map.

As I pressed the sheet to the ground everyone in camp gathered like moths to a flame. Our eager fingertips traced the trails and pointed to the stretch of dark mud where we had followed grizzly bear tracks for a quarter-mile, an oxbow where two bull moose had stood in the shadows as we passed, a spring where we found wild chives to enliven the spaghetti. The map came alive with stories, recording our journey in the language of the land.

I wondered at the map's ability to deliver the bite of wild chives, the thrill of bear tracks. Like my river inventory forms, it was only a sheet of paper, containing factual information—elevations, geographic features. Why did it hold us until dark? In simple cartographic letters, the map rendered names. Yellowstone. Thorofare. Hawk's Rest, Thunder Mountain. Names of legend, recalling the river's place in history, the passing of adventurers, the magnificence of mountain and sky. I was glad to have these names to echo in my mind.

Months after the Yellowstone River survey, I labored over the final Wild and Scenic River eligibility report, trying to describe the attributes that met the legal requirement that a stream be "outstandingly remarkable." *Outstanding* had hardly been in question the evening I perched on a rock watching the sunset burnish Younts Peak. At the same time, the Yellowstone at that far reach was just a little creek, murmuring over its cobbles as did hundreds of other streams in northwestern Wyoming. I would have trouble arguing with anyone who claimed it was merely typical.

My efforts to write an objective report made it read like a

description of the physical properties of gold—all about soft-ness, malleability, specific gravity—information that described the metal, but did not hint at the reasons it was so highly prized. Likewise the river: sterile descriptions told nothing of the way I had experienced it. Bear tracks, wild chives, and the sound of wind in the rimrock were more to the point. The topographic map had invoked these; my report did not.

For inspiration I glanced through my field notes. A creased and dirt-stained map slid from the leaves of inventory forms. As I unfolded it, a particle of sand from the Yellowstone River fell into my hand. Translucent, pale amber, and roughly round, it gathered and held the November light like a tiny sun. I sat for many minutes rolling the fragment in my palm.

On the map I fingered an egg-blue line, the Yellowstone curving past Hawk's Rest and beyond Thunder Mountain to headwaters spilling from the apron of Younts Peak. The line began to blur, replaced in my imagination by the chatter of snowmelt over cobbles and the wind moaning among basalt spires far above.

The harsh fluorescent light over my desk faded to a moon-less night in August. Frost gathered on the meadow grass as Rebecca played her guitar, laughing between forgotten, in-vented, and finally remembered lyrics. Singing to the Milky Way, we lingered late, the music mixing with horses' bells and the gentle slap of the rising Yellowstone, before it drifted into the night.

Susan Marsh lives in Jackson Hole, Wyoming where she works as recreation and wilderness staff for the Bridger-Teton National Forest. Her essays have appeared in Orion, North American Review, Bugle, *and* Talking River Review*, among others, and have been anthologized in collections including* Ring of Fire, The Leap Years, *and* Going Alone.

JENNIFER BOVÉ

⋆ ⋆ ⋆

For the Birds

I WAKE UP TO THE CLAMOR OF GLAUCOUS-WINGED GULLS just before sunrise. Their feet pound the cottage's cedar shake roof like mallets as they bicker and tussle for elbowroom along its peak. All summer, our roof has been a coveted perch for early morning eagle surveillance, and I have memorized every sound of the gulls' routine. When one of them spies the silhouette of a bald eagle slicing through the dimly-lit dawn, the roof brigade scrambles to take flight and hail a screaming legion of their kin. Opening one eye, I see the birds sweeping madly back and forth past the window, yellow beaks agape, in a desperate communal effort to overwhelm the predator. Their pulsating squall always sounds, at first, like the kind of alarm clock you would rip from the socket and slam against the wall, but when I listen deeply, I can hear a more intricate vocabulary of mews between mates, conversational muttering, and short whistles that accompany the submissive head tossing of fledglings. Today, it is cold inside the cottage, and my old dog is heavy and warm behind my knees, so I am reluctant to get up. With my ear pressed against the underside of the quilts,

I wait for the series of loud thumps that tells me the gulls have landed, and I whisper, "Good morning, Protection Island."

"How was the trip?" I call to my husband Chris as I pull the *Sea Runner* toward me and wrap the bowline in tight figure eights around the dock cleat.

He got up early this morning to meet Ulrich Wilson, the refuge biologist, at John Wayne Marina on the mainland. Days ago, Ulrich had collected the equipment that we would need to perform our latest fieldwork effort, but it was so windy all week that we weren't able to make the seven-mile trip across the water to pick up the gear until this morning.

"The water was glass the whole way. Didn't even spill a drop of coffee."

"Did you see who's in the harbor this morning?"

Chris looks past me as he steers into the dock, his hair a wind-curled mess, his forearms strong and brown. "I thought there was something suspicious about that log pile. Is it Brutus or the old guy?" he asks.

I glance back at the driftwood that's been stranded in the corner of the harbor by the tide. The bull elephant seal is asleep among the wood, his rounded back almost indistinguishable from the trunks of crosscut old growth floating motionlessly in the shallows. "Judging by the lack of scars, I'd say it's Brutus. I haven't seen his ID tags though."

Chris gets out of the boat and steps to the end of the dock for a closer look. "That's one big beast."

"He's beautiful, isn't he? Makes you want to be careful not to slip off the dock, though."

He casts me a wry grin. "Aw, the breeding season's over. He ain't out for blood anymore."

Chris barely finishes his sentence when the elephant seal rears his gigantic head from the water and bellows a warning that nearly knocks me off my feet. We both jump backward into the open hull of the *Sea Runner*, nearly falling over each other and giggling like kids who just escaped certain death. Again, the elephant opens his gaping mouth and swings his meaty snout back and forth to emphasize his displeasure at being awakened after a long night of diving for crustaceans. His throat is glistening smooth and salmon pink, and two stubby tusks jut from his lower jaw. A wet rumble echoes from within his massive gullet, but then he sinks back down into the water with a bubbling sigh and stretches his hind flippers. I spot the blue tags I was looking for, implanted in his flippers when he was a pup by Washington State biologists. The tags identify him as the young male we call "Brutus."

He watches us with one wily black eye above the water's surface, and it's obvious he just wants to be left alone to finish his nap, so we get the equipment and move out of his way.

The high sandy cliffs on the east and west sides of the island are pocked with thousands of grapefruit-sized nest burrows that are hollowed out each spring by rhinoceros auklets, small black and silver seabirds with widely webbed feet and a horn-like protrusion atop their beaks. Protection Island's auklet population (some seventeen thousand pairs during the summer breeding season) represents about half the species' entire population in the contiguous United States. Now that all of the auklets have left the island for the winter, we will determine this year's burrow density by climbing the cliffs with two-meter PVC sampling squares and systematically counting a representative sample of their recently abandoned excavations. With this information, we will be able to estimate the current population and note any changes in the numbers from previous years.

We load the unwieldy squares into the rusty bed of our island-issue Daihatsu pickup, and Chris gives its salt-crusted

battery cables a tug. I pump the gas pedal a few times, adjust
the choke, and turn the key. The Daihatsu coughs and dies, so
I start fiddling with the choke again. When the motor finally
stutters to a start, we follow the grassy roadway toward the
base of the east-facing cliff with Clarence, our gray-muzzled
Heeler, between us. The 100-foot slope, which overlooks the
harbor and the long arm of Violet Spit, is not as steep as the
one on the island's west flank, and it's only about half as high.
So, we figure we'll start with this one as a warm-up for the
other side.

After I clip a small notebook onto my belt loop and jam a
pencil through the band of my ponytail, I help Clarence out
of the cab, and he makes himself comfortable in the grass next
to the tire. He stares at his paws like all the world's answers
might be there in the spotted fur between his toes. He doesn't
concern himself with the oystercatcher following its improb-
ably long, red bill over the driftwood nearby or the northwestern garter snake curled on a flat stone beside him. It
simply doesn't occur to him, like it might to other dogs, to
bother chasing wildlife. He's got too many years of arthritis
behind him to care. His ears twitch now and then, though, so
I know he must be listening to the whirling whistles of pigeon
guillemots on the gentle surf, small creatures rustling in the
beach grass, and a bald eagle laughing on the thermals high
above us. He surely smells secrets here that I will never see.

Chris takes the first transect, near the corner of the island
where the east slope and the vertical clay cliffs of the north
face meet, and I pace forty meters southward to begin the second transect. I clamber through a thicket of Nootka rose and
position my square close to the bottom of the cliff.

After counting the burrows in my first plot (only those
holes that fall completely within the square and no shallow
excavations), it's time to move upward. I flip the square once

vertically, then over the transect line horizontally so that I'll end up with a checkerboard plot arrangement at two-meter intervals from the base of the cliff to the top. But, keeping the square under control is trickier than I thought it would be. It's taller than me, so I have to manhandle it to get it to flip in a relatively straight line, and it inevitably wants to slide downhill. Maneuvering my own body up the slope is not a graceful endeavor either. Even though there is still some grass left after the arid summer, the parched grass root system doesn't do much to stabilize the cliff's sandy loam, so the loose soil caves under my footsteps and seeps into my boots. I stagger and skid my way up the slope with clumsy persistence.

Chris and I make it to the top of the cliff at the same time and stand on level ground for a minute to catch a breath.

"I won," he says.

"You did not."

"I'll call ol' Doris over on Diamond Point and ask her." He leans on his square and looks at me like he's serious. "I've got the cell phone."

"What makes you think that she's watching us right now anyway?" I peer across the mile of seawater between the island and Diamond Point to the rows of houses lining the mainland hillside where two hundred foot trees once grew. Nearly all of the homes have picture windows facing Protection Island, and most have spotting scopes trained on the refuge that are powerful enough to pick out a song sparrow on a blade of wild rye. At any given time, somebody is bound to be watching.

"She called the other day to report some boat violation, and I mentioned we'd be doing the burrow count this week."

"You know, somehow you always end up talking to her. I don't think she's ever reported anything to me."

He shrugs and starts laughing. "She ain't sweet on you, baby."

I shake my head and start sidestepping down the cliff.

"Doris also mentioned she saw you sunbathing naked on the front porch the other day. She thought I should have a talk with you—indecent exposure on a federal refuge and all."

I refuse to turn around and call his bluff. He knows damn well nobody saw me sunbathing because I only do so in the backyard by the garden, well out of sight.

"Honey?"

"I'm ignoring you," I say, wrestling with my square to keep it from tripping me. "Hey, look." I point to the water. "Brutus left the harbor."

The elephant seal's shiny dark head is gliding slowly westward beyond the black riprap of the harbor breakwater. I puzzle over this for a minute because he usually wanders the other way, along the length of the spit, and hauls out again on Violet Point for the afternoon. There must be some subtle cue telling him it's time to go a different direction, or perhaps to move on for the winter. A sensation of change is all around us now; it is heavy on the breeze that rolls in from the east for the first time in months. Down the spit, gulls are rising and falling in great, restless clouds as if a strange September blizzard has blown in. Thousands of them still remain on the island, but I see how dramatically their numbers have decreased in the last week, and I feel how empty and still it will be once they're gone. I have noticed the faint and distant scent of imminent rains. I have noticed that the antlers on the black-tailed deer have been rubbed clean of velvet in preparation for the autumn rut. And I have also spotted a peregrine falcon, an elusive winter visitor, perched in the old cherry snag by the water tower. The animals here are the heartbeat of nature's rhythms, endlessly drumming, and they tell me the seasons are shifting.

At the bottom of the cliff, Chris paces forty meters toward me, and I pace forty farther south.

"People always have something to say about us, though, don't they?"

I'm brushing a spider web from a burrow entrance, trying to decide if it has been used this year. "Yeah, they sure do."

People we talk to on the mainland are curious about what we do all alone out here with the wild things. Most people can't believe that we would actually *choose* such an isolated existence.

"You must get so lonely," they say like we've been exiled, "so far from town and people and stuff to do."

One time, after explaining the finer points of our job to a couple in the marina store, the man remarked, "So the government doesn't even pay you kids a wage? If you ask me, that volunteer work is for the birds."

We had to laugh because he hit it right on the mark—we are, indeed, working for the birds.

Chris and I are serving a one-year term as volunteer caretakers of Protection Island National Wildlife Refuge, a job for which the qualifications include boat handling skills, a background in wildlife biology, and the ability to maintain sanity for long periods of isolation, island-style. Out here, wind and fog can strand you for days without a care about your plans or provisions, and the rain, when it lingers, can drench even the most optimistic of outlooks. It is a rather peculiar residency to say the least, but Protection Island is no ordinary wildlife refuge. It offers no visitor center, interpretive trails, or open waterfowl season. In fact, the island, within a 200-yard marine boundary, is closed to the public altogether and therefore provides true refuge for wildlife. Rising like a colossal shipwreck from the waves, swaybacked and rugged, the 400-acre island is settling back into old ways and healing the scars of previous human presence.

Understandably, tourists and locals alike are intrigued by

the island's stark beauty, its abundant sea life, and tales of its checkered past. A motley cast of characters including S'Klallam Indians, early explorers, homesteaders, military troops, sheep farmers, pheasant ranchers, nudists, and real estate developers contribute to a rich and rumored history of the island. In the late sixties, it was dissected into a neatly designed recreational community with 1,100 small lots, an airstrip, extensive roadways, and a newly dredged harbor. But when it was entrusted to the U.S. Fish and Wildlife Service in 1982, after a long and arduous struggle between conservationists and community planners, human beings at last became a much less significant part of the island's story. Wildlife populations again flourished for the first time in decades on this rare preserve of undisturbed habitat, and now more than 72 percent of the Puget Sound's sea birds breed and raise young here. The island, as they say, has gone back to the birds. Chris and I are the only people, besides a handful of refuge staff members, who are permitted to enter the closed boundary waters. We are actually allowed to *live* on the island in exchange for keeping it "safe."

As caretakers, our most important responsibility is the stewardship of the refuge, and it is no small undertaking to prevent wildlife disturbances by boaters, kayakers, jet-skiers, and impudent airplane pilots. In the summer, the spectators that swarm the island can cause beached harbor seals to crush their young in desperate lurches toward the sea. Distressed birds will also flush from their nests if they feel threatened, leaving eggs and chicks vulnerable to opportunistic predators. We've had to literally stand guard in the *Sea Runner* on fair weather days, sometimes from dawn till dusk, intercepting potential troublemakers on the water, filling out incident reports, and peering through binoculars to record the license numbers of low-flying planes.

In addition to acting as the island's sentries, we also have to maintain the few facilities on the refuge and keep the equipment running. Biological research of any kind is our reprieve from real work. Studying the diversity of life here is our means of understanding the island more intimately; it is our passion.

We undoubtedly could have made more money elsewhere, if not as biologists then as waiters or gas station attendants, but coming to the island wasn't about money. We ventured here from the high country of western Montana to explore a new life where we would be surrounded at eye-level by the ocean. Neither of us has ever lived unlocked from the land, and so it was a leap of faith to leave the firm coast of our continent. But, here at sea, we're finding out what we're really made of. The grit of who we are is settling out, and the rest is washing away with the tides.

By noon, we're finished with the eastern cliff, having each climbed up and down it ten times. We're both sweating in the glare of the high sun, and I'm so hungry I'm not talking anymore. We walk silently back along the roadway to the Diahatsu where Clarence has found a shady place to sprawl alongside the rose bushes. He wags his tail, hauls himself up to his feet, and trots after us.

We take our cooler of food around to the rocky crest of the beach where we can sit and face the wide-open blue Strait of Juan de Fuca that stretches from here to the humped backs of the San Juan Islands and Canada's hazy coastline beyond. We swig icy water from gallon jugs and eat our sandwiches and watch the waves. They tumble onto the beach just a few yards from our boots and pour playfully over one another, bubbling and frothing like champagne, and each one sizzles through candy-colored gravel as it slips back into the sea.

When I finally get enough food in me to speak, I say, "I brought the leftover brownies from last night."

"I thought you threw them to the gulls!"

"Couldn't bring myself to do it," I admit. "They were just too good."

Chris takes a bite of a brownie, and then he grabs two more whole ones from the plate. "Man," he says, chewing, "I think they're even better today."

I sink my teeth into the perfectly chewy, nutty chocolate and nod.

A harbor seal pops its head out of the surf near shore, and I give it a little wave. There are more seals farther from us, loosely strung out like silver buoys along Violet Spit, but only this brave scout dares study us at close range, its nostrils flaring to catch our scent.

"You know, I think maybe we should have done the west side first," Chris muses. "It's only getting hotter, and that other cliff's gonna be a bitch."

"Uh-huh. Whose bright idea was that anyway?"

Gripping the wheel of the Daihatsu, I concentrate on picking up speed past the storage shed so that the rickety little pickup will make it up the road that climbs the precipitous southern cliff. It's a rough ride, and it's always questionable if you're going to lose momentum halfway up the hill and roll back down. At a good clip of fifteen miles an hour, we pass underneath the cavernous cleft of pelagic cormorant nests in the cliff. The cormorants and their recently fledged brood have all but abandoned the colony to winter at sea, but the few that still linger in the nests snake their glossy black necks to watch the Daihatsu roll over the remains of two unfortunate chicks, killed by eagles or crows, that are slowly decaying into the ruts in the road. I peer out my window over the abrupt cliff edge to scan the driftwood tangle outlining the high water mark on the beach a hundred feet below. Except for a few eggshell fragments and bones, little evidence remains of the boisterous gull and guillemot nesting colonies that crowded the beach just a few short weeks ago. Fuzzy chicks have either fledged or fallen victim to nature's unforgiving hand, and the birds are now breaking their seasonal ties to the island. Unlike the concrete and vinyl development once attempted here by humans, their transient community leaves behind only shallow nests of beach grass and driftwood burrows lined with pebbles. I can only imagine how different life might be if our own species would live so lightly on the land.

Two mottled gray gull fledglings and some horned larks scatter from our path as we slowly crest the top of the hill. Here, the island's upland meadow unfolds like Eden. Sunlight is playing hide and seek among grassy knolls, a northern harrier glides over the broad valley on cinnamon-colored wings, and the gnarled woodland that hovers as dark as a secret on the island's northern rim harbors ephemeral shadows of bald eagles and timid black-tailed deer. Beyond the fringed mounds of the island's horizon, the Strait of Juan de Fuca crooks into the deep cove of Discovery Bay, reflecting blue sky like the shard of a broken mirror. Farther still, the Olympic Mountains erupt through velvet green temperate rainforest to tower above the town of Sequim. It is a view that many people would pay millions for, but on this September afternoon it is ours alone to behold.

At the top of the barren western cliff, we peer down over the wide, steep, wind-chapped grade that drops 200 feet to the short and narrow hook of Kanem Spit. Again, we have to get to the bottom before we can even begin our first transects because they must all originate from the relatively level base of

the cliff. In preparation for the descent, Chris pulls his sweat-
soaked t-shirt over his head and drops it on the ground.

"Ready?" he asks.

I'm ready as I'll ever be.

Towing the awkward squares along, we clamber over the
edge and work our way down the dusty cliff, hugging the
jagged northern edge so as not to crush any burrow entrances
that will fall within the first transect line. Chris practically runs
all the way down to the bottom, claiming it's easier on his
knees, but I like a slower pace that incorporates a good deal of
butt scooting. Granted, I may end up with shorts full of dirt,
but I'm not going to risk falling ass-over-teakettle onto that
beach so far below.

Unlike the short, sparse grass barely clinging to life on the
cliffside, the beach grass down on Kanem Spit is thick and tall,
up to my waist in some spots, and it is paper dry. Its sharp
edges slice hair-thin cuts into my bare legs, so I'm thankful
when I find a well-worn river otter trail that I can follow. The
spit itself is so narrow that there is only a strip of grass as wide
as a two-lane road between its driftwood-laden beaches. The
sheltered crescent of the south shoreline is a favorite haul-out
site for harbor seals. The seals pile up by the hundreds like big
links of sausage and bask while the surf cools their flippers.
Two pairs of black oystercatchers frequent the north side of
Kanem, plucking limpets from the rocky tide flats, and eagles
like to sit atop the driftwood where they wait for chances at
anything, feathered or furred, that might afford them an easy
meal. The forty-eight acres that comprise this spit and the ad-
joining cliffs are known as the Zella M. Schultz Seabird
Sanctuary, in tribute to the ornithologist who fought for years
to have the island declared a refuge. In 1972, the Nature
Conservancy finally purchased this portion of the island because of its critical importance to nesting rhino auklets, and

two years later, the year Zella Schultz died, the Washington Department of Fish and Wildlife reimbursed the Nature Conservancy for its purchase and commemorated Schultz by giving the sanctuary her name.

Today, Kanem Spit is conspicuously empty as Chris and I begin counting burrows again. The first two transects are long, but not quite steep enough to scare me. We climb, flip the squares, count, and climb higher in almost perfect unison, quietly lost in our own two-meter square worlds. Lulled by the sounds of distant gulls and waves washing gently onshore, I think about the birds that built these burrows.

Rhinoceros auklets resemble little air torpedoes when they fly. Though heavy-bodied like the rest of the Alcid family, in flight they are swift and streamlined, and their movements are as tight as a perfectly tuned machine. Their short wings beat furiously through the air, and when diving for fish, they propel the birds' graceful aquatic flight like paddles. It was impossible to get to know the island's auklet population the way we did the bold and ubiquitous gulls, whose company permeated our every waking moment throughout the summer, because the auklets spent their days feeding out in the Strait. Not until nightfall would the masses of football-size birds return, crashing loudly into the cliffs and the grassy dunes surrounding our cottage. Once, in early August, we made a boat trip home from the mainland after sunset with only a hand-held spotlight to guide us through the dark and misty realm that is the sea at night. When we got close to the island, we found ourselves surrounded by auklets on the water and auklets in the air. They whizzed past the boat like kamikazes with silver fish dangling from their beaks, hurrying to feed hungry chicks in their burrows, and we had to inch along toward the harbor just above idling for fear we might collide with one.

Most of our other auklet encounters were with what was

left of them after nightly raids on the colony by great horned owls. Many mornings over the summer, we'd find neatly severed auklet heads and a few wings littering the grassy path behind the cottage. Great Horned owls normally feed primarily on small mammals, but the owls on the island are the only known population to feed exclusively on avian prey during the summer months. What's more, they appear to favor rhino auklets above all the other birds. Apparently, the auklets' nocturnal activities at their burrows make them vulnerable to hunting owls because, when they return to the cliffs at night, they land several feet from their burrows, pause as still as rabbits, and then scurry into their holes. The owls need only wait to snatch them on the run.

The auklets have recently flown westward with the coming of fall. They journey for miles and miles, out past the Pacific coast, to spend a long cold winter at sea. Locals tell of fierce tantrums of wind and water that brew in November and rage on until March, though we have yet to witness this weather ourselves. How do the auklets fare in such vicious storms when there is no land to huddle against, no burrows in which to hide? Even the shelter of our sturdy cottage has seemed tenuous in gales that occasionally roar from Discovery Bay. Shingles rip from the roof and the front door strains at its hinges. When I think of the winter ahead, I realize I must still be firmly rooted to the ground, even though I've learned to love the water, because my instinct is to cling to it as if I did not know how to swim. Imagining the auklets out where there is only sea and sky, where shades of gray are all that distinguish one element from the other, stirs a sense of loneliness deep in my bones.

But now, grappling with the plot square on a near vertical face of hot bare sand, winter couldn't seem more distant. I feel as if I might collapse from bone-sore exhaustion and thirst. I reach for my water bottle on a carabineer clipped to my shorts, but it's gone. The flimsy plastic loop on the bottle must have broken. With all four of my limbs spread-eagle against the cliff, I peer over my shoulder to survey the steep and crooked path I climbed to get up this high, and I see that the chances of the bottle having landed anywhere before it hit the waves are slim.

"Shit," I groan.

"What's up?" Chris yells. He's on the other side of a massive boulder that is protruding from the cliff between our transects.

"Nothing." I clench my teeth in frustration, wiping grit and sweat from my forehead. "I lost my water bottle."

"Take it easy," he calls. "I've got plenty. If you need some, I'll try and get over to you now."

"No, it's O.K. I think this rock is just waiting for the chance to kill one of us, so I'll wait till we get back to the bottom."

I steady the square with one hand, and record the count for my plot with the other, still pressing my weight into the cliff.

"Have I ever mentioned I'm scared of heights?" I mutter.

"What?"

"I'm scared of heights!"

I hear him laughing. "Yeah, I know that."

Eyeing my next potential plot, two meters up, I decide I couldn't climb to it even if I didn't have the square to deal with.

"On that note," I say, "I'm heading back down now."

The sun is melting through the western sky, washing it in pale watercolor hues of lilac and rose, and the chiseled sand cliff is beginning to cast pools of shadow that cool me from the heat of the day as I descend the slope. With my square around my neck, I slowly plant one boot at a time, checking the stability of my footing as I go, and I claw my fingers into the crumbling sand even though it breaks into little avalanches wherever I touch it. Every few feet, I glance up at

that boulder looming above me and hope to God our movements haven't loosened its hold in the cliff. I move out from
under it when I reach the bottom and find a chunk of driftwood where I can sit and rest my legs while I wait for Chris.

He hands me his half-full bottle of water as soon as he
gets to the beach. The water is warm and tastes a lot like the
inside of the plastic bottle, but it brings me back to life, and
I have to stop myself from finishing it before he can get a
drink too.

"Better?" he asks.

"Much better. Thanks."

He takes a long draw off the bottle and gives me the rest.

"Last transect," he says.

"Yep. I doubt we'll get many plots in this run because the
cliff sheers off about halfway up."

"I saw that. Let's just go as far as we can."

"O.K. See you at the top."

I pace to my final transect. It's around the southwest corner of the cliff, and it's marginally climbable. My feet keep
slipping in the loose sand, so it takes me forever just to get up
to the second plot, using the burrows I've already counted as
footholds. Balancing the square with one hand and one foot,
I count six burrows inside it, and then I rest my notebook on
my thigh and scratch the number on the page with the dull
piece of a broken pencil I have left. Two more plots are all that
I can reach, so I finish them and sidle along the cliff to a deer
trail that appears to ascend to the top of the island. Before
climbing the trail, though, I sit down to take off both of my
boots and dump a good cupful of sand and gravel from each.

We sit on top of the cliff. The light breeze is cool from its
passage over the water, and it rouses scents of fading flowers
and humid earth in the meadow behind us where deer are

emerging from the woods as silently as stars to feed in the twilit grasses.

I'm watching the far off beacon from the Dungeness Lighthouse blink hypnotically against the fiery western horizon with my arms wrapped around my legs and my chin on my knees. Although my muscles are swollen and warm, my skin feels cold to the touch.

Chris shakes the grass from his t-shirt and pulls it back on. "I'm starving," he says, reading my mind. "Let's go home."

An eagle glides easily along the cliff as we wade back through the grasses toward the Diahatsu, and I find myself thinking of an old Sandy Denny song, "Across the evening sky, all the birds are leaving..." Time on this island does seem to move on wings, and I know our own future is out there somewhere, waiting like weather on the far horizon. But, at the moment, I can't say I care. Right now *tired* and *hungry* are the things that matter. A fire in the woodstove. More brownies. Even when most of the birds have gone, we'll stay here a while longer, riding out the storms of the coming winter until our year comes full circle, and it's time for us to go.

Jennifer Bové also contributed "First Night in Field Camp" to this collection.

✴ ✷ ✴

Milk

I BORE DOWN ONE LAST TIME, MOANED AS DEEPLY AS I
could muster, and pushed my first baby into a November day
that had alternately pressed snow flurries and sunshine around
our bedroom windows. Cheers erupted from those standing
in a half circle around the foot of the bed—my mom, my husband's parents, my sister-in-law—as if I had just broken a
marathon winner's tape. I squatted upright between the pillars
of my brother and dad, and, while my legs trembled with fatigue, my cervix no longer felt as if it were going to be ripped
in half by a grizzly bear. I recall feeling surprised, not daring
to expect relief so soon. I had only labored for four nights, and
all of the fourth day, after all.

Our eyes focused on a wet, little pile of arms and legs and
a blue, still face. Midwife Dolly swiftly placed an oxygen mask
over the baby's nose and mouth, while my people shushed and
held their collective breath.

"Talk to your baby, Mom," our midwife coached.

"Welcome to this world, Sweet Pea," I said. "I'm so glad to
finally meet you. Breathe little one, breathe."

Suddenly our baby sucked air, and again the room resounded in cheers and laughter. I was told later that Dad cried, but I was too busy watching my daughter to notice. I lay back on the pillows. Midwife Dolly handed our baby to my husband, Scott, who set her onto my belly. I touched her blood smeared skin, marveling at its softness, and the way our daughter's face looked like that of an old woman. Dolly placed a little hat on her head and a blanket over her back, and said that I could nurse. I pulled baby higher onto my chest. Scott touched her back.

During pregnancy I had worried about how breast-feeding would work. I studied the benefits for nutrition, immunity, and bonding, had witnessed friends nursing their infants, but had tried and been unable to imagine this moment for myself. Mom had chosen to bottle feed me in an era when most doctors thought that modern formula contained everything a baby needed, and my grandmother had bottle fed her. The best information I received as a girl about milk production came from our family milk cows.

Each morning and night of my childhood Dad walked to the barn with a pail of warm water, for udder washing, and returned with frothy milk. Sometimes I went with him, watching over his shoulder before trying it myself. I learned that it took a minute of rhythmic tugging before the cow "let down" her milk, and that she would "dry up" if not milked for consecutive days. The most surprising thing about udders was how much they felt like human skin.

I hoped now that I could feed the way mammals were intended. My baby bobbed her head back and forth a few times, located a nipple and grabbed hold. As it turned out, she needed no instruction.

Two months after birthing Freya, I finally pulled my chin once over the bar hanging in our porch and began completing shaky push-ups from my toes instead of from my knees, as I had done during pregnancy. I would need to be able to do seven pull-ups, twenty-five push-ups, forty-five sit-ups, and run a mile and a half in less than eleven minutes if I wanted to return to my job as a U.S. Forest Service smoke jumper. I walked Freya around town for errands, took turns with Scott running after dark each night, and cross-country skied weekends with baby swaddled against my chest. Between three and four months old her painful gas episodes began to subside.

My sister-in-law sent me her old breast pump—a double-barreled, electric, Medela "Pump In Style" bearing the subtitle: "Professional Performance for Today's Active Mothers." Since I did want to return to woods work some day, it was time to practice. On the box a woman wearing high-heeled sandals and a short-skirted business suit slung the faux leather briefcase containing the breast pump over her shoulder. This depiction of the "active mother" didn't take into account my work as a wielder of Vibram-soled boots and chainsaws. For two summers Scott and I had earned our paychecks jumping from Forest Service airplanes to fight remote wild fires, and previously on other kinds of fire crews.

I had spent a pregnant 2003 season working in an office, unwilling to expose my developing infant to inhaled smoke, and other hazards. One early July night Scott received the summer's first dispatch by telephone. I had visualized this moment and how strong and sweet I would be. But, when Scott told me he would be flying to a fire in Northern Montana's Bob Marshall Wilderness early the next morning, I bawled.

It had been a year and a half now since I had swung a Pulaski—a combination hoe and axe—in the flames. I had wanted badly to get pregnant and wasn't regretting it, but this pump contraption stood between me and my hope of getting back out there this spring, 2004. While I knew moms who had continued to fight fires, I hadn't known or heard of anyone negotiating breast pumping in the field. I hoped it would prove possible—and I wanted to test it with some pre-season projects.

I spread out the "Pump In Style" parts onto the table a couple different times, and re-read the directions. My sister-in-law had handwritten her own additions in the margins: "When in a bind, pumped breast milk can put out a small wildland fire," and "It's hardly even noticeable when jumping out of airplanes. People will just think it's your lunch."

Finally I got brave enough to "hook up." Freya gazed at me from her bouncy chair on the floor and I wondered if I was being untrue to her in some manner. Was I a bad mother for wanting to return to my job, or for resorting to technology for help?

I plugged the long plastic tubes into the mechanism and turned the switch to "on." The faux briefcase sprung to life with a noise like high-speed electric windshield wipers. After using her pump, a friend joked that now whenever she drove in rainstorms she would probably leak milk. I awkwardly positioned the clear plastic "shields" over my breasts then watched, fascinated, as my nipples got sucked forward, and then released, forward and then released. After a minute a thin strand of white liquid squirted forth into the shield, through the valve and dripped down into the storage bottles. I beamed in triumph. Lori's dairy was open for service. Freya swatted at toys hanging over her bouncy chair, apparently unperturbed.

She turned five-months-old in April, and over the course of a scream-spewing, tear-gushing weekend, she finally drank breast milk from a bottle. Monday I awoke to a pre-dawn alarm and pulled her close once more. Sensation tingled like warm electricity as milk moved through the ductwork in my breasts. I closed my eyes for ten more minutes while Freya drank her belly full, and then left her to snuggle against her drowsy father. He had worked the past three months, and now it was my turn.

I pulled on my pants and, even after months of closet residence, the smell of smoke and diesel met my nose. Today I would walk on pine needles. I had become a firefighter after four years of college and three more of graduate school. The transition back to life in the woods, after a childhood spent there, had been like going home.

The burn boss explained that we would be lighting a fire on a unit in the foothills of the Bitterroot Mountains. It was intended to be low intensity, to clean out the underbrush, kill unhealthy trees, and provide greater space and nourishment for the survivors to thrive. I went through a checklist in my brain of important equipment to carry: Pulaski, drip torch, radio, water, lunch, hand operated breast pump, empty milk bottles that would hopefully be full by days' end and an ice pack to keep them cool.

Five other guys and I carried our giant Thermos-shaped drip torches a mile across our designated unit's upper edge. There were still a few patches of snow spotting the north-facing slope. One by one we walked slowly through the forest, dripping burning diesel and gasoline into brush piles and onto pinecones that looked likely to burn. My small dabs of flame sometimes blossomed into leaping red and orange dancers, but mostly reached blind fingers around looking for dry fuel to combust. It reminded me of Freya her first month, all mouth and instinct, searching for food. I could feel milk expanding my breasts and hoped Freya and Scott were doing all right, and that she missed me at least a little.

Midday orders came over the radio for our group to halt while the team on the south side continued lighting. As we waited the pressure in my breasts increased to uncomfortable. We could get called back to work any moment, or end up sitting here for an hour. I felt slightly self conscious as I told the man I'd been working next to that it was milking time, and asked if he could please holler at me if we needed to move anywhere. He looked confused, then realized what I meant and agreed.

There is a macho ethic among wildland firefighters, but there is also largely a caring and down-to-earth attitude, and a lack of pretense among us. We generally mean to help each other out, if we understand that help is desired.

I walked a few hundred feet away from the others and sat near a large ponderosa pine. I pulled my yellow Nomex shirt free from my pants, brushed twigs and pine needles out of my sports bra, and put the manually held pump on my sweaty breast. With the other hand I pushed the spring-loaded, bicycle pump-type handle in and out and in and out and in and out. After a couple minutes I was sweating as hard as I had been while hiking and no milk had surfaced. In and out and in and out and in and out. Would the milk turn sour if I cussed? In and out, in and out. I pumped harder. Finally an eyedropper worth of white liquid squirted into the shield and dripped down the bottle's interior. In and out and in and out. After fifteen minutes of this I had less than an ounce of milk, I was shaking from exertion and I worried that it would be time to go back to work. The electric pump would have sucked out three times as much in half the time from both breasts. Until now I'd always been grateful that pine trees didn't come with electrical outlets. I packaged both pump and my breasts into their respective holders.

Most of my life I had merely tolerated my breasts, which developed late in high school and never could fill a B-sized cup. As an athlete I appreciated their lack of interference, but disliked trying on swimsuits and formal dresses because disappointing puckers formed where the chest fabric hung loose. Now, suddenly, I found myself sporting grapefruit shaped orbs with cleavage as distinct as an avalanche chute. Fine blue veins, branching like mapped rivers, showed through pale skin, advertising that these glands were working gals. Just the sight of my breasts sometimes sent Freya into spasms of giggles or anticipatory pants.

Orders came for us to light another swath. In a few places we produced flames toasty enough to consume, but other areas could not be coaxed to burn. We encountered snow patches in the unit's northernmost corner.

Early afternoon my co-workers drew together to compare their lunch contents and trade gossip. I walked away to give this miserable excuse for a pump another try. Milking was proving lonely business. By this time my breasts were taut as water balloons, and hurt. I spent twenty minutes working at it, and got a couple more ounces, not enough to satisfy my fifteen-pound daughter for even a single feeding. I worried my way through the remainder of our shift.

When I parked in front of our home that evening, Scott walked onto the porch holding Freya. She saw me, smiled, and began pumping her arms up and down in excitement, whether more for me or for milk, I don't know; it's not a distinction my daughter would make. Scott exclaimed about how good and smoky I smelled, then handed Freya into my sooty arms. I pulled her close, sat on a step, unbuttoned my shirt, and offered her a breast.

The following week I trotted and slid down the steep edge of another Bitterroot National Forest unit, dripping fire in my wake. On my Nomex lapel I wore a 1940s gold-painted pin reading "Mother" in cursive, and in my backpack rested the $80 battery-operated "Single Deluxe Breast Pump," compliments of my thoughtful husband. Unlike the previous week, dry sticks cracked under my boots, and the temperature looked likely to break 70 degrees by midday. The inside acres had already been lit from a helitorch, a fuel scattering contraption that hung below a helicopter's belly, and now we were lighting the edges with drip torches.

Over my radio I heard the team from the other ridge reporting fire jumping their lines. My three-person group had now reached the dirt road serving as lower boundary of our unit and looked back at our handiwork to see whorls the size of small homes churning skyward in orangey-red cartwheels. Without a quick weather change for the cooler, our boundary lines were not going to contain this dervish fire.

The smoke grew so thick that we could no longer see the interior. We drove our pickup a half-mile away to a safer vantage point. The two men I had lit the line with got out so I could pump in private. I was finding that the battery powered version functioned better than the hand model, but still only one breast at a time, and not as thoroughly as the electric, like the difference between a cheap blender and a good Cuisinart. Also like a blender, it made a *buzz-thrum* noise in which the volume pulsed louder every couple seconds, advertising to any within earshot that something somewhere nearby was being mechanically either chopped or sucked upon.

I preferred a log to lean on with a view, but today settled for the cab to perform my chore as quickly as possible. Soon my co-workers grabbed their Pulaskis and went to scout the damage. Adrenaline charged through my muscles and I wondered if it would change the milk's flavor. I carefully transferred the bright white milk from the receiving bottle into a storage bottle, put it inside an insulated sack, shoved the whole thing back inside my field backpack, tucked my shirt, shouldered the pack, and hiked back up the road to help chase flames.

I met a 500-gallon carrying engine rolling slowly towards a trampoline-sized patch of dried grass and logs burning below the road. The engineer tossed me the nozzle and asked if I would operate the hose. I began spraying at the base of the flames, remembering how much I loved the *thunk-sizzle* of pressurized water hitting hot coals. In fifteen minutes steam replaced smoke and we moved to the next hot spot. The burn boss collected a list of those needing to inform spouses that we'd be home late, and relayed them to forest dispatch to make the calls.

The clock read midnight as we drove back into town, and the Bitterroot's Fire Management Officer declared our intended thirty-eight-acre burn officially "escaped."

For a week I rose at four-thirty A.M., coaxed groggy Freya to nurse, then drove back to fight fire. I contributed ideas at tactical briefings, flung dirt over flames, stirred hot ash, made and received radio calls, and expressed milk every four or five hours. The battery pump worked barely well enough to provide next day's drink for Freya, and sometimes not quite enough. In gradual increments the frozen supply I had stored the previous month decreased. Scott wanted to take the $80 pump back and demand a refund, but as far as I could learn, there was nothing better on the market not requiring electricity.

For three consecutive days I didn't see my daughter fully awake. Missing her hurt me like a toothache lodged somewhere in my center. At the same time I loved lacing my black boots mornings and pulling them off tired feet each evening. I fell happily back into the banter of people who liked each other and their work. It felt good to be contributing to the family bank account, and to be giving Freya and Scott this opportunity to know each other better. I breathed in the smell of rocks heating in the sun and felt energy return.

Then spring snow fell and extinguished the remainder of our heat. We had lost an additional thirty acres, which isn't much as forest fires go, and everyone had gotten a chance for some early season fire fighting practice. We rolled up our hoses and returned to ten-hour workdays, clearing a fuel break between private and Forest Service property and piling the brush.

One day I spent my entire half hour lunch break pumping and didn't produce a drop. I tried again a couple hours later and expressed only a trickle. It wasn't a life-or-death situation; Scott could come back out to the field anytime and I could stay with Freya, but even more important to me than this clearing project would be getting through our yearly Refresher Training and practice parachute jumps at the beginning of June.

Acquaintances frequently asked me if I shouldn't be looking for a career more compatible with raising a family. I explained how my husband and I were getting to job-share the off-season, how I was being encouraged to bring our baby to work as a tour guide at the Smokejumper Visitor's Center this summer. Another co-worker who had her baby a couple months after ours was planning to jump fires already, while her mom cared for her daughter during absences. I knew of three other pregnant smokejumpers, all being offered creative flexibility in figuring out what would work for them. I asked the skeptics if they knew of any other employer as supportive as ours was proving. No one had yet offered another idea.

When I got home I dialed Community Hospital in search of a lactation consultant. She said she had a cigarette lighter adapter that would probably work for my electric pump.

The following morning on our way out of town, I drove our green work truck to the hospital, apologizing to my co-workers for dragging them along on my errand.

"No problem, Lori. We don't mind starting work fifteen minutes later," they assured me.

The lady at the OB-GYN counter said that the cord cost $3, and would I like a receipt; since it was related to work it could be a tax write off. "Don't bother," I told her, and jogged back out to the truck, clutching the cord like hope.

Lunchtime the guys wished me luck and I hiked back up the ridge the half-mile to our truck. I plugged the shiny black adapter into the cigarette lighter on one side and my "Pump in Style" on the other, then placed double shields over double breasts, wondering if there was any truth to Amazon legends of women warriors chopping off a breast in order to be able to better aim their crossbows. I stood on the dirt road facing my chest into the cab, my temporary barn, and flipped the switch. "*Varoom, varoom,*" thrummed the pump, here on a ridge overlooking the Bitterroot Valley. White liquid squirted forth. Freya would drink fresh stuff another day.

The last week of May my parents arrived to watch Freya during the days while Scott and I went through our annual smokejumper Refresher Training.

"Our goal this year is to get you five jumps," our trainers told us during orientation. Since I had been three months pregnant at this time last year, I hadn't jumped, making it closer to two years since I had fallen through sky. Everything that took place in my life prior to giving birth felt like it had occurred in a previous life. I wanted to jump again and I was scared. This was a different kind of fear than when I was a rookie; Freya needed her momma whole. Was I being too selfish? By the end of every summer a few jumpers hobbled around the base on crutches, relegated to answering phones and helping with paperwork, and since the program's 1939 conception three have died in parachute-related incidents. At the same time, people died daily in car wrecks; living was risky. I wanted my daughter to see me reaching for the life I wanted.

My first three jumps were not elegant, but I made it to the ground, executed my landing rolls, and walked away healthy. I'm not sure that a trainer could have said anything looked wrong about my performances, but I didn't feel sharp.

Number four I fell too far forward while exiting the aircraft, and nearly somersaulted before my chute opened and stalled the flip. The lines connecting my harness to the nylon parachute were twisted terribly, and for at least twenty seconds I kicked my legs in order to spin my body back the other way and unwind the lines. Only then could I aim my parachute at the landing zone, a meadow surrounded by pine, fir, and larch. My brain was having a difficult time adapting to my descent speed.

"Drive, Lori, drive," Scott hollered from the clearing, running toward me. Too late I realized that I wasn't going to make the landing zone and no longer had time to reach an alternative clearing. I would either encounter a tree or barely squeeze through them. I steered for an alley of smaller trees but missed it. My chute's skirt caught a tall, skinny fir, and there I dangled, thirty feet above terra firma.

Up to that point there had been no time for panic, and my fuzzy brain had been unable to accurately register my predicament anyway. Now it all came clear. Before anyone arrived from below to tell me, I knew that my parachute must be barely holding its branch, and that if I fell to the flat, rock-studded ground from this height I would break something. I grabbed the closest limb and pulled my two hundred thirty pounds (body weight plus gear), as close as I could to the trunk, unsure how long the puny-looking branch would hold me. *Freya,* I thought, *life is too good to let yourself tumble now, Momma. Hold on.*

Scott reached the tree's base at a run, "Careful, Lori, you're barely hung up." All he could do was offer moral support and be ready to pick up the pieces if I fell. Three years previous, on his first fire call after completing rookie training, he had shattered his wrist falling from a similar height.

There was nothing uncommon about tree landings as a smokejumper, and we had practiced the procedure early that week: pull the 150-foot length of tubular webbing out of your jumpsuit leg pocket, tie off to your harness, unbuckle your parachute, and rappel down. But that procedure only worked if your chute would hold your weight. I was pretty sure that in this case, mine wouldn't. I would have to tie my rope off to the tree's trunk. One problem, among many at the moment, was that my parachute capped a higher branch at just the right angle to prevent my reaching the trunk. The only solution I could fathom entailed holding myself to the branch with my left hand, and lunging hard towards the trunk so that I could swing the rope end around it with my right hand.

The first two tries I failed. *Birth, Lori, you gave birth just six months ago. Push. Concentrate.* My left arm grew numb, and didn't feel strong enough to hold much longer. This was why we had to be able to do seven pull-ups minimum for our physical test each spring. *Breathe, Lori, breathe.* I yanked my body toward the bole as hard as I could with my left arm, while simultaneously flinging the end of my webbing. I wish I could say that I unleashed a full labor groan to focus my strength, but even in my predicament I knew this was not the social environment for such behavior. Two more jumpers had joined Scott on the ground beneath my tree. Nevertheless, my rope wrapped the trunk and I caught the tail. Scott shouted up that someone had called my mom and dad to let them know that we'd be home late, and that everything was fine.

One half-hitch. Two half-hitches. Painfully slowly I tied the knots with my right hand and shaking fingers, while somehow still clutching the branch with my other.

"I'm tied off!" I hollered down. As we had trained to do, I executed the final safety checklist out loud. "Through my rings; under my leg; through my carabineer; no parachute lines around my neck."

I unclasped parachute from harness and rappelled, weaving my gear-inflated body through tight branches. My feet touched the earth. With trembling fingers I unzipped my Kevlar, foam-lined, jumpsuit and peeled it from sweat-sopped clothing. Scott packed my gear while I strapped spurs over my boots, chunked the points into the wood, and climbed back up to retrieve my parachute.

When I reached my knots I tethered myself in, untied them, and then retied the same rope end to the parachute lines. A squad leader on the ground tugged the other end of the rope, and my parachute slid down in a silky blue and white cascade.

"I've never felt a chute come out of a tree that easily," he told me. "It wouldn't have held your weight." Everyone but Scott headed away to load the vans. Darkness eased itself into the woods as I climbed down. Increasing humidity intensified the scent of fir where I bruised the branches. This time when my feet touched the dirt they got to stay there for a while. My husband wrapped his arms around me.

Two days later the airplane circled the selected jump spot for our fifth and final training flight, an even smaller meadow than the last one. I squeezed onto my knees next to my jump partner so that we could both study the ground through the window. To our south strode the Bitterroot Mountains, and closer, to the west, rose the curvaceous, pyramid-tipped peak that I had taken to calling fondly, "The Tit."

Strangely, I felt more relaxed than I had during all of Refresher Training. When my turn came I leapt into the airplane's 100-mile-an-hour slipstream, pulled my knees into tuck position, and counted, "one one-thousand, two one-thousand, three one-thousand." Once again I had committed to air. "Four one-thousand." My chute snapped open before I reached "five" and I reached up for steering toggles. The plane's engine passed from hearing range and all was quiet except the soft flutter of nylon. In a controlled corkscrew, I maneuvered to earth, landed with no more force than if I had jumped from a bar stool, and rolled through last season's blond grass.

Scott's parents, who had traded mine out for childcare this week, walked through the meadow toward me, carrying Freya and snapping pictures. I pulled off my helmet to feel the sun-warmed breeze touch my damp cheeks, and coiled my parachute. Her grandpa handed Freya to me and I hugged her close. She bounced in my arms and pointed at the sky, then Scott thumped down and they went to greet him. We carried our backpacks to the clearing's edge, where we would be out of the way for the next load.

Once the excitement of people dropping from the sky like bloated raindrops had worn off, Freya looked at me with a familiar expression of impatience that said something to the effect of: "Here are you with milk, mom, and me with hunger, and why don't we do something about it now before I have to get all wound up and cry." I sat down on my pack, lifted my shirt, and offered her a gummy-textured raspberry of a nipple. She heaved a couple of excited breaths, latched on, and drank.

Lori Messenger lives in Missoula, Montana with her smoke-jumping husband Scott Jones and their daughter Freya, who to date jumps on beds but not from airplanes. When not chasing fires—metaphorical as well as actual—for the U.S. Forest Service, Lori writes, reads, and plays outdoors as much as possible.

Radiant Lives

YEAH, WE'RE WILDERNESS WOMEN.

You can tell from the well-loved leather boots. They've been waxed half a dozen seasons. The scuffed toes and cracked sides show the miles traveled. The laces, looped through rusty eyelets are frayed and knotted. These boots guide us through deep puddles without straying off trail. They walk in the dark over icy lakes and through thick sand. They post-hole up winter slopes.

Out of the storm, the boots come off. We dry our socks by the fire. They're hand-knitted socks with grey wool-darned crosses on the undersides. Our socks are stiff from days of sweat and mud. Peeled off, our toes are free.

Strong toes. Tough soles. Pine needle, glacial water, hot rock feet. We compare fading tan marks from summer sandals. We massage the firm, calloused pads and tickle each other's arches.

Muddy pant cuffs rolled, we push up the thermal layer. Matted hairs stand up on end, glistening in the firelight. The skin is so alive, experiencing the extremes of hot and cold. Our calf muscles are burly, always walking or pedaling to get where we're going.

The room warms and we shed our outer layers, unbuckling thick leather belts, a pocketknife case looped on one. Our heavy canvas trousers also show signs of our work: sap on the rump, grease and paint on the thighs, worn knees, snags from thorns.

Off come the down vests, moth-holed wool sweaters, fleece layers. We strip down to tank tops that cover our loose breasts and show our fuzzy underarms. Our shoulders have been shaped by lifting and hauling. Scratches, bruises, and scabs will heal.

The radiant fire warms our hands. They are texture-sensitive hands that reach out to touch rough and smooth tree bark, soft and waxy leaves, moist and dusty soil. Hands adept at building a fire and tying knots. We flex our fingers. Exposure to the elements has dried and cracked the skin. Scars shimmer in the flickering light. We stare at our clipped fingernails and unattended cuticles. These creative hands and fingers repair and restore gear, knead and bake bread, pluck and strum guitar strings.

We remove our fleece and knit hats. Our hair is wind-blown and wild, curled by salt water and rain, dusted by sand and ash, and decorated with twigs and lichen. The easiest style is no style; hair of one length ties back with an elastic band. Let loose, we pull our fingers through the threads and hook them behind our ears. Firelight glistens off the natural oils.

Rosy cheeks, sun-freckled and wind-burned faces glow. An ashen smudge or muddy streak is a beauty mark.

Our ears burn as blood courses back into them. In the wilderness, these ears are attentive to waves lapping, trees creaking, winds howling, and cricket trills. They are appreciative of silence. Tiny stud earrings of dragonflies, frogs, amber or turquoise stones stay in for weeks as if tattooed on the lobes.

We snap chunks off raw carrots and rip bites out of organic apples. Our diet is simple and natural. Each bite is chewed well to allow the full sweet, sour, bitter, salty flavors to penetrate the taste buds. Food and drink are the building blocks of our bones and muscles, never to be compromised.

Herbal tea, prepared from native plants warms the nostrils as we inhale the steam. Mint, sage, lavender, rose are some favorite smells, as well as rain-touched soil, wild mushrooms, a storm on the horizon, musky skin, the sea.

Our mouths are loose with smiles and expression. We read poetry aloud and make up song lyrics. Selective with speech, we just as often whistle, hoot, and bugle. Echoes bounce off canyon wall, travel down valleys, and get sucked away by the wind. Among friends we compliment and comfort.

Deep in each other's eyes, reflected flames dance. No color goes unrecognized, unappreciated. The world is a visual spectacle, from the scale of an insect wing to the breadth of an ecosystem. The moon phases, tidal cycles, wave sets, weather patterns, sunrise and sunset are important.

Our minds are clear so we act from the heart, without worries of social consequence. We value the freedom of natural places, warmth, simplicity, and friendship.

We know who we are. We are wilderness women.

Deborah McArthur is the Education Coordinator at the Northwest Fisheries Science Center. A biologist and educator, she has worked in the backcountry of California, Montana, and Washington. She enjoys world travel, bike touring, and sea kayaking. Currently, she lives in the Puget Sound area with her partner, Thomas, and Border collie, Cascade.

Acknowledgments

My greatest, biggest thanks go to the women who wrote this book. On top of being wild, tough, and brimful of guts, you're awesome storytellers. Of course, my appreciation also extends to those of you whose stories didn't make it onto the book. I loved reading your adventures and wish I could've included them all. Each of you is an inspiration to me.

Contributor MaryJane Butters ("Caught for Sure") has been a friend and steadfast supporter of the book from the get-go. Talk about an inspiration. If you don't know MaryJane yet, I encourage you to visit her online at www.maryjanesfarm.org. Even better, head out to Moscow, Idaho in person and revel in the warmth and hospitality of her farm. With her new book, her own magazine, and a line of self-produced organic backpacking food, MaryJane is at the helm of the burgeoning organic agriculture movement. She is a powerful and eloquent voice for small farms (and the women who either own or dream of owning them). She's as generous as she is smart, and she absolutely embodies the phrase "down to earth." MaryJane connected me with Erik Jacobson, visionary photographer, who created the ideal cover image for *Boots*. Isn't it gorgeous? Infinite thanks, Erik and MJ. I am so grateful to you both.

I want to mention a handful of women with whom I've shared some of my most memorable outdoor experiences. LeAnn Kramer and I learned the ropes of fish work together in the Ozarks, suffering and laughing our way to sisterhood. Dana Huffman of Paris, Missouri may never know how much I cherish the brief friendship we forged on the Amazon in '94. Nor does Becca Chapa probably have any idea how fondly I remember our season with the Wind River Ranger District in Carson, Washington. I grew up wild and wooly with my sister, Erica, who has recently rediscovered her love of the woods in the spirit of Artemis, the huntress. Thank goodness our mom was willing to wield canoe paddles and walking sticks so that we were able to take the whole idea of "women in wilderness" for granted.

Thank you, James, Larry, Susan, and the rest of the Travelers' Tales staff for seeing the merit of this collection and making it happen. Your books are gifts to the planet.

Lastly, I wouldn't be a writer if it weren't for my husband, Chris. His "real job" sacrifices have given me the freedom to work at what I love. Our relationship could be compared to a perfectly broken-in pair of boots—the kind that make you feel strong, secure, and damn sexy when you put them on. Our luscious little girls are blossoming wilderness women themselves, all tender budding green and huckleberry sweet. They know how to talk to elk, listen in the woods, decipher poop, and keep trudging on (even through tangles and tears). Rita and Sophie, I hope you always know the wonders of the world around you.

About the Editor

Growing up, Jennifer Bové lived in Missouri and Colorado, and she traveled with her family to many wild corners of the continental U.S. Along the way she caught a serious case of wanderlust, learning just how easy (and how hard) it can be to fall in love with every place you go.

After graduating from the University of Missouri, Jennifer and her husband-to-be Chris packed up their degrees and headed west to pursue a nomadic, competitive, and often extraordinary career in field biology. They've wandered back and forth along the Lewis and Clark Trail, studying everything from skinks to salmon and searching for a place to settle down.

In recent years, Jennifer ventured into the uncharted territory of full time motherhood, and parenthood has proven to be a wild and challenging adventure of its own. Her daughters Rita and Sophie are eagerly awaiting a new sibling, due to arrive this summer.

Jennifer's writing has appeared in various magazines and anthologies. Her first anthology, *The Back Road to Crazy: Stories From the Field*, was published by the University of Utah

Press in February, 2005. She dreams of growing up to be a children's book writer/illustrator and successful business owner.

For book news and other info, visit her online at www. bovesboots.blogspot.com.